Ewa Nowak

Experimental Ethics

Development in Humanities

edited by

Zbigniew Drozdowicz
(General Editor)

and Sławomir Sztajer

Volume 6

LIT

Ewa Nowak

Experimental Ethics

A Multidisciplinary Approach

LIT

NARODOWY PROGRAM
ROZWOJU HUMANISTYKI

The present thesis has been financed as a part of a programme of the Ministry of Science and Higher Education, which is called: the National Programme for the Development of Humanities (NPRH)

Typeset by Michał Staniszewski

This book is printed on acid-free paper.

Bibliographic information published by the Deutsche Nationalbibliothek
The Deutsche Nationalbibliothek lists this publication in the Deutsche Nationalbibliografie; detailed bibliographic data are available in the Internet at http://dnb.d-nb.de.

ISBN 978-3-643-90375-4

A catalogue record for this book is available from the British Library

Klosbachstr. 107
CH-8032 Zürich
Tel. +41 (0) 44-251 75 05
Fax +41 (0) 44-251 75 06
E-Mail: zuerich@lit-verlag.ch
http://www.lit-verlag.ch

LIT VERLAG Dr. W. Hopf
Berlin 2013
Fresnostr. 2
D-48159 Münster
Tel. +49 (0) 2 51-62 03 20
Fax +49 (0) 2 51-23 19 72
E-Mail: lit@lit-verlag.de
http://www.lit-verlag.de

Distribution:
In Germany: LIT Verlag Fresnostr. 2, D-48159 Münster
Tel. +49 (0) 2 51-620 32 22, Fax +49 (0) 2 51-922 60 99, E-mail: vertrieb@lit-verlag.de

In Austria: Medienlogistik Pichler-ÖBZ, e-mail: mlo@medien-logistik.at
In the UK: Global Book Marketing, e-mail: mo@centralbooks.com
In North America: International Specialized Book Services, e-mail: orders@isbs.com
e-books are available at www.litwebshop.de

Contents

Introduction

This book creates a space where ethical reflection "on a trial basis" – that is, experimentally – deals with research findings, observations, and experiences that since several dozen years ago have become the domain of scientific disciplines. It is at this level that ethical reflection is to be conducted: the cognitive definition of personal morality and the normatively and affectively founded definitions are crucial to consider the following question: Why are people unable to follow the values, norms and ideals they declare? Why do they conduct themselves in ways that contrast with their (sometimes well elaborated and highly rational) reasons? One possible answer is that their cognitive skills of judging and decision making need to be strengthened or the values and principles they declare affect them in an contingent, uncoordinated, and dispersive manner only. Contemporary culture seems to be dispersive and "liquid" (Z. Bauman's metaphor), which suggests that the social environment cannot increase the consistency and integration of moral personality. Public education should offer opportunities for personal betterment,[1] but it does not because it belongs itself to the dispersive culture. However, several studies proposed in this volume do not concentrate on the sociological and cultural; rather they focus on personal and interpersonal development as well as on the selected professional and normative contexts.

Ethical reflection also deals with issues that have become excluded from the discourses hedged with claims of rationality and universalism as in, for example, affectivity, emotionality, and preverbal communication. Classical ethics, from the start, pursued regularity, consistency, harmony and universality,

[1] The term *strengthening* replaces the more and more popular biotechnological enhancement here, see I. Peterson, J. Savulescu, *Unfit for the Future. The Need for Moral Enhancement*, Oxford 2012, p. 121: "In our view it is a serious mistake to reject moral bioenhancement [...]. Significant moral enhancement of the human species appears to be necessary in order to ensure the survival of human civilization in the longer run."

reliability, and predictability. This desire still meets the human mind's desire for inner harmony and consistency, pointed out long ago by Plato. At the same time, in light of new challenges coming today from science and rapidly evolving human relations, ethics – unlike legal discourse, which is rigid due to conventions and procedures – can and should consider experiences that are *new, significant, and problematic for individuals*. Such experiences may be of a professional character, such as in the medical and legal professions, where risky decisions are made suspended in a regulatory vacuum, related to a difficult dilemma, or requiring critical social engagement. They can be also of a personal kind when an individual comes into contact with something radically *different and strange*. For a rationalist, this could be affectivity, and for myself – another self. Several such situations are considered in this volume in an attempt to build a bridge of understanding and mediation where for many individuals exists a deep abyss. Ethics assumes that we deal with what is strange, new and unknown not by exclusion and turning our back to express indifference (or fear or contempt), but by careful observation and dialogue. The results of this dialogue can be surprising and informative, making this aspect of ethics investigational and quite experimental.

Experience, observation, and experiment as part of ethics might surprise a "legitimate" philosopher-theorist, but were once well established in ethics and philosophy. It is no coincidence that in this book there are many references to Aristotle. In the history of philosophy a thinker who carefully clears the spiritual and scientific issues occurs rarely. When English philosophers F. Hutcheson, D. Hume, and A. Smith took experience as one of the main reference points for reflective moral self-evaluation and started talking about reflected moral feelings, their method was indeed recognized as genuinely experimental. Yet at that time, professional research methods that allow for making repeated, independent observations and interventions, and for collecting and evaluating data, were still largely unknown and not used. The object of observation could not be defined exactly, although hypotheses were proposed. These experimental philosophers were later called "psychologistics" and "irrationalists." Shortly after W. James (1884) published his ground-breaking article "What is an Emotion?" in the philosophical journal *Mind*, continental philosophy distanced itself from psychology. The time for thoughts thinking themselves had arrived (L.S. Vygotsky). An anti-psychological turn found its expression in G. Frege:

> For Frege, even the "thought," *der Gedanke*, wasn't a mental event, but an abstract object. To have thoughts without thinkers: it's hard to get more anti-psychological than that! [There was a time when] Philosophy was struggling to define itself, crucially, by contrast with psychology.[2]

[2] K.A. Appiah, *Experiments in Ethics*, Cambridge, MA – London 2008, p. 15.

Indeed, philosophy was seen to have the right to discuss only abstract ideas. The same would be the case with ethics insofar as it examines decision-making processes, incentives, and special circumstances for the formation of special judgments, which include moral and normative judgments and their impact on personal moral performance and practical efficacy in social contexts. Ethics needs some kind of philosophy of psychology. Again, the development of research on normativity has given us a wealth of normative ethics. However, the lack of research on moral judgment and decision making is still quite apparent.

The experience of war, and later the continued expansion of science and technology, have eroded the belief that only purely rationalist, objective, and true doctrines and claims can create a supportive framework for the fragile and vulnerable human condition in all its integrity. Therefore, the experiences that H. Arendt's, E. Lévinas', and even L. Wittgenstein's works talk about have sown the seeds from which ethical interest in what is important and meaningful to a person, and not just to the system or project, has sprung up. G. Radbruch's work is also within this trend, thanks to whom in legal theory legal intrinsic values arise as a counterweight to legal positivism. However, the value, importance, and significance of great differences in preferences do not always undergo con-sensualisation and universalization. Individuals must be able to (as I. Kant would say) identify and realize what is valuable and meaningful for them autonomously, but this autonomy must be the subject of legal protection. However, no law monitors us twenty-four hours a day to ensure that our choices are not accidentally harmful to other individuals. The only guarantee lies in some personal moral culture, or individual competence in forming moral judgments. I present their importance in at least two chapters of this volume.

It is not neutrality or abstract rules, but it is the value, importance, and perfection identified by humans that cause the emergence of moral judgments and decisions of such a quality that rises above the criteria such as fear of punishment, conformity, and profitability. In order to make difficult decisions and face the conflicts, dilemmas, and challenges of today efficiently, it is necessary to strengthen the cognitive structure related to making judgments, as it has been stated by experienced cognitive-developmental psychologist G. Lind, who also created a unique method to develop competence in moral judgment. Our own experiments with his method are described in two chapters of this book. In the final analysis, it is moral cognition (strengthened by repeated exercises, discovered and described by Aristotle in his theory of virtue) that is critical to the implementation of what is valued and significant to a person in action. In the social context, action is based on the right balance between mutual respect, empathy, dialogue, and rationality is required. But still it is hard to maintain this balance in the practice of social life; in this book, I try to show where this difficulty comes from and why it is reoccurring.

The essays gathered in this volume illustrate the triple-stage research process, which I started in 2008 and which was inspired through cooperation with Professor Georg Lind (University of Konstanz, Germany) and an international group examining the parallelism between affectivity and cognitive processes. Parallelism has its immediate effect on the formation of moral judgments and decisions, especially in the face of such difficult situations as moral dilemmas. In using the term "affectivity," I am in no way referring to so-called emotivism – a traditional notion in metaethics that supposes that moral evaluations "express" emotional approval or disapproval in an irrational way.

Affectivity plays a very different role in the formation of moral judgments: namely, the values and ideals of a person, to varying degrees, activate, facilitate, and support a number of cognitive processes, which in turn enable the construction of logically correct moral judgments providing further argumentative justification, correction, legitimization, etc. It's about moral judgments in the normative and evaluative sense. In the scope of my interest, there are origins of such judgments that can be found in light of moral psychology. The origins are of a distinctly mixed nature, or hybrid: we cannot conclude that, from the very beginning to the end, moral judgments arise in a way determined by reasons and the medium of discourse because affectivity plays a significant role in the initial stage of moral judgment formation. This stage was exhaustively but briefly recounted by J. Habermas in an interview published in the book *Autonomy and Solidarity*. On the other hand, reasons and communicative actions may reflexively stimulate affective processes, which again cause moral judgment formation. Surely they can help one develop sensitivity and the ability to perceive moral issues, and may also (which we know from everyday experience) evoke hostility and aggression when in contact with someone else's beliefs that are radically different from our own. The latter problem can be due to an underdeveloped democratic competence – i.e., the ability to deal with the judgments and reasons of other thinking persons.

The following chapters present various aspects of the parallelism between affectivity and cognition: *How does affectivity contribute to moral judgment making?* (Chapter I) and *Normative dissonance vs. the order of argumentation* (Chapter II).

Subsequent chapters consider the repercussions that the above mentioned parallelism may evoke in experiencing otherness, starting from the identification of another person's mental state through to attempts to universalize certain patterns of relationships, such as conflict and mutual recognition. The following chapters are dedicated to these issues: *Facing otherness as ethical and aesthetical experiment* (Chapter III), *The concepts of respect revisited* (Chapter IV) and *What is universal? Between subjectivity and intersubjectivity* (Chapter V).

Still other chapters examine the consequences that values and, in particular, value judgments – provided sufficiently educated social cognition – could have on the legitimacy of legal norms and other social and political institutions. These include the following chapters: *Experimenting with values in legal contexts: Hegel and Radbruch* (Chapter VI) and *Democracy begins in the mind. Developing democratic personality* (Chapter VII).

The reader's close inspection will reveal that the findings of neurocognitive sciences are discussed in this volume and they confirm a number of independent hypotheses raised by such authors as J. Piaget, L. S. Vygotsky, L. Kohlberg, G. Lind, and A. Honneth. In this volume, a *cognitivist* approach is strongly advocated instead of the promotion of the newest "postcognitive" theories suggesting that social cognition (at the skills level) is solely owing to the self-evident existence of mirror neurons. The cognitivist approach, both in its psychological and philosophical aspects, presupposes that social cognition – i.e., the ability of social performance (like intentional principled moral behaviour, which solves conflicts in a rational way) and of bonding relationships with others – is not just innate or given together with a set of specified neurons that are ready to lead a human through social paths. Human social cognition relies on the evolutionary youngest areas in the brain. These areas still need to be strengthened through educationally supported socialization. Constant deep differences in human behaviour are proof of how much social cognition is new and still unfixed, especially conscious moral cognition, which is capable of critical and corrective reflection over itself (amounting to ethics in the sense given to it by Socrates). The vast majority of people declare a variety of values, ideals, and meanings, and identify with them with complete confidence. However, observations show that not all people are able to follow even their best intentions. By taking on issues such as affective and cognitive development, I remain distant from an annoying (and thankfully now widely rejected) manner of reducing complex social phenomena, such as morality, to the existence of a set of neural networks. But I am convinced that properly stimulated growth of social cognition guarantees the consistency and quality of principled moral judgment making, commonly regarded as one of the indicators of social morality in a democracy. Democracy not only trusts its citizens, allowing them to openly formulate independent judgments, but also strengthens their ability to think and judge.

Many ethicists ask themselves why so carefully formulated and constantly improved normative systems do not have the expected effect on human performance. Many share the prevailing belief that there is still something wrong with accepted norms and values – that there has been a "collapse" of norms and values. Only a few have realized the fact that people have different abilities to follow norms and values. Ethics should aim at understanding the causes of this difference, and perhaps developing effective normalization tools, where this goes beyond mere rational legitimacy. Some new measures are certainly needed that differ from the increasingly stringent legal penalties demanded by societies, which are desperate in the face of new problems and moral challenges posed by – and will be continuously posed by – the economic crisis, the expansion of technology, and rampant consumerism. These challenges are exacerbated also by the revival of fundamentalism and the decreasing quality of education.

Acknowledgments

I would like to thank the following professors: Georg Lind, Anna and Wojciech Jamroziak, Klaus Helkama, Piotr Przybysz, and Andrew Wierciński for inspiration, fruitful discussions, and helpful criticism. Thanks also to Agnieszka Wróblewicz, Jason Matzke, and Gosia Dereniowska for helping me to share complex, cross-disciplinary issues in English. Special thanks go to Professor Zbigniew Drozdowicz for motivation and inviting me to his project. This volume is the result of research started in 2008–2010 and supported by the Alexander of Humboldt Foundation, whom I would also like to acknowledge.

Chapter I

How does affectivity contribute to moral judgment making?[1]

Is the rationalist model of personal morality, with its primacy of reflected judgment making and critical self-reference, passé in light of the contemporary findings of neurocognitive science and biotechnological experiments? Why is the tendency to overestimate the intuitionist model growing? Or should deontology and emotion go together, as J. D. Greene purposes. "First, moral emotion provides a natural solution to certain problems created by social life. Second, deontological philosophy provides a natural 'cognitive' interpretation of moral emotion. [...] Deontology [...] is a natural 'cognitive' expression of our deepest moral emotions,"[2] Greene claims. There is a difference between expression and interpretation: emotions can be voiced, memorized, remembered and yet still not interpreted. Interpretation is a narrative work of cognition. If one voices or describes his or her own emotions as providing guidance for his or her judgments or decisions, the uniqueness and contingency of emotions does not allow us to assume that they are the foundations of deontological statements. To elaborate, deontological statements, values, discourse, and a consensual approach are needed with respect to truth claims. From the emotivist perspective (which will be not a concern of this chapter), moral judgments might express "one's attitudes for and against"[3] moral issues. Deontology, however, is more than

[1] The author is grateful for permission to publish this paper in extended version by P. Juchacz (ed.). The paper first appeared in *Filozofia Publiczna i Edukacja Demokratyczna*, vol. I (1), 2012, pp. 26–47.

[2] J. D. Greene, "The Secret Joke of Kant's Soul," in W. Sinnott-Armstrong (ed.), *Moral Psychology*, Cambridge, MA – London 2008, p. 59.

[3] G. Harman, *Explaining Value and Other Essays in Moral Philosophy*, Oxford 2000, p. 80.

a mental act, more than a narrative about a mental act, and more than an expression of positive or negative attitudes. Thus, I disagree with Greene's ultimate conclusion that "deontology [...] is a kind of moral confabulation."[4] It is rather that making deontological constructions by cognitive skill is rooted in judgments and decisions that are facilitated by affective processes. Moral affects may guide humans' judgment behavior in some, but of course not all, situations (in particular, not in the complex situations). Sometimes cognitions and emotional processes compete during the moral judging process and sometimes they harmonize. In this chapter, I try to reconstruct the historical narrative toward affectivity in philosophy, and then in psychology and neuroscientific approaches too. By considering moral judgment making, ethics can no more ignore the relevance of affectivity.

1. Learning affectivity

Even Aristotle considered one's affective self-awareness and self-regulation as evidence of a developed moral personality, the predisposition to which is admittedly innate but its development depends on adequate support through education, and the latter contributes to the flourishing of *virtue*. In the following passage, *virtue* seems to be defined similarly to cognition in modern cognitive psychology:

> The impulses of incontinent people move in contrary directions [...]. We feel anger and fear without choice, but the virtues are modes of choice or involve choice. Further, in respect of the passions we are said to be moved, but in respect of the virtues and the vices we are said not to be moved but to be disposed in a particular way.[5]

Uncontrolled fluxes of emotions can be either creative or destructive; it does not allow for self-disposition, or autonomy. But can we make any decision without being affected by emotional attribution? To paraphrase Kant, one must admit that feelings that lack reflection are blind and thoughts devoid of feelings are empty and calm.[6] If one is committed to the position of extreme dualism, one depreciates feelings in favour of thoughts or thoughts in favour of feelings. Breaking the one-sidedness of the Cartesian rationalist model,

---

[4] J. D. Greene, "The Secret Joke of Kant's Soul," op. cit., p. 63.

[5] Aristotle, *Nicomachean Ethics*, transl. W. D. Ross, 1994. Retrieved from http://classics.mit.edu/Aristotle/nicomachean.1.i.html [21.05.2009]; compare R. C. Solomon, *Not Passions' Slave. Emotions and Choice*, New York 2007.

[6] M. Ratcliffe, *Feelings of Being. Phenomenology, Psychiatry, and the Sense of Reality*, New York 2008, p. 232.

Condillac was allegedly to say, *je sense donc je suis*. After all, human motivations, judgments, encounters with someone or something, interests, wonders, surprises, commitments, current impressions, or recently memorized or just sensed experiences are all embedded in feelings, emotions, or moods. This occurs especially though teaching: "Teachings go deep when carried into the human being by deep affection,"[7] as A. Zajonc assumes. How we experience affects and emotions may have different colours and intensities, and their impact on personal judgment and decision-making is immense. Turning the tradition on its head, A. Damasio says that today "we think with our fingertips and we feel with the mind." When we do not understanding the manifold role or affectivity for personal performance and interpersonal relations, we are incapable to properly use the potential of affectivity as the completion of cognition, in particular in the formation of moral judgments.

I acknowledge the ability to identify, understand, and tune one's own emotions in a reflective way and to share and respect emotions (especially empathy and affective self-regulation), in particular when being confronted with demanding social situations (conflicts and dilemmas), as one of the key cognitive skills. The described ability enables one to look at social issues from the perspective of other participants[8] and to solve them without excluding or discriminating against anyone, for the benefit of everyone. This skill requires special educational care, especially in the age of highly promoted individualism, authenticity, and selfish personality, because it not possible in an emotional social limbo when elemental attention, respect, and a sense of support and solidarity remain dim. Among others things, we should educate in order to open individuals to the other, and to make entire communities able to open up to otherness and diversity. The ability to construct one's own basic moral emotions of approval and disapproval, and those expressed by others, in a preconscious but cognitive way has been analyzed by W. James. He discusses the importance of the ability to accurately identify what such an emotion "says" in a preverbal but not voiceless way about human evaluations, interests, priorities, and preferences. An evaluation can be verbalized, purified from affectivity, and therefore treated as a judgment, regardless of its subconscious prehistory. "Our mental condition is more allied to a judgment of

[7] A. Zajonc, "Cognitive-Affective Connections in Teaching and Learning: The Relationship Between Love and Knowledge," *Journal of Cognitive Affective Learning*, 2006, vol. 3 (1), p. 1. Retrieved from: https://www.jcal.emory.edu//viewarticle.php?id=82layout=html [20.05. 2013].

[8] R. L. Selman, *The Growth of Interpersonal Understanding*, New York – London – Toronto – Sydney – San Francisco 1980, pp. 245–263.

right than to anything else. And such a judgment is rather to be classed among *awareness* of truth: it is a *cognitive* act,"[9] James claims.

At early stages of infancy, before the development of awareness and self-awareness, humans seem to share an "emotional vision"[10] with others. Following A. N. Schore, infants learn at first

> [...] proto-communications [...] [that] are accompanied by gestures, affectively salient tones, and facial expressions. Such emotional communications occur within the context of dialogic "face-engagements" between mother and child who share "intimate connections." [...] Infant research now highlights the principle that an event achieves significance when it is amplified by an affective response [...].[11]

Affective development requires sufficiently early affective interaction with a facilitator.

In his paper entitled *Intelligence and Affectivity*,[12] J. Piaget indicates the *affective primacy* in learning and other cognitive processes. Among other things, affectivity includes the innate human properties of a *feeling of respect* and *feeling of justice*, as well as *interpersonal* feelings. The key role played by moral feelings is that of facilitating the development of cognitive structures of moral behavior.[13] On the other hand, in the affects Piaget sees "interests," "energetics," and "motions" of human judgments and decisions. Decisions are made neither only because we "theoretically" realize which option for action is the right one, nor because it can be fully justified by rational arguments. The key to judgment is a relatively strongly felt belief in the rightness of the options in a situation requiring action. The rational-communicational way of human functioning in the world requires, however, the additionally abilities of calling forth linguistically articulated reasons for judgments – i.e., the social norms that justify judgments in the eyes of other persons who don't have direct access to our mind and to our subjectively self-evident, simple judgments. Some people seem to make judgments by rejecting, at the same time, the normative reasons and justifications for them. In his latest book, A. Honneth calls this phenomenon a normative "pathology." However, neuropsychological research has shown that "the capacity to accept norms is peculiarly human and depends on language,"[14] that is, on the linguistic cognition that needs to be strengthened. Sharing our motivations and justifications with other people demonstrates our

[9] W. James, "What is an Emotion," *Mind*, 1984, vol. 9, no. 34, pp. 201–202.
[10] A. N. Schore, *Affect Regulation and the Origin of the Self*, Hillsdale, NJ 1994, p. 109.
[11] Ibidem, pp. 108–110.
[12] J. Piaget, *Intelligence and Affectivity*, transl. T. A. Brown, C. E. Kaegi, Palo Alto, CA 1981.
[13] Ibidem, p. 15.
[14] A. Gibbard, *Wise Choices, Apt Feelings. A Theory of Normative Judgment*, Oxford 1990, p. 61.

social preference in understanding, articulate reflection, and linguistic communication as a measure of rationality. Its durability is based precisely on the fact that we let each other understand our reasons for action, and in the case of social issues we try to develop such reasons that everyone could share in order to solve common problems and fulfill collective interests.

> Signals given by our feelings and thinking strategies are not yet rational in themselves. They can be considered rationale only if they are consistent with the conventions, social norms [...]. Their source is in the culture.[15]

According to Piaget, affectivity significantly facilitates cognitive processing and the intellect, which because of our rationalist heritage we value more than affectivity. We can continue to do so, but we must not ignore the role of affectivity in the development of intellectual and moral human beings. If we identify respect for social rules as a key element of morality, we should be aware that "Standards are not just there to be used and believed in. [...] They are also there to arouse feelings."[16] A feeling evoked and related to morally valuable content (moral choice, problems, or conflict) indicates that some proto-judgment[17] is being already pre-consciously formed in the mind, whose shape will later be affected by already aware and reflective work involving precise articulation, understanding, argumentation, justification, etc. A feeling indicating the formation of judgment starts and facilitates this work, which in turn allows a person to become aware of and develop a judgment that is based on reasons in favour and against it, or – what is of considerable social importance – that is being corrected by the "reasonable force" of arguments (Habermas' term). Articulation, understanding, and rationalization of the proto-judgments and judgments can be made only at the level of language, through conscious cognitive processes. In a situation of boredom, inattention, indifference, or lack of affective "motion," it is difficult to trigger effective moral consideration and ethical discourse.

Whereas cognitive processes can cause feedback stimulation, the development of moral sensitivity and affection is desired at every stage of socialization and in re-socialization. Society, after all, cares about strengthening the feeling of empathy, respect for social rules, and a sense of justice, deepening personal commitments to principles and values, and having individuals follow their commitments in their daily lives, relationships, and institutions. "Interpersonal

---

[15] I. Stamm, *Zwischen Neurobiologie und Sozialethik*, Oldenburg 2007, pp. 133–134.

[16] Ibidem, pp. 128–131.

[17] Or several proto-judgments when one is confronted with a dilemmatic issue as shown in the chapter *Normative dissonance vs. the order of argumentation* in this volume. Compare A. Zajonc, "Cognitive-Affective Connections in Teaching and Learning...," op. cit.

feelings," which involve the development of affective and discursive interaction, are also needed here. Between affectivity and cognitive processes there exists some kind of effective feedback to facilitate learning processes that include the formation of consistent cognitive structures. Piaget calls this feedback the "affective-cognitive parallelism." In *Intelligence and Affectivity* he states:

> Today no one would think of denying that there is constant interaction between affectivity and intelligence. To say that they are indissociable can mean two very different things, however. In one sense, it could mean that affectivity speeds up or slows down intellectual functioning without modifying the structures of intelligence as such. This stimulating or hindering role is incontestable. Students who are eager to learn have more enthusiasm for studying and learn more easily. [...] In the second sense, the indissociability of intelligence and affectivity could mean that affectivity changes intellectual structures and is, therefore, the source of new knowledge or new cognitive operations.[18]

To A. Honneth, the "social significance and visibility"[19] of others develops thanks to bodily expressions, facial expressions and gestures, an affective (preverbal) relationship of mutual attention, and trust and empathy in early childhood. Even infants perceive and appreciate other people from their immediate surroundings as significant figures (and eventually learn to perceive in this way also those distant and fictional characters from literature, film, etc.). Thanks to "social visibility" they expand their commitment to willingness and "participation."[20] Thus, even at the preverbal stage of affective socialization, other persons become "significant"[21] in infants' eyes, and in turn, infants become significant for other people. All is about "[...] mutual, reciprocal adjustment at the level of affective attention paying to another. [...] This adjustment takes place mostly by means of gestures."[22] Honneth assumes that this elementary form of mutual human "perception in terms of meaning and validity has enormous impact on the interactions between adults, too."[23] The fact that others gain significance for a child is the result of the developmental

---

[18] J. Piaget, *Intelligence and Affectivity*, op. cit., p. 1.

[19] A. Honneth, *Unsichtbarkeit. Stationen einer Theorie der Intersubjektivität*, Frankfurt am Main 2003, pp. 14–16; see also J. Habermas, *Autonomy and Solidarity. Interviews with Jürgen Habermas*, ed. and introduced by P. Dews, London – New York 1985, p. 270; A.I. Goldman, *Simulating Minds. The Philosophy, Psychology, and Neuroscience of Mindreading*, Oxford 2006; T. Breyer, *Attentionalität und Intentionalität. Grundzüge einer phänomenologisch-kognitionswissenschaftlichen Theorie der Aufmerksamkeit*, München 2011.

[20] A. Honneth, *Unsichtbarkeit*, op. cit., p. 13.

[21] Ibidem, p. 15.

[22] Ibidem, p. 17.

[23] Ibidem, p. 26.

process, which, in the first place, occurs at the affective (emotional) level. Without paying attention to others – and gaining from them – all communication and understanding emerge with difficulty, if they emerge at all. But therefore, still "in childhood a man would have developed the first germs of self-esteem and respect for himself by experiencing himself as a partner in an interaction of a collaborative merry-making."[24]

2. Linking affectivity, interest, and value: Piaget

Let us take – says Piaget –

> [...] the meaning of the word "interest." Latin *inter-esse* means to be in between, to oscillate between [...] to build the relationship between a subject and an object by the fact that the object of interest is included into the area of subjective activity, it means that assimilation takes place, assimilation in the mental, spiritual sense. [...] Emerging interest mobilizes energy reserves, and this alone is enough to draw a man to work and make it seem even easier for him, and fatigue to be overcome. That is why some students achieve incomparably better results when we meet their interests, when we convey them the message that they hunger and need. On the other hand, the interest brings about a whole system of values, popularly also known as "interests." These are derived in the course of spiritual development, when a man sets himself increasingly complex goals to be achieved. [...] The interests and values that we aim at, are also closely related to self-esteem: the famous complex of inferiority or superiority. We constantly tend to record our activity on the inner scale of values. Successes increase and failures in turn lower our self-esteem (in comparison to their own expectations). This is where an individual derives his self-esteem from [...]. The system built on these different values affects first of all the emotional relationships between people [...] the feelings between one person and another. [...] The feelings that arise in interpersonal relations [...] include the feeling of respect feeling – a feeling by all means unique. [...] The resulting values are normative in the sense that they are not called just sympathy, antipathy, etc., but they become the rules and principles, required by respect.[25]

In other words, the feelings of approval or disapproval are further translated into normative grammar, words, and expressions that are as meaningful as they can be. In this way, the human mind is able to reconstruct preconscious

[24] A. Honneth, *Das Ich im Wir. Studien zur Anerkennungstheorie*, Frankfurt am Main 2010, p. 266.

[25] J. Piaget, *Psychologie et pédagogie*, Paris 1969, pp. 222–224 (free translation); compare M. Nussbaum, "Emotions as Judgments of Value and Importance," in R.C. Solomon (ed.), *Thinking About Feeling. Contemporary Philosophers on Emotions*, New York 2004.

proto-judgments. Even simple perceptions seem to be guided by interests generated by subconscious processes of the mind, including memory: a subject perceives what is, in a particular way, relevant to him or her.

> Our perceptions are emotionally coloured. In our opinion, the surroundings always gain some value, meaning. In this way, emotions are also involved in our thinking and decision-making. [...] The ability of rational action, learning the rules and standards of proper behavior depends in great extent on the ability to feel,[26]

Stamm emphasizes.

The people and things that bother a person are not indifferent to him or her. Who intends to do anything that means nothing to him? The human mind is led by interest, respect, and other interpersonal feelings that distil from the world what is important for his or her own vision of the world. This cognitive constructivism is a learning process (the growth of social cognition) when consciously stimulated, the learning process can be more efficient. Learning may be lifelong, provided that the person resides in a socially supportive learning environment.

3. Linking affectivity and rationality: Habermas

In philosophy and discourse ethics, rationalism is still far from reconciled with the "misguiding" power of affectivity, although there is an appreciation of the relevance of moral emotions. Habermas also does justice to the moral emotions, especially as they relate to the process of cognitive construction of moral issues – the genesis of moral commitment that is difficult to talk about in terms other than self-commitment, mutual respect, and the grounding of social rules. Following values, Habermas also excludes moral feelings from the orchestra of justifications, because within social discourse practice values and feelings are not universalizing. As such, they belong to private biographies. Let us consider the relevance of moral feelings in Habermas:

> First, moral feelings play an important role in the *constitution* of moral phenomena. We would not even perceive certain action-related conflicts as morally relevant if we did not *feel* that the integrity of a person was being threatened or harmed. Feelings provide the basis for our *perception* of something as a moral issue. A person might lack the sensorium, as we say, for the suffering of a vulnerable creature who is entitled to the preservation of his or her integrity, both personal and corporeal. This sensorium is obviously connected with capacities for sympathy and empathy.

[26] I. Stamm, *Zwischen Neurobiologie und Sozialethik*, op. cit., p. 109.

> Second, and above all, moral feelings [...] give us an orientation for the *judgment of morally relevant individual cases.* Feelings build the experiential basis for our intuitive judgments: shame and guilt are the basis for self-reproaches, pain and the sense of injury for our reproaches against another person who has harmed us, indignation and rage for the condemnation of a third person who has injured someone else. Moral feelings are reactions to disruptions of patterns of intersubjective recognition, of interpersonal relations, in which the actors participate from a first-, second-, or third-person standpoint. For this reason moral feelings are so structured that the system of personal pronouns is reflected in them.
>
> Third, of course, moral feelings play a role not merely in the application of moral norms, but also in their grounding. Empathy, at the very least – in other words the capacity to transport oneself by means of feelings across cultural distance into alien and *prima facie* incomprehensible life conditions, patterns of reaction, and interpretative perspectives – is an emotional precondition for the ideal taking over the roles, which requires each person to adopt the standpoint of all the others. To see something from a moral point of view means that we do not elevate our own understanding of the world and our self-understanding to the status of criteria for the universalization from the perspective of all others. This demanding cognitive achievement would scarcely be possible without that generalized sympathy which becomes sublimated into a capacity for fellow feeling, and points beyond our emotional ties to those closest to us, opening our eyes to "difference" – in other words, to the individuality and autonomous significance of the other who remains in his or her otherness.[27]

Some contemporary philosophers follow Habermas in considering emotional bond between individuals and the social rules.[28] Basing decisions to act only on emotions (without reflection) is not possible, and can certainly be misleading and quite dangerous for a number of social relationships. Misunderstood or poorly understood feelings cannot be the unique guide for human decisions and actions (Piaget said that "love is not blind either"). We can however learn how to reconstruct the feelings in the reflection follow-

[27] J. Habermas, *Autonomy and Solidarity*, op. cit., pp. 269–270.

[28] See J. Deigh, *Emotions, Values, and the Law*, Oxford 2002. A stronger hypothesis toward the cognitive role of "intelligent feelings" in the socio-normative contexts has been proposed by: J. Elster, *Alchemies of the Mind. Rationality an the Emotions*, Cambridge, MA 1999; R. de Souza, *The Rationality of the Emotion*, Cambridge, MA – London 1987; R. C. Solomon, *On Emotion as Judgment*, in idem, *Not Passions' Slave...*, op. cit.; J. Beane, *Affect in the Curriculum: Towards Democracy, Dignity, and Diversity*, New York 1990; M. Nussbaum, "Emotions as Judgments of Value," *The Yale Journal of Criticism*, 1992, vol. 1 (5), pp. 201–212; M. Boler, "Disciplined Emotions: Philosophies of Educational Feelings," *Educational Theory*, 2005, no. 47 (2), pp. 203–227; A. Ben-Ze'ev, *The Subtlety of Emotions*, Cambridge, MA 2000. "Emotions are often rational in the normative sense: frequently, they are," Ben-Ze'ev highlights.

ing it. We can also learn to assess their colour, intensity, and direction better, and above all, to translate them into speech, reasons, and verbal arguments, making feeling and thinking become more harmonious, parallel processes, which in turn will more likely lead to the reconciliation of heart and mind, and contradictions and conflicts rarer. Such harmony is envisioned by Solomon and Ratcliffe when they speak of "the inestimable importance of emotions in our lives, with an intelligent commitment that must be nurtured and strengthened."[29] For years, many researchers have emphasizes the need for reconciliation between affect and cognition also in disciplines such as rationalist ethics and the psychology of moral development. Such reconciliation has taken place in recent years on the basis of phenomenology, ethics, experimental psychology and neurosciences.

4. Linking affectivity and meaningful thinking: Vygotsky

The fact that emotional and reflective processes are closely related to each other was already noted by L. S. Vygotsky, whose hypotheses were for a few decades ahead of discoveries in modern science. Following him, we might note, the irreducible interdependence of affects and intellect as they relate to all mental activities that contribute to the genesis of meaning for both human cognitive activities and social practice. This would include its cooperative and social contexts:

> Their separation as subjects of study is a major weakness of traditional psychology, since it makes the thought process appear as autonomous flow of "thoughts thinking themselves," segregated from the fullness of life, from the personal needs and interests, the inclinations and impulses of the thinker. Such segregated thought must be viewed either as a meaningless epiphenomenon incapable of changing anything in the life or conduct of a person or else – some kind of primeval force exerting an influence on personal life in an inexplicable, mysterious way. The door is closed on the issue of the causation and origin of our thoughts, since deterministic analysis would require clarification of the motive forces that direct thought into this or that channel. By the same token, the old approach preludes any fruitful study of the reverse process, the influence of thought on affect and volition.[30]

Humans do not think about meaningless issues. Vygotsky's viewpoint corresponds with that of H. Arendt, as found in her book *The Life of the Mind*:

---

[29] Cf. M. Ratcliffe, *Feelings of Being*, op. cit., p. 21.

[30] L. S. Vygotsky, *Thought and Language*, newely revised, transl. and ed. by A. Kozulin, Cambridge, MA 1986, pp. 10–11.

"The need of reason is not inspired by the quest for truth but by the quest for meaning. And truth and meaning are not the same."[31] On the one hand, thinking processes might be affected by impulses from the external environment that attract attention. On the other hand, they might be affected by the impulses streaming from one's own mind, from experiences, memories, and already processed issues that have become meaningful to the person, for reasons of any kind. The affection occurs at the sub-conscious level: a subject only observes reflection as a conscious process. So the fact that humans think is a meaningful fact in itself. Additionally, humans have the specific ability to consider thoughts as linguistically articulated wholes in a relevant respect – namely, as meaningful – by viewing them from the perspective of their own interests, from the interests or engagement they share with other fellows, and, finally, from their interpersonally and socially engaged viewpoint (compare Piaget's and Habermas' hypotheses quoted in this chapter). Affected by a meaningful linguistic form, it is affectivity that affects the subjective (always "mine") construction of the meaning corresponding to the meaning expressed in the original linguistic form. This "new" meaning is brought to light in new notions, thoughts, and linguistic expressions, in the narrative interpretation that reveals the meaning, or in the thoughts that affect, again, decision making process and activity.

Vygotsky's own approach demonstrates

> [...] the existence of a dynamic system of meaning in which the affective and the intellectual unite. It shows that every idea contains a transmuted affective attitude toward the bit of reality to which it refers. It further permits us to trace the path from a person's needs and impulses to the specific direction taken by his thoughts, and the reverse path from his thoughts to his behaviour and activity.[32]

To be aware that thinking reveals and bears witness to the specific effects of affective processes implies not only a cause-effect relationship between a subject and some external or internal reality and reflective processes. Inner reality may be a constellation of experiences evoking newer and newer mental processes. This constellation itself cannot fully reach the surface of consciousness to be considered or fully thought through. Affective and reflective processes can take place on two parallel paths, though their interdependence and mutual relations have not yet been fully explained by science. Perhaps an explanation will be developed solely on the level of brain activity but not on the conscious mind level. Awareness does not "observe" affective processes. Additionally, affective processes occur at a faster rate than do the reflexive processes, which

[31] H. Arendt, *The Life of the Mind*, part I: *Thinking*, New York 1978, p. 15.

[32] L. S. Vygotsky, *Thought and Language*, op. cit., p. 11.

gives rise to the impression that they precede thinking, rationality, and any controlling influence of a subject on his or her decisions. There are a multiple of influences on human decision making, including both intrinsic and extrinsic factors of which we are unaware.

5. Distinguishing between feelings and emotions: Damasio and Craig

Terms for feeling, emotion, and affect do not always mean the same. Their meanings depend on various research disciplines and methods. In light of the present research findings, emotions are something different from bodily feelings (e.g., warm, cold, pain, and pleasure), moods and affective traits (e.g., depression, sadness, happiness), or sentiments (e.g., nostalgia). By "emotions" B. Craig means "emotional feelings, including maternal and romantic love, anger, fear, sadness, happiness, sexual arousal, disgust, aversion, indignation, uncertainty, disbelief, social exclusion, trust, empathy, a 'state of union with God,'"[33] care, responsibility, contempt, disappointment, feelings of respect and disrespect, feeling of rightness, helplessness, etc. – all feelings we can have "emotional awareness" of. In this chapter I follow Damasio's and Craig's definition insofar as it distinguishes feelings and emotions by giving feelings an awareness-similar role: "Humans perceive 'feelings' from the body that provide a sense of their physical condition and underlie mood and emotional state."[34] In this way humans are able to feel their emotions, which can be complex mental experiences and "objects" of perception and "self-directed recognitional [introspective, phenomenal] concepts."[35]

Emotional feelings have affective and motivational content and they contribute to socio-moral judgment formation. This kind of emotion, on the one hand, and moral reasoning, judging, decision making, conflict solving, etc., on the other hand, belong together. Moral emotions directly refer to the

---

[33] A. D. Craig, "How Do You Feel Now? The Anterior Insula and Human Awareness," *Nature Reviews in Neuroscience*, 2009, no. 10, pp. 59–70. Retrieved from doi: 10.1038/nrn2555 [7.09.2012]. Craig briefly defines basic emotional awareness in humans: "I regard awareness as knowing that one exists (the feeling that 'I am'); an organism must be able to experience its own existence as a sentient being before it can experience the existence and salience of anything else in the environment. One proposal holds that awareness of any object requires first, a mental representation of 'me' as a feeling (sentient) entity, second, a mental representation of that object, and third, a mental representation of the salient interrelationship between me and that object in the immediate moment ('now')." Ibidem, p. 8.

[34] A. D. Craig, "Interoception: The Sense of the Physiological Condition of the Body," *Current Opinion in Neurobiology*, 2003, no. 13, pp. 500–505.

[35] A. I. Goldman, *Simulating Minds...*, op. cit., p. 265.

justice and rightness of judgments. How do emotions "know" the difference between right and false? Internal moral principles, norms, and values can guide personal judgmental behavior only if one has an affective "bounding" to his or her internal moral orientations. Moreover, experiencing moral emotions and bodily feelings seems to be based on the same neural and somatic processes, as neuroscientific research in the last two decades shows. Compared to philosophy and psychology, this research has brought about new discoveries on the role of emotions.

In his book *Looking for Spinoza*, Damasio reports on the experiences of one of his patients who suddenly has "emotion-related thoughts" that:

> [...] only came after the emotion began. After she reported feeling sad she began having thoughts consonant with sadness. [...] The sequence of events in this patient reveals that the emotion sadness came first. The feeling of sadness followed, accompanied by thoughts of the type that usually can cause and then accompany the emotion sadness. [...] She had no thoughts causative of sadness. [...] At this point one should ask: Why would this patient's brain evoke the kind of thoughts that normally cause sadness considering that the emotion and feeling were unmotivated by the appropriate stimuli? The answer has to do with the dependence of feeling on emotion and the intriguing ways of one's memory. When the emotion sadness is deployed, feelings of sadness instantly follow. In short order, the brain also brings forth the *kind* of thoughts that normally cause the emotion sadness *and* feeling of sadness. This is because associative learning has linked emotions with thoughts in a rich two-way network. Cognitive and emotional levels of processing are continuously linked in this manner.[36]

Learning process occurs efficiently if emotional engagement is provided. A similar effect can be demonstrated in one of P. Ekman's experiments. He asked individuals to move certain muscles of their face in order to imitate sad or happy facial expressions without explicit awareness of. Damasio elucidates the mechanism of emotionally-based learning:

> [...] the subjects came to feel the feeling appropriate to the emotion displayed. [...] In their minds there was no thought capable of causing the portrayed emotion. [...] Psychologically unmotivated and "acted" emotional expressions have the power to cause feeling. Thee expressions conjure up the feelings and the kinds of thoughts that have been learned as consonant with those emotional expressions.[37]

Ekman explains that the interpersonal perceptions of facial expressions can stimulate the mirror neurons to represent feelings that the observer sees

---

[36] A. Damasio, *Looking for Spinoza. Joy, Sorrow and the Feeling Brain*, New York 2003, pp. 68–71.

[37] Ibidem, p. 71.

in another individual.[38] Further, the sensual-affective transactions can stimulate the personal affectivity that facilitates understanding and reasoning processes. Facial expressions, gestures, and tones have a strong impact on the development of moral awareness even in the preverbal periods of infancy

6. Training[39]

The ability to understand one's own and others' emotional states is still explored by experimental sciences. Its development can be highly important in school communities, physician – patient relationships,[40] and in other social contexts. Profession-related semantic and taxonomic tools and trainings[41] are developed. Members of communities and institutions are often confronted with interpersonal misunderstandings and their consequences they must cope with. "Affective confusion"[42] and emotionally based pluralistic ignorance may disturb the communication process. "With the ability to identify emotions early on, we may be better able to deal with people in a variety of situations and to manage our own emotional responses to their feelings,"[43] Ekman states. One must not share emotions with others in all social situations, but one needs to identify them and react adequately to support educational processes. The quality of education strongly depends on the quality of interpersonal relationships and the community. "We do not need to feel another person's fear to accept it and help the other person cope with his or her fear."[44]

---

38 Ibidem, p. 116.

39 This part of chapter is based on the paper presented at the 5th International Symposium Moral Competence and Brain, on 26-27.06.2011, Konstanz (Germany).

40 A. I. Goldman, *Simulating Minds...*, op. cit.; T. Breyer, *Attentionalität und Intentionalität...*, op. cit.; H.-G. Gadamer, *Schmerz. Einschätzungen aus medizinischer, philosophischer, und therapeutischer Sicht*, Heidelberg 2003; N. Grahek, *Feeling Pain and Being in Pain*, Oldenburg 2001; R. Sachse, *Therapeutische Beziehungsgestaltung*, Göttingen – Bern – Wien – Toronto – Seattle – Oxford – Prag 2006; H. Plügge, *Wohlbefinden und Missbefinden. Beiträge zu einer medizinischen Anthropologie*, Tübingen 1962; F. Overlach, *Sprache des Schmerzes – sprechen über Schmerzen. Eine grammatisch-semantische gesprächsanalytische Untersuchung von Schmerzausdrücken im Deutschen*, Berlin – New York 2008.

41 See S. Baron-Cohen et al., *Mind Reading. Emotions Library*, London – New York 2002[1], 2003[2]; T. Breyer, *Attentionalität und Intentionalität...*, op. cit., Section "Experimenting with Phenomenology;" S. Gentsch, M. Gordon, *Organization Roots of Empathy*, after M. Dworschak, "Die Macht des Mitgefühls," *Der Spiegel*, 2013, no. 29, pp. 118–121.

42 R. L. Selman, *The Growth of Interpersonal Understanding*, op. cit., p. 259.

43 P. Ekman, *Emotions Revealed. Recognizing Faces and Feelings to Improve Communication and Emotional Life*, New York 2003, p. XVI.

44 Ibidem, p. 153.

Picture 1. Troubled

Picture 2. Shocked

Picture 3. Thoughtful

Picture 4. Joyful[45]

Of course, philosophers are very limited in conducting psychological experiments. However, being inspired by psychological research findings and training programmes, they can develop training courses like I did. In 2011 I offered a pilot training course for two separate groups: pupils and teachers. The training consists of 6 sections, about 10 minutes each; for

[45] All pictures retrieved from http://www.harrycutting.com/; http://ruff-draft.tumblr.com/; http://harrycutting.blogspot.com/ [17.05.2013]. My thanks go to Harry Cutting for his kind permission to apply his pictures as training stimuli.

each section one photograph showing a facial emotion must be provided. I asked American artist Harry Cutting for didactic licence for a set of his professional photographs because they show emotional states of children and adolescents representing different cultures and ethnic contexts, and are highly impressive. They show facial and bodily expressions of elementary emotional states like joy, sadness, fear, embarrassment (or feeling troubled, shocked), curiosity, frustration, surprise, mistrust, embarrassment, anger, thoughtfulness, etc. Additionally, they show full facial expressions and can be applied in an educational training. Pictures showing partial expressions, posed expressions, or weak expressions[46] would not be useful. The proper role of the pictures is to activate one's affectivity and not to be merely "a still photograph on the page of a book." A given emotion should be unavoidably expressed on each picture. Participants in the training will "respond with emotion to emotion"[47] as far as it is possible within their relationship to a pictured person. Of course, this relationship is limited to the time set by the trainer. Although the relationship is one-sided, it is sufficient to affect the process of identifying emotions in participants. Of course, identification of emotions can be limited for subjective and objective reasons. To diminish the objective reasons for the training aims, it is important to select expressive faces.

The most important limitations in identifying facial expressions have been called by Ekman:

> No one knows exactly what message we get automatically when we see someone's facial expression. [...] Or we may feel the appropriate emotion, but we show it in the wrong way. [...] We share some triggers, just as we share the expressions for each emotion, but there are triggers that are not only culture-specific, they are individual specific. [...] It is important to remember that emotional signals do not tell us their source. [...] Some people have very subtle signs of how they feel [...] while another aspect is how clearly we signal others how we are feeling.[48]

Thus, being confronted with someone else's actual emotional behaviour does not provide a full foundation for recognizing emotions. Within such superficial relationships, others' actions and verbal expressions cannot be observed repeatedly to gain information about emotional states. How we understand facial and vocal expressions often creates the only foundation we are equipped with to make moral judgments and decisions. It drives our behaviour. This may occur in an unconscious, uncontrolled, unreflective way, or alternatively in a conscious, reflective, more intentional, attentive, and rational

[46] Ibidem, p. 102.

[47] Ibidem, p. 92.

[48] P. Ekman, *Emotions Revealed...*, op. cit., pp. 13, 17, 57.

way. Within demanding social situations the second way is preferred. In the training reported below, pictures of facial expressions suggesting ambiguous interpretations have been avoided. Advanced training would be needed to learn to recognize them, which is possible, Ekman states. I propose a first-step training course with a guided reflection component on the basic emotions that can increase "emotional behaviour awareness"[49] in participants.

The training I developed has been inspired by Selman's "clinical-affective approaches,"[50] Ekman's emotion research and multimedia training,[51] and S. Baron-Cohen's multimedia training.[52] In the philosophical part of the training, three sets of questions have been developed: the phenomenological, hermeneutical, and analytical. Inspiration came from authors working with E. Martens' Five-Finger Method[53] because it offers efficient instruments to facilitate the phenomenological, hermeneutical, analytical (and other kinds of) reflection in participants. They are treated as members of the "community of inquiry." Some questions used to facilitate the taking of an interpersonal perspective by participants relate to Selman's questionnaires.[54] Phenomenological questions let us examine how exactly participants perceived the facial features of the pictured persons. They also facilitate identifying the emotions. According to Ekman's suggestion that one has to learn others' facial or bodily expressions to recognize his or her emotions more easily and widely, stimulation through questions and providing time for contemplating and processing are recommended. Showing photographs offers more time for participants than showing movies. This is important if attentiveness as "knowing that one is emotional"[55] has to be strengthened. Real-life experiences do not always offer such learning opportunities. A sample set of phenomenological questions:

– What can you see in the picture?

– What do you notice about the features of the pictured face? (The next questions are generated by the participants, and the instructor must attentively follow them and involve them in the session).

---

[49] Ibidem, p. 221.

[50] Ibidem, pp. 244–263.

[51] P. Ekman, *Emotion in the Human Face – Guidelines for Research and an Integration of Findings*, New York 1972; idem, "Facial Expressions of Emotion: New Findings, New Questions," *Psychological Science*, 1992, no. 3, pp. 34–38.

[52] S. Baron-Cohen et al., *Mind Reading. Emotions Library*, op. cit. The researcher engaged 6 professional actors to illustrate 412 human emotions through their faces, voices, and narratives.

[53] See E. Marsal, "A German Framework for Philosophizing with Children. The Five Finger Method Model of Ekkehard Martens," in E. Marsal, T. Dobashi, B. Weber (eds.), *Children Philosophize Worldwide. Theoretical and Practical Concepts*, Peter Lang, Frankfurt am Main – Berlin – Bruxelles – New York – Oxford – Wien 2009, pp. 503–512.

[54] Cf. R. L. Selman, *The Growth of Interpersonal Understanding*, op. cit.

[55] P. Ekman, *Emotions Revealed...*, op. cit., p. 78.

– What about the mouth, lip corners, eyebrows, eyelids...?

– What about how his/her eyes look? Are the eyes moistened? (e.g., in Picture 2, showing sadness).

– Let us imitate (mirror) the main features of the pictured faces (participants may start to share emotional states with the pictured persons).[56]

Hermeneutical questions have been used to decode the meaning of feelings and personal emotional states that participants have perceived, identified, and interpreted. By applying hermeneutical reflection to the facial expressions, one can foster the process of understanding, construction, and interpretation of the meaning of emotions.

A sample set of hermeneutical questions:

– What does this face express?

– How sure are you that it is the feeling of...?

– Please identify the facial and bodily signals of sadness (Picture 1), joy or amusement (Picture 2), fear (Picture 3), curiosity (Picture 4), frustration (Picture 5), surprising (Picture 6), etc.

– Have you ever seen such a facial expression?

– Can the identified feelings tell us anything of their sources?

– Can words be helpful to express feelings? Say they do so more than feelings about human condition?

Analytical questions are asked to stimulate participants to reflect on the already identified emotional states and to provide adequate verbal articulation of the emotions. Self-correction of verbal expressions and the "social-cognitive tutoring" (Selman) are conducted in this session. Participants have an opportunity to verify their constructions about feelings, and to learn skepticism by making judgments about other people's emotional condition. In this part of training, elements of Selman's[57] method were inspiring. In the section on joy, Ekman's research findings concerning actual joy, *Duchenne smile*, have been adapted in order to make participants sensitive to the truth revealed by facial movements that are typical for joy.

A sample set of analytical questions:

– Can we understand how other person feels? How good?

– Did you find accurate words to describe the feelings of the pictured person?

– Does smiling always mean enjoyment? Is it always true?

– Can smile be confusing? When can it be so?

– What is easier: describing how we feel or how others feel?

– How important is it to recognize emotions in others adequately?

---

[56] Ibidem, p. 135.

[57] R. L. Selman, *The Growth of Interpersonal Understanding*, op. cit., pp. 244–263.

– Can we better cope with interpersonal problems if we are aware of how others feel?

Self-evaluation questions:

– What was interesting about the feelings and their facial expressions?

– Are feelings important within interpersonal relationships? Why is this so?

– Imagine that there are no feelings and emotions in the world. What would happen to people?

Section: Pupils (N = 28, 12 year old)

The full training session has been offered to pupils at the age of 12 years. In the beginning children were fully impressed and became silent. This means, they became open to experiencing other human beings. They needed time to find words to express their experiences. Some of them needed more time to identify, in particular, the expressions from faces coming from another ethnic contexts. According to Ekman, media offers opportunities to be confronted with facial and bodily expressions or persons representing other cultures and ethnic groups, but Polish media still offers relatively few. Yet Polish society is not as multi-ethnic as are other European countries. Children have few opportunities for multi-ethnic or interracial interpersonal relations with peers. This was, in my eyes, why participants in my session needed more time to become familiar with the pictured faces. Moreover, for some reason, it is not easy to identify another person's emotions by following their facial expressions only.

Participants initially formulated judgments constructed as follows: "This person feels good/not good." After each question, they identified, evaluated, and described the emotional states of the pictured persons. They seemed to do a "reflective appraising"[58] with the pictures. Children adequately answered phenomenological, hermeneutical, and analytical questions. They were able to guess emotional states from all the pictured faces, to reflect on them, and to make judgments about the pictured persons that seemed to be guided by emotional states they earlier recognized and (partially) shared with the pictured persons. They showed mature judgmental behavior. Nevertheless, at the age of puberty, the ability to identify another's emotional state is still developing. But it may be underdeveloped in adults and developed enough in children; social experiences and supportive learning opportunities instead of age factor are deciding here. This ability is more than an affective responding to another's emotional states with similar emotional states. Complex cognitive operations

[58] Ibidem, p. 25.

are required to interpret human emotions, their personal and social contexts.[59] Finally, we changed to a picture of plants with the children, allowing them about minute to contemplate this last, very special picture of dark roses. "The roses put down their heads from sadness... because they are dying," they claimed. The mood in the group changed, according to the picture.

Section: Teachers (N = 36, 26–60 year old teachers, 70% active teachers, 30% students of faculty of pedagogy and ethics)

The same programme has been conducted with a teachers' group studying as post-graduates at one of the Polish universities. After being instructed by the first phenomenological questions, participants immediately began to interpret the facial expressions shown in the photos. However, the participants did not provide proper descriptions. They viewed each picture only briefly and constructed complex, sophisticated stories about the pictured persons' mental condition, moral intentions, personal problems, etc. In the participants' judgments, actual observations have been somehow replaced by prejudices, beliefs, and ready-made answers they had attained from handbooks or literature. They seemed to pay more attention to details like clothes and other circumstances than to a children's facial expressions. Then I offered participants additional time to consider the pictured faces again and to respond with emotion to emotion, without speaking for a period of 3–5 minutes. This exercise was repeated four times. Participants slowly learned to stop reporting on their theories and, instead, to start to identify emotional states of the pictured persons. Over 70% of participants identified the pictured children's expressions, but their answers were wrong. Some of them signaled their uncertainty about whether their interpretation was right. For example, when looking at the faces expressing sadness, fear, embarrassment, or even excitement, participants showed their mistrust and identified them mostly as "morally negative" or "destructive" (by following the original expressions) emotions like anger, aggression, or arrogance. Some of participants suddenly began to react highly emotionally with the "aggression" they believed to have recognize. This is in accordance with Ekman's research findings demonstrating that being confronted with another's aggression may evoke aggression in the beholder. "Anger is the most dangerous emotion to others,"[60] he claims. Why did participants recognize anger in the facial expressions of young persons in the pictures? Maybe because some

---

[59] J. Moll, R. de Oliveira-Souza, R. Zahn, J. Grafman, "The Cognitive Neuroscience of Moral Emotions," in W. Sinnot-Armstrong (ed.), *Moral Psychology*, Cambridge, MA – London 2008, pp. 1–17.

[60] P. Ekman, *Emotions Revealed...*, op. cit., p. 142.

of the people were photographed while learning, thinking, or finding an issue difficult. As Ekman clarifies, some people use similar facial signals (for example: lips pressed together, brows drawn together, tensed lower eyelids, etc.) as a sign of concentration and thinking, "while in other people it is a frequent mannerism."[61] So in the mind of the beholder, concentration in pupils' faces might be associated with slight anger. A hooded man's photo provoked irritations because hoods are frequently considered as a stereotypical accessory of hooligans, terrorists, and "bad guys." Only a photo of happy teenager was not confusing by most of the participants.

Surprisingly to me, the training revealed a higher level of socio-emotional cognition in students than in teachers.[62] In a school community, one of a teacher's tasks is to establish an atmosphere of mutual trust and understanding, which is highly supportive of the learning and teaching process. Teachers' professional experience in creating supportive relationships needs to be strengthened in each country. After having completed the courses (including the training) with the group of teachers, I was frequently asked for similar training courses addressed to new groups. In sum, the training described above enabled us to consider a hypothesis about pluralistic ignorance concerning human emotions from a new perspective. Despite the psychological theories, for members of an educational community the ability of attentiveness and correct identification of others' facial and bodily expressions seems to have a strong impact on the quality of social relations, on the effectiveness of education, and last but not least, on the moral judgments people make about one another.

---

61 Ibidem, p. 141.

62 R.L. Selman, *The Growth of Interpersonal Understanding*, op. cit., p. 261.

Chapter II

Normative dissonance vs. the order of argumentation[1]

1. The social need for validity and arguing

"How to educate citizens in critical adherence when as citizens they are never in the position of engendering the political sphere of themselves?"[2] P. Ricoeur is correct that as citizens of a self-founding democracy we are deficient with respect to argumentative abilities. Instead of solving practical problems together and seeking comprehensive, rational argumentation, people adopt the strategies and semantics of domination from politicians and pragmatists,[3] together with the habit of making arbitrary decisions. Because of this, vertical, hierarchical, and unilateral channels of pressure exerted by political authorities change, in a democracy, into a network of microcapillaries, in Michel Foucault's terms. Mutual pressure flows through them and a permanent *agon* weakens and slows down individuals in their striving toward consensus. With certain practical decisions individuals remain isolated because they lack reflective and argumentative competence. In particular, professionals in certain decision contexts, such as applied medical sciences, are isolated when forming practi-

---

[1] The author is grateful for permission to publish this paper in extended version by P. Orlik and K. Przybyszewski (eds.). The paper first appeared in their volume *Filozofia a sfera publiczna* [Philosophy and a Public Sphere], Poznan 2012, pp. 141–159.

[2] P. Ricoeur, *Critique and Conviction*, transl. K. Blamey, New York 1998, p. 102.

[3] Cf. M. Brugidou, "Argumentation and Values: An Analysis of Ordinary Political Competence via an Open-Ended Question," *International Journal of Public Opinion Research*, 2003, vol. 15 (4), pp. 413–430; W. Outhwaite, *Habermas. A Critical Introduction*, 2nd edition, Stanford, CA 2009.

cal judgments. On the one hand, these contexts may contain new practical challenges and moral dilemmas; on the other hand, there might continue to be a lack of legal regulations and ethical codes of conduct, as is the case with bioethics law in Poland. In such a situation, the agents making decisions refer to their own moral or cultural axiologies and their private consciences. Instead, what is not subjective and open to collegial decision making is reflective and argumentative competence – i.e., reflective and argumentative cognition. This competence needs to be strengthened by offering professionals tools, typologies, and samples of argumentation that could be instructive if one is interested in learning how to make well-argued and valid practical decisions in demanding, or even risky, contexts.

Why are personal axiologies not the proper tool of for argumentation and validity? If the validity of the results of social discourse is not relative to cultural values, what are contemporary social discourses based on? "The type of validity claim attached to cultural values does not transcend local boundaries in the same way as truth and rightness claims."[4] Values are not the proper objects of deliberation and universalization; they belong solely to life forms. Social discourses are "oriented to achieving, sustaining and reviewing consensus – and indeed a consensus that rests on the intersubjective recognition of criticizable validity claims."[5] According to H. Joas,

> Discourse ethics is characterized by a sharp distinction between values and norms and by the view that moral objectivity can be reached on the level of norms, but not on the level of values. Norms, according to Habermas and Apel, can take on the character of universally valid statements of obligation, but values are said to remain in the necessarily subjective and contingent sphere of individual or collective commitments.[6]

Normative argumentation should be relatively independent from culture-related axiology (it can never be fully independent) so that deliberation and social will formation can reach conclusive and universal solutions in spite of particularisms and axiological differences, while at the same time not diminishing anyone's rights to realize specifically defined values in a particular life form context. Because the discussion here concerns pluralistic contexts of decision-

---

[4] J. Habermas, *The Theory of Communicative Action*, vol. 1, transl. T. McCarthy, Boston 1983, p. 42.

[5] Ibidem, p. 17; see also J. Habermas, "Werte und Normen. Ein Kommentar zu Hilary Putnams Kantischem Pragmatismus," in M. L. Raters, M. Willaschek (eds.), *Hilary Putnam und die Tradition des Pragmatismus*, Frankfurt am Main 2002, pp. 280–305.

[6] H. Joas, "Values versus Norms. A Pragmatist Account of Moral Objectivity," *The Hedgehog Review*, 2000, Fall 01, p. 44. Retrieved from http://www.iasc-culture.org/THR/archives/Pragmatism/3.3EJoas.pdf [15.05.2013].

making, the available tools of argumentation must be differentiated according to rank, and decision making subjects must be able to recognize and distinguish the rank of arguments. In this study I consider sets of argumentation exhausting two models of reasoning: normative and normative-procedural. Deliberation related to the two models takes place in particular institutions which make decisions regarding social life, and the objective of that deliberation is to gather a set of arguments and order them according to the two models. None of the models precludes the existence of other typologies of normative argumentation. They only indicate that typologies are possible, supportive, and socially useful.

When we state that one practical rule should be preferred over another, we can free our statement from arbitrariness in only one way: by arguing with all participants of the discourse and gaining their potential approval. Approval is the source of legitimacy – i.e., the *relative* validity of judgments and normative decisions, which in turn can be addressed to many entities as judgments that are shared and approved by a multitude of entities (the judgments then cease to be mere opinions). A true judgment and a valid judgment are not the same; there is no direct connection between them. A valid judgement requires agreement from all relates; a true judgement must be shared by all relates (everyone must "hold a thing to be true," in Kant's words) because the truth cannot be transferred. It is, on the one hand, based on the agreement between a subjective judgment and its object, and, on the other hand, on mutual agreement. In his *Critique of Pure Reason*, Kant clarifies why a universal truth cannot be achieved within a discourse:

> The holding of a thing to be true is a phenomenon in our understanding which may rest on objective grounds, but requires also subjective causes in the mind of the person judging. If a judgement is valid for every rational being, then its ground is objectively sufficient, and it is termed a conviction. If, on the other hand, it has its ground in the particular character of the subject, it is termed a persuasion [...]. Hence a judgement of this kind has only private validity – is only valid for the individual who judges, and the holding of a thing to be true in this way cannot be communicated. But truth depends upon agreement with the object, and consequently the judgements of all understandings if true, must be in agreement with each other [...]. Opinion is a consciously insufficient judgement, subjectively as well as objectively. Belief is subjectively sufficient, but is recognized as being objectively insufficient. Knowledge is both subjectively and objectively sufficient. Subjective sufficiency is termed conviction (for myself); objective sufficiency is termed certainty (for all). I need not dwell longer on the explanation of such simple conceptions [...].[7]

[7] I. Kant, *The Critique of Pure Reason*, transl. J. M. B. Meiklejohn, Pennsylvania 2010. Retrieved from http://www2.hn.psu.edu/faculty/jmanis/kant/Critique-Pure-Reason.pdf [15.05.2013].

Let us conclude Kant's passage with Habermas' claim: "The universality of the claim to truth is an illusion; what is accepted as true at any given time is a matter of convention."[8] If, indeed, one cannot seek justifications either in political power or in universal cultural values and absolute truth, "a considerable burden of proof is placed upon the theory of argumentation; it has to be in a position to specify a 'system of validity claims'"[9] instead of truth claims. Truth, however, is still the key criterion for expressing personal intentions and constructing statements that are "true" and "right," or at least are approximating the truth within communicative action (i.e., the "value-orientation implicated by the speech act"[10] that is a preparatory task to starting interpersonal discourse). In the argumentation context, the notion of truth is still a relevant criterion if the opponents strive with solidarity to reach a consensus that is, according to Habermas, synonymous with the truth established throughfully-inclusive and free argumentation discourse. "In argumentation, proponents and opponents engage in a 'competition with arguments' in order to convince one another, that is, in order to reach a consensus. This dialectical role structure makes forms of disputation available for a cooperative search for truth."[11] In his *Theory of Communicative Action*, Habermas adds: a "criticizable validity claim derives from an assimilation of the truth of statements to the validity of norms [...]."[12]

In applied sciences, in particular in medical research, prescriptive judgments are formed. But are they elaborated in a cooperative and discursive way? Do doctors and patients, presupposing they are engaged in a deliberative model of doctor-patient relationship, participate in the same way in the mutually truthful and collaborative search for truth, or more precisely, for the right clinical recommendations? Both participants can propose "truthful intentional expressions" but only one of them is a professional, with the second advancing "intuitive evaluations" basing on "pretheoretical knowledge," as Habermas puts it. Doctors and patients do not share "universal capabilities" – i.e., "a general cognitive, linguistic, or interactive competence"[13] – so their speech actions are not consensual. Sometimes they relate to different normative backgrounds

---

[8] J. Habermas, *The Theory of Communicative Action*, vol. 1, op. cit., p. 126.

[9] Ibidem, p. 38.

[10] L. Kohlberg, *Essays on Moral Development*, vol. II: *The Psychology of Moral Development*, San Francisco 1984, p. 377; compare J. Habermas, *Communication and the Evolution of Society*, transl. T. McCarthy, Boston 1979, pp. 3–6.

[11] J. Habermas, *Moral Conciousness and Communicative Action*, transl. Ch. Lenhardt, S.W. Nicholsen, introduced by T. McCarthy, Cambridge, MA 1990, p. 160.

[12] J. Habermas, *The Theory of Communicative Action*, vol. 2, transl. T. McCarthy, Boston 1981, p. 70.

[13] J. Habermas, *Communication and the Evolution of Society*, op. cit., pp. 3–4.

too. Furthermore, clinical or therapeutic prescriptions cannot achieve validity before being applied and before their implications can be experienced. Thus, their validity (rightness) depends on the empirical efficiency (from descriptive statements) and, partially, on the right diagnostics (descriptive statements, too). But clinical decisions and prescriptions are made prior to this, in a high-risk space. Their validity is in the professionals' pragmatic hands.[14] This is a much more difficult situation than that of making a sentence valid during a trial, which is in a judge's hands[15] because he or she is applying objective legal norms.

In order to achieve argumentative legitimacy of clinical judgments in medical professions, ethics can be helpful in working out new, so far nonexistent, tools of argumentation and decision making procedures. Numerous clinical prescriptions are made within new and risky situations by way of insufficient argumentation. The public health care system, even as it is based on potentially dependable experiences and their consequences, which constitute the touchstone of the rightness of judgments, cannot allow fully "monologously"[16] made clinical decisions. Surgeons and therapists cannot justify their decisions using only morality, or culture-related axiologies not subject to deliberation (this in the critical tradition, as a result of the separation of norms and values proclaimed by Habermas and Joas). In the medical profession, however, argumentative discourse is mostly replaced by ethical codes of conduct and collegial proceduralism. Ethical codes promote universally recognized axiologies combined with various intrinsic medical values and procedures. In the medical professions, K. Helkama indicates that, referring to the Finnish Code of Medical Ethics,

> [...] professionalism could be seen as an implicit contract between the profession [including intrinsic medical values] and society [i.e., a set of values that are highly

[14] I. Kant describes a similar case in his *Critique of Pure Reason*, op. cit., p. 546: "The physician must pursue some course in the case of a patient who is in danger, but is ignorant of the nature of the disease. He observes the symptoms, and concludes, according to the best of his judgement, that it is a case of phthisis. His belief is, even in his own judgement, only contingent: another man might, perhaps come nearer the truth. Such a belief, contingent indeed, but still forming the ground of the actual use of means for the attainment of certain ends, I term pragmatical belief."

[15] Cf. J. Habermas, *The Theory of Communicative Action*, op. cit.; W. Outhwaite, *Habermas. A Critical Introduction*, op. cit.

[16] Biotechnological development called the decision making sovereignty of physicians into question, David R. Rothman suggests. "Physicians turned to a lay commitee because they realized that the traditional medical ethic of each doctor doing everything possible to enhance the well-being of the particular patient could not operate in these circumstances," the author explains. D.R. Rothman, *Strangers at the Bedside. A History of How Law and Bioethics Transformed Medical Decision Making*, New York 1991, pp. 149–151.

estimated in a society]: the profession commits itself to high ethical principles and the society guarantees the status of the profession.[17]

This implies exchange and the equilibrium between professionals and laypeople or, as K. Wunder claims, an intersection between the "inner circle" (directly involved professionals) and the "outer circle"[18] (experts, ethicists, etc.).

Even when not being confronted with new challenges and risky decision contexts, it seems effective to strengthen argumentative competencies in those areas of practice in which new problems arise that require urgent and ethically legitimate decisions, and to develop a moral and procedural consciousness that can form the basis for the ability to argue. Making decisions of this kind is usually the responsibility of expert collegial bodies, individual experts, and managers of institutes, teams, and research projects. It is impossible to avoid them, in particular when confronting new problems and dilemmas for which there are no legal or intra-institutional regulations yet developed (social practice and progress are always ahead of legislative processes[19]). In order to be able to make risky decisions and carry the burden of responsibility for it, experts must hone their ability to argue in a rational manner. That ability comprises such competences (in Habermas: attitudes) as differentiating arguments on the basis of their weight, or – in Habermas' words – rational force: "In discourse what is called the *force* of the better argument is wholly unforced. Here convictions change internally via a process of rationally motivated attitude change."[20] The consideration of an exhaustive number of arguments *for* and *against*, independently of one's own particular beliefs;[21] an analysis of the con-

---

[17] From the Finnish Medical Ethics Textbook, K. Helkama, *Change in Moral Judgment in Medical School*, in E. Nowak, D. Schrader, B. Zizek (eds.), *Educating Competencies for Democracy*, Frankfurt am Main 2013, p. 98.

[18] K. Wunder, *How Ethical Standards Can Be Put Into Practice: Ethical Decision Making in Neonatology Intensive Care.* Paper presented at the 7th International Symposium Moral Competence and Behavior, on 25–26.06.2013, Konstanz (Germany).

[19] Cf. G. Radbruch, *Rechtsphilosophie*, eds. R. Dreier, S. L. Paulson, Heidelberg 2003.

[20] J. Habermas, *Moral Consciousness and Communicative Action*, op. cit., p. 160.

[21] Fairness in the meaning of the quality of a discourse demands arguing *fully and completely* for and against, i.e., having a so-called dispute, (a) independently of our personal moral beliefs, and frequently against them, and (b) independently (and frequently against) the moral beliefs of the discourse participants (or their representatives) who will be impacted by the judgment. An example of an (a) type situation is the situation of a physician who considers performing an abortion and is personally attached to a definite axiological/ideological/confessional option, and an example of a (b) type situation is that of a physician who considers a blood transfusion for a Jehova's Witnesses' child. In both cases it is the task of a discourse to successively broaden the argumentation so as to put aside the axiological convictions of the participants of the decision-making process and to arrive at reasoning more universal than the reasoning marked by the rationales of both sides. Fairness is required, among other areas, in rabbinical

sequences of the accepted (or rejected) judgement from all agents' points of view (the so-called *perspective-taking competence*[22]), on a short and long-term basis; and finally, following the principle of the highest level of reasoning, regarding which Kohlberg, Habermas, and Outhwaite agree that "a higher level is preferred as more 'objective' or more 'adequate' because of particular moral criteria"[23] – i.e., criteria that make, in fact, the claims of validity.

Concluding the introductory remarks, I would like to note that the democratization of social life can proceed from the bottom up if we strengthen the ability to argue, targeting the areas of practice in need of rational-discursive cooperation for the sake of achieving the best-argued decisions. In the technologically and culturally expanding world, especially in the young and educationally deficient Polish democracy, appropriate professional groups will most probably have to assume responsibility for risky but inevitable decisions concerning the practical use of scientific and technical achievements. Intra-institutional regulations and independent ethical committees will assist the professionals on condition that they continue to increase their normative-procedural consciousness.

2. Moral dilemmas and decision making

A moral dilemma[24] is an axiological or normative conflict with the following properties:

exegesis and judges' ethics. As I will demonstrate later on, the psychology of a moral judgment refers here to Habermas' statement that the greatest trial of human democratic competences is a confrontation with our enemy's arguments or opinions and the ability to adequately evaluate their axiological quality. As regards axiology, pro and counter arguments must be of equalized strength, cf. G. Lind, *Moral ist lehrbar. Handbuch zur Theorie und Praxis moralischer und demokratischer Bildung*, 2nd updated edition, München 2009.

[22] Cf. R. L. Selman, *The Growth of Interpersonal Understanding*, New York – London – Toronto – Sydney – San Francisco 1980.

[23] W. Outhwaite, *Habermas. A Critical Introduction*, op. cit., p. 50.

[24] Not every controversy, conflict, or either-or alternative is a proper moral dilemma. Not all dilemmas are of a moral nature. Some of them remain unrecognized – people perceive and become conscious of dilemmatic issues in varying degrees. Many morally sensitive people attempt to solve a dilemma by disqualifying one of the options as wholly useless. This is because, as Plato and Kohlberg pointed out, the human mind strives at innert consistency and harmony between value-related options. There are also false dilemmas: "to be or not to be," "to do or not to do," "good or evil," and other, rather banal choices between something and a lack of something, positing and negating, etc. Some of them have a technical solution; e.g., the alternative "to do or not to do" can be solved by postponing an activity until a later, more convenient moment.

1. A decision-making agent recognizes a choice of two possible solutions to a problem and experiences cognitive dissonance.

2. The choice is inevitable and urgent.

3. There is no third solution which would save the entity the choice.

4. None of the solutions is absolutely right.

5. The entity bears social responsibility for the solution.

6. The entity can only choose one of the two solutions.

7. Each of the two available solutions has a strong justification in social rules.

8. Each of the available solutions raises strong moral controversies because it entails breaking social (moral, legal, or cultural) norms; moreover, the cancellation of values and rules justifies the choice of the other, unselected solution.

9. From the moment of recognizing and becoming conscious of the "dilemmatic character" of an issue, through cognitive processing of the short and long-term consequences of the choice, to the moment of articulating the decision, the entity experiences normative dissonance on the cognitive level – i.e., he or she is confronted with contradictory contents and moral judgments, arguments, rules, and ideals.

10. From the beginning to the end of the decision-making process, the entity faced with a moral dilemma experiences contradictory feelings and emotions. This shows that the decisive problem (context) engages the decision-making entity on the level of internal moral principles, ideals, and beliefs important to that person.

In everyday life, principles, values, and virtues may collide. The human mind strives for moral consistency and demands, at the same time, ordering preferences hierarchically, free of contradictions. This culturally strengthened ordering-tendency seems to be responsible for creating regulative systems too.[25] Certain norms developed by human reason show high universality; for example, Aristotle's golden rule and Kant's categorical imperatives, whose usefulness lies in seeking right maxims and performance ways, have been proven in ethics. But humans still do not have principles that are helpful in solving dilemmas. What happens when a decision-making agent tries to make decisions in agreement with his or her internal principles or values, but they collide? Individual moral sensitivity allows for the experience of varying degrees of normative dissonance. Some people do not hesitate to pick one or the other option, claiming that the decision is obvious, while others feel ashamed of

---

[25] L. Kohlberg, *Essays on Moral Development*, vol. II: *The Psychology of Moral Development*, op. cit.

their "inability to accurately point to the final solution."[26] Meanwhile, a moral dilemma is such precisely because it does not have a final solution. Other participants, when confronted with a dilemma, hesitate long before evaluating the protagonist's decision, and upon making a choice experience discomfort related to the evaluation and its consequences for a longer period of time. Another group of people try their best to abstain from making a choice and do not "get into the protagonist's skin," even when the discussion is about a semi-real social dilemma. "The dilemma is in the eyes of the beholder,"[27] and a number of observations point to the fact that decision-making in a dilemma situation is a huge challenge for an individual's competence in forming moral judgments and inevitably leads to a sense of responsibility. The practical use of scientific and technical achievements generates many, yet unknown dilemmas. They usually involve important and complex controversies with long-term social ramifications. Habermas emphasizes that although a person can change professions and "distance oneself from the institutions of the social world [...] it is impossible to distance oneself from values."[28] In some professions responsibility for difficult choices and risky decisions are unavoidable. Scientist have one advantage over non-scientists, namely, that they have at their disposal the newest knowledge, discoveries, and technologies. As scientists (and in the case of applied sciences, whole societies) gain knowledge about developing technologies, and especially as they put these into practice, they are confronted with ever new ethical problems. In order to make decisions in a justified manner, with correct risk evaluation – that is, in order to cope with normative controversies – a scientist should learn to problematize troubling issues in a variety of ways, from the level of facts to the level of norms and meta-normative criteria. This will allow him or her to skillfully form reasons or arguments with different strengths, appropriate to a given situation and the social importance of the problem. To realize how varied the strength of arguments can be, it is sufficient to form three arguments for or against a decision and ask other people which of them they consider to be inconclusive (weak), moderately conclusive (medium-strength), and the most conclusive (very strong, decisive). While preparing for difficult decision-making, it is worth classifying the best available knowledge about the topic – both normative and procedural – differentiating arguments with respect to their quality

[26] To quote from participants of the discussion conducted by the author according to the Konstanz Method of Dilemma Discussion with the view to foster moral judgment competence).

[27] G. Lind, *Moral ist lehrbar...*, op. cit.

[28] J. Habermas, "Philosophical Notes on Moral Judgment Theory," in G. Lind, H. A. Hartman, R. Wakenhut (eds.), *Moral Judgments and Social Education*, New Brunswick – London 2010, p. 9.

(strength). This will allow us to argue in a comprehensible manner, precisely, and in a way that allows, if not achieves, democratic legitimacy. We could then at least obtain validation for new, difficult decisions that evoke strong emotions in society when knowledge and technology are about to be used to solve important individual or social problems. Ethics has at its disposal tools which assist in such ordering. They allow us to work out argumentative typologies that are more inclusive than the classical theories of intention, utilitarianism of goods and preferences, contractualism, consequentialism, etc. The reflection of contemporary ethics is situated at the boundaries of practices requiring normative justification, forming a bridge between the areas of duties and of practical needs.[29] It responds, in a way, with the *supply* of norm-creating tools, to the *deficiency* of normative regulations that persists especially in the areas in which scientific and technical innovations are used. Ethicists can propose more if they are ready to cross between ethical reflection and the related research problems. I would like to show the work of an ethicist, understood in such a way, using a case involving resocialization, neurodiagnostics, and neurosurgery. It is a semi-real case (the situation and the dilemma are real, although the protagonists are fictitious). In order to emphasize the supra-cultural, universal character of the case description I will remove it from its ideological context. Its different variants are currently being discussed all over the world: the possibility of "adjusting" criminal offenders by causing a permanent dysfunction in the part of the brain cortex responsible for misunderstanding, disrespecting, and persistently breaking basic social rules. In order for the system to do more than penalize, isolate, and inefficiently rehabilitate such people, ethicists have considered the possibility of returning the offenders to society with the help of new methods discovered by science. Societies face a dilemma: exclude or include these methods?

> Erroneous interpretations, i.e. disturbances on the level of reflexive internalizing of social practices, generate individual and collective ways of performing which hinder the participation in a social process. That is because people who cannot adequately grasp the normative meaning of socially institutionalized practices isolate themselves from the rest of society which integrates itself by mastering all forms of mutual recognition.[30]

---

[29] And sometimes even reversing the traditional primacy of duty over being, and deriving the former from actual social practices in such a manner as if Hegelian phenomenology had priority over Kantian pure deontology, which has been organizing normative ethics for over two hundred years while also separating it from social context, as argued by A. Honneth in his newest, provocative book *Das Recht der Freiheit*, Berlin 2011.

[30] Ibidem, p. 206.

Modern society cannot get rid of the problem just through isolation and exclusion. It has to educate, re-educate, and re-adjust to social life those individuals whom it had previously deprived of proper education; when that is impossible for objective reasons, it has to consider regulations that would enable the use of the scientific methods.

Later in the chapter I will present sample scales of argumentation together with the criteria for evaluating the degree to which an argumentative order can strengthen the normative self-consciousness of a contemporary scientist and help him or her make risky decisions. When doing so, I will share textbook criteria, such as good intentions.[31] Although the road to hell is paved with good intentions, as the saying goes, ethicists would not want to throw the researchers who use their discoveries in institutionalized social practice on such a road.

3. Case study: Neurosurgeon's decision

Dr. Scott manages a renowned team of neurosurgeons and has made discoveries about the sources of aggression. He is studying the inmates of a youth correctional facility. In one inmate's verdict the following justification for punishment is provided: *The offender was raised in an orphanage. He hurts his victims in a particularly cruel, emotionless manner. The violation of rules does not evoke any interest in him, he shows judgmental indifferent behavior.*

While studying those documents, Dr. Scott suspects that it is a case of proactive aggression.[32] He wants to have certainty, though. He watches the patient's brain many times on the screen. He performs several brain imaging

[31] In his *Psychology of Moral Development* Kohlberg says: "Kleinberger attributes to me the Kantian (and Christian) view that the only thing that counts in evaluating a moral action is the intention or principle that lies behind it, not the consequences, or the ability to foresee the consequences, which determines the good effects of the action upon other people. [...] In fact, I [...] rather hold a modified version in which a distinctively moral judgment is a necessary component of an action judged moral, but it need not to be sufficient for evaluating the morality of an action or actor [...] it is our position that moral judgment is a necessary factor, and other factors are not necessary to the definition of an act as moral." Ibidem, vol. 2, pp. 512–513. Actually, Kohlberg does not represent the Kantian view. "Hence [...], moral judgment principles may not be sufficient for good action or good character." Ibidem, p. 512. Kohlberg promotes judgments as a full expression of moral agency, however, arguments are needed when individuals start to legitimize their judgments in the eyes of other individuals – i.e., when the communicative action and interpersonal discourse occur as the key social institutions in a democracy.

[32] A. Raine, K. Dodge, R. Loeber, L. Gatzke-Kopp, D. Lynam, C. Reynolds, M. Stouthamer-Loeber, J. Liu, "The Reactive–Proactive Aggression Questionnaire: Differential Correlates of Reactive and Proactive Aggression in Adolescent Boys," *Aggressive Behavior*, 2006, vol. 32, pp. 159–171; R. W. Novaco, J. L. Taylor, "Anger and Assaultiveness of Male Forensic Patients

studies on the tomograph. He subjects his patient to a test which evaluates the reaction to drastic pictures of suffering. The pictures do not evoke any reactions in those regions of the cerebral cortex in which in a typical brain of that age should contain both specialized cells and neural networks responsible for evaluation and moral decision making.[33] Neither these areas nor the amygdala (the most important emotion-related area in the brain[34]) are found to be developed in this patient. Moreover, the doctor discovered a local disturbance in the firing process localized between the medial and dorsolateral prefrontal cortex area. Consequently, an emotional response to the pictures of suffering is missing in the young patient. Electric impulses get dispersed instead of reaching their aim – the dorsolateral prefrontal cortex where judgments are made. Even if the patient has any feelings which could stop him from hurting the victims and violate basic rules, the feelings have no impact on either his decisions or his motoric activity. The boy is not able to develop compassion and empathy and so nothing stops him from cruel behaviors. Additionally, impulses dispersed in improper directions create tension in other areas of the brain. That makes the patient nervous.

Dr. Scott knows that the results of numerous studies demonstrate that a deficiency of sensitivity and empathy goes hand in hand with a dysfunction of the prefrontal cortex and amygdala. A teenager with a distinct tendency to such behaviors usually becomes a habitual offender before reaching adulthood. A small but significant percentage of offenders are people with such a tendency, and are described as pathological. Rehabilitation therapies are useless.

Taking all that into account, the doctor thought that it would not be difficult to remove the dysfunction of the medial prefrontal cortex. If the operation is successful and the boy is subjected to a few months of therapy, there would be a strong chance of permanent improvement of his behavior. Moreover, such an operation would be important for the development of neurosurgery and for the future of the physician's research team. However, the doctor hesitates, and all the more so since in his country the law does not yet say anything about these newest possibilities offered by medicine.

---

with Developmental Disabilities: Links to Volatile Parents," *Aggressive Behavior*, 2008, vol. 34, pp. 380–393.

[33] D. Knoch, A. P. Leone, K. Meyer, V. Treyer, E. Fehr, "Diminishing Reciprocal Fairness by Disrupting the Right Prefrontal Cortex," *Science Express*, 5.10.2006. Retrieved from www.sciencexpress.org/5October2006/Page1/10.1126/science.1129156 [12.04.2010]; E. Nowak, A. Urbańska, "Can the Konstanz Method of Dilemma Discussion Support an Emotional-Cognitive Balance in Aggressive Juveniles?," *Journal of Strategy and Decision Making*, October 2011, pp. 77–85.

[34] W. Sinnot-Armstrong (ed.), *Moral Psychology*, vol. III: *The Neuroscience of Morality: Emotion, Brain Disorders, and Development*, Cambridge, MA – London 2008.

The matter, however, is urgent. This morning the doctor was informed that in a few days the boy's group will be directed to a top security prison. The doctor called an anesthesiologist and the operation theater. In two days, at the latest, the boy will be operated on.

*

Why did Dr. Scott hesitate? What had he thought about before making the decision? Before reconstructing the spectrum of arguments for and against the operation, on different levels, let us consider what the argumentation process involves in the first place, and what mistakes we must avoid in order to argue in a comprehensible, clear, and concrete way.

4. What do we do when we argue?

We argue when we share our judgments with others and we participate in the communicative interaction. We may have self-evidence concerning our private judgments. But sometimes we make judgments that address other persons, groups, or institutions, which requires arguments or reasons to make our judgments (or decisions) reasonable, and, finally, to make them valid (or invalid if an opposing argument is deemed stronger). We must be able to deal with others' arguments and counterarguments, too. Arguments are the kind of judgments that must be explicitly based on normative criteria (except when discourse participants try to improve existing normative criteria through post-conventional reasoning, as Habermas describes it in his *Moral Consciousness and Communicative Action*). When confronted with new problems (dilemmas), sufficient criteria are not always accessible in the institutionalized regulatory systems, such as in laws and professional codes of conduct. From the psychological perspective, when we articulate reasons – i.e., statements explaining and justifying, or subverting the rightness of, for example, Dr. Scott's decision – we articulate various intuitive prejudgments which originate in a more or less clear, and thus a gradable, feeling that the decision was or was not right. That feeling could be measured on a rightness scale of, say, –4 to 4 points, and on a difficulty of the decision scale of, say, 0 to 5 points (in such a case the affective, very personal aspect of a moral judgment in sensu Lind and his Moral Judgment Test can be measured[35]). If, however, we want to justify our evaluation of the rightness or wrongness of the decision, we have to form arguments as strong as possible

[35] G. Lind, "The Meaning and Measurement of Moral Judgment Competence. A Dual-Aspect Model," in D. Fasko, Jr., W. Willis (eds.), *Contemporary Philosophical and Psychological Perspectives on Moral Development and Education*, Cresskill, NJ 2008.

for the respective judgments. These arguments will justify our evaluation and they themselves will have a meta-justification in social norms, moral and legal norms, and intra-institutional regulations and procedures. Dr. Scott's patient and his legal guardians, the physician's colleagues from the research team, and observers of the decision-making situation can form very different judgments on the basis of normative criteria with different weights and persuasive power; they will, however, always choose the most valid criteria from those which they can understand and evaluate in an adequate manner.

A difficulty consists in the fact that the dilemma situation presupposes two equally wrong solutions, both of which imply some negative consequences and break some norms or values better supported by the other option. Both operating and not operating on the juvenile offender raises strong controversies. Therefore, the situation requires argumentation of the highest moral quality so as to take the steam out of Dr. Scott's opponents' weaker arguments.

When making such risky decisions we should be able to classify, evaluate, and distinguish among arguments with regard to their rational "power," not to mention adequate application to decision-making and discourse. "The power of arguments" has an ethical advantage over the "argument of power"[36] (Habermas).

5. Hypothetical argumentation scaled with the use of a "six-stages" scale

The pre-conventional level (1–2)

Legitimacy (foundation, source) of rightness is located beyond conventions.

1. Norms, rules, and laws should be abided by because they have been established by a person in a privileged position – an authority – and people who do not abide by them will be punished (orientation toward fear of punishment and toward obedience to the provider of norms).

A sample hypothetical argument for Dr. Scott's neurosurgical intervention: (a) with respect to punishment: *Dr. Scott's team need not fear any punishment from the supervisors for operating on the boy;* (b) with respect to authority: *The authorities of the institution have threatened that if researchers do not patent and implement at least one new therapeutic method a year they will lose their professorial positions.*

[36] To Habermas, argumentation takes place at the meta-level of criteria and procedures that make universal discourse possible too: "Argumentation serves to focus on and test validity claims that are initially raised implicitly in communicative action and are naively carried along with it." J. Habermas, *Moral Consciousness and Communicative Action*, op. cit., p. 178.

2. Norms and rules should be abided by if one gets something in return (orientation toward benefits).

A sample hypothetical argument for the neurosurgical intervention: *Such operations should be performed because they will advance scientists' careers (important publications, points, patents, and grants for further research).*

The conventional level (3–4)

Legitimacy of rightness located in others' expectations or conventions. Norms, rules, and laws should be abided by because other people do so and because they are as they are (orientation toward conformism and/or legal ramifications, legalism).

A sample hypothetical argument for the neurosurgical intervention: (1) With respect to conforming to the expectations of others: *Dr. Scott's operation will certainly be appreciated by his colleagues.* With respect to legal regulations: *As no act of law forbids such operations and there is no bioethics act, the operation can be made.* (2) With respect to the medical code of ethics, the insurance act, and other regulations: *The operation is acceptable.* With respect to intra-institutional regulations: *The operation can be made because a statute of the clinic says that due to the research and development character of the institution, it is permissible to employ new therapeutic methods in medical practice. However, the institution must provide risk insurance against adverse effects for the patient, find an insurance provider for that purpose, and bring about an agreement between the insurance provider and the insured party.*

The post-conventional level (5–6)

Legitimacy of rightness located in the social agreement to norms, in ethical, universalizing values and rules such as justice and the dignity of every person, autonomy, equal rights, and equality legitimized by rational procedures and universalizing reasonings such as the categorical imperative, the golden mean, the veil of ignorance/fairness, maximizing common good (e.g. the quality of life), minimizing damage and suffering, etc. On the post-conventional level there is strict ethical reflection on the principles and practical choices with respect to the necessity of perfecting norms in a democratic culture (social and ethical orientation).

Sample hypothetical arguments for the neurosurgical intervention: (a) With the view to an improvement of the quality of life: *All patients, including prisoners, are entitled to the use of methods available to science.* However, (b) With the view to autonomy and a patient's sense of dignity: *One must obtain the patient's agreement to the operation.*

6. Hypothetical argumentation structured with Georg Lind's pattern of moral judging

In his Moral Judgment Test (MJT), the German moral psychologist, Georg Lind used Kohlberg's six stages model to develop a set of criteria (orientations) that allows us to differentiate and order arguments from the most pre-social and subjective (pre-conventional), through the socially actual and conventionalized, to the post-conventional, which allows people to improve and universalize the still inadequate social conventions. Post-conventional criteria such as the social contract (in Habermas' language: permanent democratic will formation process) and universal, chiefly procedural ethical rules are particularly valid today when the multicultural, secondarily stratified social crucible is boiling with dilemmas, particular claims, and new, burning issues. On the basis of Kohlberg's six stages, Lind created a sequence of arguments for and against the decision made by the protagonist of a dilemma. For each moral dilemma that concluded with a decision it allows one to form 12 arguments (6 pro and 6 counter) concerning the decision. The pro and contra arguments make us aware of the controversial nature of a decision in the situation of a dilemma, much better than Kohlberg's earlier pro argumentation. A dilemma presented in the light of pros and cons appears to be a clearer and, in a pluralistic context, even paradigmatic situation of decision making. The knowledge of Lind's argumentative model can be highly educational for everyone who is frequently confronted with socio-moral dilemmas. It allows for independent evaluation and consideration of the normative weight of the reasons necessary for justifying ethical judgments, regardless of one's own position regarding the dilemma and the decision made in it. Below I give sample arguments for and against neurosurgeon Scott's decision. Readers can evaluate their weight while pausing at each of them to ask themselves how strongly they agree or disagree. Approval and disapproval, as affective aspects of moral judgment, are gradable: arguments can be "weighed" and can "outweigh" one another. Their weight (or validity) can be highly variable from the perspective of the evaluating subject but they built a structure. That exercise enables us to become aware of the strength of many other arguments considered in the context of a given decision. Reflection on a possibly comprehensive set of arguments lets us consider, verify, and distinguish their value. In that way the reflecting participants of a deliberation learn to recognize, appreciate, and take into account new, so far unnoticed or depreciated arguments. By opening themselves to new arguments and subtle, but sometimes socially crucial differences in their weights, people can develop and even change their positions. Convincing one another, which is a frequent topic in the ethics of discourse, is not exhausted by a purely rational exchange of information, as it involves ethically relevant information, and relevance is nothing else but a *feeling* of the strength of an argument applied to our convictions. The process of convincing must, of course, be mediated in discourse and its rational constraints, because it is also aimed at articulating a decision, recording it for a decisive subject, reaching mutual understanding, justifying a decision, and agreeing within a society on their ultimate shape and recognition.

Sample arguments for the performance of the operation by Dr. Scott:

Pre-conventional level:

– No punishment will be leveled at Dr. Scott for performing the operation.

– The physician and his team can receive awards and additional grants for performing the pioneering operation.

Conventional level:

– As his colleagues have already performed similar operations, it is now Dr. Scott's turn.

– The physician is not breaking the law. There is no legal prohibition against neurosurgeries on prisoners for therapeutic purposes.

Post-conventional level:

– As the criminal code does not solve the problem, Dr. Scott is only doing what rationally thinking citizens of a democratic society allow him to do.

– Children who have been victims of fate deserve the opportunity to be included in the social life and to have a dignified human existence.

– Dr. Scott thinks that the patient has been socially disadvantaged by fate, due to the atypical structure and dysfunction of his brain. He deserves to live the life of a conscious, autonomous human being.

"Counter" arguments (sample):

1) Pre-conventional level:

– Dr. Scott is afraid that the Supreme Medical Council will punish him or will hinder his career when it finds out about the operation.

– It does not pay for Dr. Scott to perform the operation or to risk its adverse effects. The patient is not even insured.

2) Conventional level:

– Colleagues and related experts would hold it against Dr. Scott that he decided to perform such an operation.

– Regulations and instructions in the health care system forbid the performance of pioneering operations – they are treated as experiments on humans.

3) Post-conventional level:

– It is better to wait with the operation if neither the patient has agreed to it (the patient is not capable of making such a decision) nor have his legal guardians, and there is no other socially legitimate reason for such an act,

– It is doubtful whether all people with an atypical brain structure should be subjected to neurosurgeries. It is better not to violate the principle of the autonomy and integrity of a human being (Kantian argument).

7. Hypothetical argumentation scaled according to Sonja Wrobel's method

Sonja Wrobel[37] proposed an interesting classification of argumentation in institutional, norm-establishing, and political contexts. I have adapted Wrobel's criteria to a decision-making situation in which a person is making a risky decision, the results of which are socially highly relevant and the space for decision-making is not strictly regulated. In Poland (where there is no act on bioethics) this is not so much the case whenever *new discoveries and technologies are made use of* and legal regulations remain behind the development of such social practices.

Under such legal conditions argumentation must always take into account the following aspects of acting:

1. The objective aspect (What is the situation? What is the state of affairs? What do we have at our disposal?),

2. The performative aspect (Which agents have undertaken which actions? Which actions should be undertaken? What should not be done? What actions should be stopped?),

3. The procedural aspect (The basis for an action; the correctness of the procedure of decision-making; the adherence to the regulations, codes, and policies; the conclusion of an agreement; the issuance of a permit; and the performance of the agreement, authorizations, etc.).

Wrobel applied the aspects mentioned above to five types of argumentation, thus obtaining fifteen variants of argumentation. I have used them all to model sample arguments which should be taken into consideration in neurosurgeon Scott's decision-making situation. Obviously, the discussion which the head of a research team and an employee of a clinic must hold with other entities co-responsible for decision making is not only clinical (diagnostic)

---

[37] S. Wrobel, "Es ist notwendig und wir werden es machen. Basta! Legitimationsstrategien in sozialpolitischen Reformdebatten," in G. Drews-Sylla, E. Dütschke, H. Leontiy, E. Polledri (eds.), *Konstruierte Normalitäten – normale Abweichungen*, Wiesbaden 2010, pp. 243–258.

but also legal-procedural and ethical in nature. One needs to bear in mind the specifics of diagnostic argumentation which is characterized by therapeutic prescriptiveness.[38]

Wrobel assigned the highest rank to *performative* and *procedural* arguments because of *norms* and situation dynamics-related necessity. Her combination of criteria, however, allows the creation of many other precise and valuable arguments for various situations of decision-making.

> The first category of arguments, *factual* in nature, encompasses descriptive statements in an objective meaning, free of value judgments, having the nature of a constitution. They result in a certain, limited number of potential options of acting [something has been done, something has not been done, etc. – E.N.]. An example: the statement that for a few years nothing has been done to advance the reform of social insurance. The second category of arguments of *causal* nature encompasses statements based on the knowledge of causes and effects of particular actions or states of affairs. [...] Causal arguments have greater normative value than factual arguments as they concern particular options of human activity more strictly and clearly. An example: the difficult situation on the job market has for a few years been making the reform of social insurance impossible. [...] The third category of *utilitarian* arguments invokes the benefits which maximize the good or welfare of a given social group, which benefit is to be the aim of the considered regulations, reforms, operations, etc. An example of an argument based on benefit can be the statement that families will profit from social insurance because people who tax themselves together with a spouse will be able to deduct the insurance from the tax. [...] The *explicit normative* arguments in the fourth category are not for a gradual improvement of the existing state of affairs but for achieving a specific ideal, e.g. the ideal of justice. That form of argumentation is close to the highest degree of normativity because the considered regulation is very closely related to the said ideal. [...] Finally, the fifth category comprises arguments based on *necessity*. They have the highest degree of normativity of all five categories. The argument of necessity excludes an alternative for a given action. [...] An example is the statement that demographic growth enforces the introduction of private retirement insurance plans. [...] In the argumentation based on the notion of necessity it is not objectivity but a special argumentation technique that is vital – it allows the adoption of a particular option of action [...] as an option for which no alternative is in sight.[39]

---

[38] L. H. Eckensberger, U. Gähde (eds.), *Ethische Norm und empirische Hypothese*, Frankfurt am Main 1993, p. 285.

[39] Ibidem, pp. 246–247.

Table 1. Argumentation sensu S. Wrobel

The type of argument	The objective aspect (policy)	The performative aspect (politics)	The procedural aspect (policy)
Factual arguments (a description of facts)	Example *In the patient's right prefrontal cortex a dysfunction has been diagnosed which disperses neural impulses to other brain regions.* Example *The patient's brain has atypical structure.*	Example *The neurosurgeon has fully diagnosed the patient, the team has exhibited very high neurosurgical competences on numerous occasions.* Example *The neurosurgeon takes the risk of injuring other tissues which may cause further dysfunctions.*	Example *The ethics committee has given an approval. An agreement has been signed with the patient / his legal guardian. A case conference has been held.* Example *The neurosurgeon made the decision about operating without approval.*
Causal arguments	Example *The operation will contribute to unblocking the flow of neural impulses in the prefrontal cortex and to the development of sensitivity in the patient.*	Example *An assistant who has conducted a simulation of the operation on a scanned image of the brain demonstrated that the operation should not have negative side effects (side-effects probability is law).*	Example *Because of the lack of an insurance policy for the patient the hospital must be prepared for actions for compensation in the case of complications after the operation.*
Utilitarian arguments	Example *The operation is much more beneficial to the patient than penalization.* Example *The operation will facilitate the development of research and technology. Neurosurgeon Scott's team will be able to test their operating techniques, strengthen their scientific position, and gain new research grants. Science and society will benefit.*	Example *Neurosurgeons will use a technology which gives the patient an opportunity to gain full psychomotor skills. The operation will be performed by experienced specialists, at the patient's optimal age (time of fast development of brain cortex) when it will have the greatest therapeutic effects.*	Example *The law allows neurosurgical operations on condition that they return basic psychophysical functions and are not the tool of eugenic engineering.* Example *The penitentiary system, society, and state treasury will save money.*

Normative arguments	Example *A neurosurgeon bears the responsibility for the consequences of the operation, he is motivated by the good of the boy and a sense of duty resulting from the medical code of ethics.*	Example *A neurosurgeon should not take such a great risk knowing that the patient's brain does not have a typical structure.* Example *He should not perform the operation because documented studies have shown that a lack of sensitivity and empathy is caused not only by the area in the prefrontal cortex but also by underdeveloped amygdala etc. There are multiple influences that he is still not aware of. Therefore, an operation will not bring about the expected effects.*	Example *A neurosurgeon should adhere to the medical code of ethics and to international standards of good medical practices. He should obtain written permission for the operation from the patient and inform the patient about all possible effects of the operation.*
Arguments justified by a state of necessity	Example *There is no other solution – the operation is the only opportunity for the underage patient to avoid the fate of a serial killer and for society to avoid the danger.*	Example *The neurosurgeon is the only expert with the necessary qualifications for operating on a patient with such a complex defect.*	Example *As there is no law on bioethics the ethical committee must immediately give an opinion. A meeting should be called on an extraordinary basis.* *It must be verified whether the decision is in agreement with EU law.*

Source: own elaboration (by following Wrobel's criteria).

8. The argument of social responsibility. Conclusions

Because decision-making and executive competences are deployed in a particular fashion in hierarchical institutions, planning the areas of competence would require separate, complex studies. In the case described above, the physician undertakes, on his own authority, efforts aimed at returning another person, his teenage patient, to full self-control and self-responsibility. If he does not make the efforts, the young offender will be repeatedly prosecuted by the court system of a democratic society that is unaware of the fact that resocialization or "repair" of the perpetrator can only be successful if he is capable of being held accountable for his behavior toward other people. That presupposes that the perpetrator has the ability to read, share, and respect other people's feelings, which would prevent him from hurting them. That is why the society, the educational culture of which virtually generates the development of sociopathy and which subjects mentally disabled people to resocialization, will have to consider returning such people to normal social life at some point in the future. A citizen who reacts emotionally to the problem of sociopathy and demands the return of the death penalty can "easily invoke moral abomination or the threat of social stigma, but do you prefer to have blood on your hands because you did not agree to a procedure which could save human life?"[40] – asks J. Fischman. Ethics does not provide ready answers. Neither does it take over citizens' right to rationally co-decide which solutions are the best for the whole, diversified and pluralistic, society. Rather, it is the source of normative tools and argumentative procedures that allows agents to reach their independent conclusions. At least this is what it should look like in a democratic society.

[40] J. Fischman, *Criminal Minds. The Chronicle of Higher Education*, 12.06.2001, http://chronicle.com/article/Can-This-Man-Predict-Whether/127792 [24.05.2013].

Chapter III

Facing otherness as an ethical experiment

> The Other is metaphysical. The Other is not transcendent because he would be free as I am; on the contrary his freedom is a superiority that comes from his very transcendence... If I have no longer have power over him it is because he overflows absolutely every idea I can have of him.
>
> Emmanuel Lévinas[1]

1. The other – the same

An encounter with the other is by far the most difficult challenge for the person who comes to meet this other. The situation of a contact with the other includes the unknown, with which we cannot deal in a routine, learned, and common manner. The unknown is the other him or herself, and is unknown in a scale that is beyond any notion that the mind itself is capable of producing about him or her. This situation is invariably new and surprising – and the more surprising, the more deeply we are confident that we can tame what is strange and different and that we can be in control of it. In this situation ethics is ready to emerge, and happen, and in this situation ethics is an experiment conducted by people who meet one another and start a conversation and a relationship of one kind or another. This is comprehensive, since in leveling hostility and alienation ethics cannot be based on a "imperialism of the same."[2] Relations with the other in his or her impenetrable otherness are, indeed, possible and inevitable, just as the pluralism-founding social life is possible and inevitable. "The relationship with the Other does not move

---

[1] E. Lévinas, *Totality and Infinity. An Essay on Exteriority*, transl. A. Lingis, The Hague – Boston – London 1979, p. 87.

[2] Ibidem.

(as does cognition) into enjoyment and possession, into freedom, the Other imposes himself as an exigency that dominates this freedom. [...] The Other, whose presence is exceptionally inscribed in the ethical impossibility of killing him in which I stand, marks the end of powers," Lévinas claims. People are endowed with an inner life, the secretive, mysterious modus that provokes all sorts of strategies to tame, control, socialize, or unify.[3] Those strategies do not spare for us within social and political philosophy, which is often more like social engineering than ethics – the ground in which the pluralism is rooted. What kind of ethics is it, which Lévinas (as well as Ricoeur) excavates from the mass of ideas of the cognitive-collective order known to us as rational normalization, routinizing relationships between people similarly to physical relations, where freedom is portioned, rationalized, utilized, and traded within the frames of mutual exchange?

> The existence of the Other does not concern us in the collectivity by reason of his participation in the being that is already familiar to us all, nor by reason of his power and freedom with which we should have this subjugate and utilize for ourselves, nor to virtue of the difference of his attributes which we would have to surmount in the process of cognition or in a movement of sympathy merging us with him as though his existence were an embarassement. The Other does us as what must be surmounted, enveloped, dominated, but as other, independent of us: behind every relation we could sustain with him. [...] It is this way of welcoming an absolute existent that we discover in justice and injustice, and that discourse, teaching essentially, effectuates.[4]

2. Mystery of mind and body

The problem, from which the ethics outlined above arises, the problem with which such an ethics must deal with, is the limited experience of the other because of the body-mind separation and the imminent risk of experimenting with the other on the epistemic and ethical level. Encountering the other, in the first moment of experiential character, turns the imperceptibly to the participant into an encounter of experimental character. This happens when we start looking for some certainty and rules as to how we should behave towards otherness and interact with him or her in a situation that for us is located in the future (as a challenge or task), and which such an encounter only opens, promises, or designs. The responsibility inherent in

[3] Ibidem.

[4] Ibidem, p. 89.

a human, designing modus of being tells us to prepare for the meeting in advance and reduce the risks included in the meeting with others. We are not responsible for the other person, but for our own performance towards him or her – once it is within our range of responsibility, we can only prepare for it.

As we try to find out as much as possible of what is hidden in the otherness, our cognitive capabilities face barriers. One of them is the body, which in its expressions opens minimal access to the psyche. Another barrier is the limitations of our cognitive abilities. Finally, we encounter a barrier in speech, which – although it is the most perfect medium of communication – reveals less than the truth: it can also hide and obscure the truth and even confabulate and lie. Within the mysterious fault between body and mind oscillates our cognitive curiosity when we face Otherness in other people as well as in our fellows since physical and psychological closeness is not the same. Intersubjectivity gives only partial insight into the other's innert life, and how we interact with others is due, however, to that only fruitful but, at the same time, burdensome fault and tension between the psyche and physicality, by the expression: facial, bodily, motoric, etc. Psyche makes itself felt. And in the words of L. Kołakowski, even if we looked into it, who knows how deep is the well; at the bottom we always discover our own face.

Insight into the mental life of others has interested many thinkers, including Aristotle, St. Augustine, Hume, Smith, Spencer, Wittgenstein, Austin, Arendt, and Lévinas. At the same time it fascinated and impassionated quite a few psychologists, psychiatrists, and neuroscientists from James[5] and O'Connor Drury to Mead, Selman, Ekman, and Damasio. The availability of cognitive mental life is only possible for beings who are also endowed with a mental life, and even then to only a very limited extent. Psychology is still not yet a science, but "only the hope of a science. [...] There is indeed a science of experimental psychology, this science will continue to grow."[6] According to O'Connor Drury, one may assume that the growth of human sciences heavily depends on their openness to experimentation. There is nothing surprising also for philosophy. After all, Aristotle's *De Anima*, St. Augustine's *Soliloquia*, Descartes' *Treatise on the Passions of the Soul*, d'Espinoza's *Ethica More Geometrico*, Wittgenstein's *Philosophical Investigations*, Arendt's *The Life of The Mind*, and Lévinas' *Totality and Infinity* confront us with deep introspection into the human psyche. In the final paragraph of his *Critique of Pure Reason*, Kant describes a "foreign thought," i.e., a specific subjective faith that accompanies one's way of understanding the world, preventing investigation into "common" truths

[5] W. James, "What is an Emotion," *Mind*, 1984, vol. 9, no. 34, pp. 188–205.

[6] M. O'Connor Drury, *The Danger of Words and Writings on Wittgenstein*, Bristol 2003, pp. 25–29.

with others mainly because of the specific language (usage of language) of different people. Language seems to be an instrument that governs thinking: thinking is in its hands. The ability to think and linguistic skills belong together. But speaking one's own language allows us to follow the meanings constructed in a way of anamnesis. By contrast, speaking a similar language to others' allows us to seek truths. The same is the case with morality in Kant: one's own guidance (i.e., autonomous moral lawgiving) is governed by universal imperatives. We speak the same moral language and are understood and accepted by others by following universal principles. When we only speak a subjective moral language (i.e., the language of our individual maxims), something meaningful to us is not always right from others' or, in particular, a universal perspective.

By using the word "experimental" in relation to the experience of other mental life, I do not mean either psychological investigations or mind reading technologies. Rather, when confronted with the psyche, one is confronted "with the immeasurable"[7] and "infinity" (Lévinas) in a way that requires opening to the otherness and respecting it as transcending our cognitive capacities. But experiencing otherness challenges us to explore it by, among other things, giving testimony and examples. Following the voice of his teacher, Wittgenstein, O'Connor Drury asks for examples: "Give examples, give examples, do not just talk in abstract terms, that is what all these present-day philosophers are doing [...]."[8] It is, as he would prefer to experience the human condition instead of investigate it. "We live in an age of investigation, everything is investigated. [...] And so we go through routine procedure. [...] There is no more dangerous phrase in philosophy than to investigate perception and memory and the true nature of the self 'in the same way,'" O'Connor Drury claims. Otherness must be investigated in another way. Any experience with the other and otherness in any universal methodology or words is not existent. We become conscious of otherness by experiencing sensations through the appropriate patterns of neural activity, as "a private perceptual world which is an interpretation of specific events in the brain."[9] This constructivist approach does not, however, remove all restrictions concerning perception and, in particular, understanding of such a radical otherness as incorporated in persons living their own mental life.

In the twentieth century, treating the psyche as opposed to the body, and completely detaching it from the body as an inner world[10] has ceased. It has been stated that the mind is rooted in the brain somehow, and the only mystery

[7] Ibidem, p. 42.

[8] Ibidem, p. 38.

[9] Ibidem, p. 63.

[10] S. Overgaard, *Wittgenstein and Other Minds. Rethinking Subjectivity and Intersubjectivity with Wittgenstein, Lévinas, and Husserl*, New York 2007, p. 126.

we have yet to solve is how it is thus rooted. There is an illusory hope that "the mysteriousness of our present being" will disperse and that we will be able to speak from the outer point of view about the interior life, so far still latent to someone else's (and often also your own) view. The reckless use of the terms "outer" and "inner" has been pointed out by Wittgenstein and O'Connor Drury. "The words compelled [in] us this picture of a boundary which had to be crossed and yet somehow we were to be conscious of both sides of this boundary. There is no such boundary,"[11] O'Connor Drury concludes. There is instead "a mystery of mind and body"[12] and we must be careful of missing the fault between them and of speaking it too.

3. Expression and perception

While asking whether it is possible to adequately look into a person's mental life, Wittgenstein paid close attention to face expressions and body shape, allowing capture of the affective-emotional signals by an outside observer. The expressions and motor activity of the body are directly related to the dynamics and complexity of the affective-emotional processes at the neural level. Wittgenstein concluded that our mental life is largely expressed in the way our body moves.[13] It manifests itself in body language, in the eyes and facial expressions, in speech and in silence, and in the no less inseparable and no less significant act of speaking.[14] Despite this, there is still a gap between expressions and the inner life, raising the question of how it is possible that something internal is manifested outside. Or perhaps it is our ability to perceive or being so sensitive to subtle signs, or rather to their meanings? Because we usually do not interpret facial and body expressions consciously, they reach us rather unconsciously and work ahead of conscious reflection (which – as we have shown in another chapter – can be helpful in the development of this sensitivity). Wittgenstein explains it:

> "We see emotion. – As opposed to what?" – We do not see facial consortions as make the inference that he [or she] is feeling joy, grief, boredom. We describe a face immediately as sad, radiant, bored, even when we are unable to give any

---

[11] M. O'Connor Drury, *The Danger of Words...*, op. cit., p. 78.

[12] Ibidem, p. 95.

[13] S. Overgaard, *Wittgenstein and Other Minds...*, op. cit., p. 121.

[14] On the expressive role of being silent and its supportive function for mutual understanding: P. Freire, *Pedagogy of Freedom. Ethics, Democracy, and Civic Courage*, transl. P. Clarke, Lanham – Boulder – New York – Oxford 1998.

other description of the features. – Grief, they would like to say, is personified in the face.[15]

This approach can, however, contribute to cognitively objectivizing mental states (assigning them independent existence, as when we speak of sadness or melancholy visible in someone's eyes, as if they were objects instead of fleeting emotional states or moods). As a result, we are on track to reduce mental states to physical and physiological descriptions, or to reproduce dualistic patterns. On the other hand, many researchers have gone too far in the belief that "what you see is always a behavior, not a pain [...]."[16] While emotional states to a large extent can be translated to facial expressions and motor activities, and can be submitted to some interpersonal game of reading other people's feelings, the more thoughtful face – although thinking puts a distinctive shadow on a human face – is not always easy to distinguish from the face not showing, or concealing, any mental activity or intentionally (the so-called "poker face" indicates a special focus on not showing tension and nervousness). Thinking deeply about an issue puts on a human face a distinctive look of concentration, forgetfulness, and momentary absence in the external world, which – as H. Arendt would say in her book *The Life of the Mind* – is a testimony to the fact that when I think, I am following the thoughts as being representations of things. Mentally, I am getting involved in the absence of things: I deal with absences, as Arendt puts it. Getting to the thoughtful person can be as difficult as getting to one who is strongly emotionally engaged. Deep reflection and a certain kind of affection are closely related. Wittgenstein was aware of this relation. But when he gives advice to his friend – psychiatrist O'Connor Drury – "to look more closely"[17] into his patients' faces, he means a nonverbal completion of the communication between doctor and patient and its therapeutic effect rather than the sharing the reflective moods with someone else and the contemplation of such an experience (as will be shown in the final part of this chapter). To an experienced psychiatrist, it is unnecessary to translate the language of feelings into the language of words. However, communication between physician and patient provides the development of specific verbal

[15] L. Wittgenstein, *Culture and Value*, ed. G. H. von Wright in colaboration with H. Nyman, rev. A. Pichler, transl. P. Winch, Oxford – Malden 2004, § 570. See Overgaard's analysis of the quoted passage in his *Wittgenstein and Other Minds...*, op. cit., p. 128.

[16] S. Overgaard, *Wittgenstein and Other Minds...*, op. cit., p. 130.

[17] Wittgenstein in one of his letters to O'Connor Drury: "Look at your patients more closely as human beings in trouble and enjoy more the opportunity to say 'good night' to so many people [...]. I think in some sense you don't look at people's faces closely enough." M. O'Connor Drury, *The Danger of Words...*, op. cit., p. 96.

semantics (including metaphorical expressions) in order to create effective therapeutic relationships.[18]

4. Face to face as phenomenological structure of reciprocity

The ability to mental align with another person and his or her mental states has already been established in preverbal infants, initially as a capacity for empathy, which Schopenhauer had already written about. As described in the literature, the prominent role in this process is played by mirror neural networks and a number of processes initiated by them. The early phase of socialization relies on, among other things, the fact that others gain "social significance" for an infant (in Honneth's terms). The ability to treat others as "significant" because of their subjective status, that is, the inner life typical of only higher living beings, develops unevenly and depends mainly on the quality of a stimulating social environment. Differences suggest that some children are randomly given a more stimulating interpersonal environment than are others who often experienced, if not indifference from their loved ones, hostility, rejection, and "insult" understood as a denial of significance resulting from being a person of his or her own, sovereign inner life and his or her outer expression. No child should be held accountable for his or her social environment.

The inability mentioned, which can affect people of all ages – also called a pluralistic ignorance – is manifested in a superficial perception, lack of attention to another person, and incorrect reading of the mental states (especially emotional) in other people, in addition to a number of behavioral and relational consequences. From the lack of sensitivity and tact, and assigning intentions, attributes, abilities, and qualifications to other people (or alternatively: denying those present), and depreciating their values, one is quite close to taking advantage and dominance over the Other and using this domination to legitimize exclusion, oppressiveness, intolerance, manipulation, and verbal, emotional and physical abuse. "Asymmetry of recognition"[19] is the most suitable field for the

[18] See F. Overlach, *Sprache des Schmerzes – sprechen über Schmerzen. Eine grammatisch-semantische gesprächsanalytische Untersuchung von Schmerzausdrücken im Deutschen*, Berlin – New York 2008; G. Brünner, E. Gülich (eds.), *Krankheit verstehen. Interdisziplinäre Beiträge zur Sprache in Krankheitsdarstellungen*, Bielefeld 2012. The authors are looking for language of pain but not for rhetorics of pain. A patient just is to reveal his psychosomatic experiences and make them understandable instead of to convince the doctor, deliver evidence, etc.

[19] B. Zachariah, "On Not Understanding the Stranger: Histories, Collective Victimhood and the Futility of Postcolonialism," in B. Weber, K. Herb, E. Marsal, T. Dobashi, P. Schweitzer (eds.), *Cultural Politics and Identity. The Public Space of Recognition*, Zürich – Berlin 2011, p. 102; see

arising of tensions, conflicts, and harm, especially for the instrumentalisation of another person, appropriation, control, and manipulation of her inner life. What – if not asymmetry of recognition and pluralistic ignorance – authorizes us to openly express verdicts and diagnoses such as: "I see that you are back in the same mood as...," "I see no reason to agonize so over..." (which at the epistemological point of view, is true), or questioning "why you look away, are you hiding something?, admit to...," etc.

If these problems seem trivial to someone who decides that they fall under a spontaneous, sociable, and blunt disposition, we can indicate more "extensive" social reasons why it makes sense to undermine the legitimacy of any asymmetric recognition among people. The very first would be that expressions of topoi are culturally determined and the force of counterclaims (including exuberance and restrain, submission and domination, etc.) is also specific to certain cultures and circles. Meanwhile, more and more people have found in themselves performance within intercultural social contexts. Naturally, the open access to one's own mental life rather than to someone else's leads me to ask: Why am I surprised at this, that in another culture, along with welfare, fulfillment, and other "hard" values, more subtle ones are also appreciated, such as (unknown to carefree risk-takers) a sense of security, comfort, and harmony, preferred by many to feeling of anxiety and distress in relation to chaos and bustle?

In a multicultural reality, psyche is at risk already if someone's specific expression, partly showing presents the psyche to be at the mercy of the environment.[20] This is especially true for expressions of feelings and emotions:

> [...] our expressions of feelings and emotions are culturally transmitted to us, and some may vary quite extensively from culture to culture. We do not create our own expressive patterns; we learn them as we are initiated into what Wittgenstein calls a life-form. And those patterns of expression that appear to be innate rather than culturally transmitted (the smile of joy, the cry of pain, etc.) are, of course, not our personal creation either. And in any case [...] they are later supplemented and to some extent replaced by linguistic expressions. [...] But [...] every expression in the face of another, being the expression of *another's mental life*, is also a creative event that reveals an alien source of meaning; a source that is extremely present.[21]

P. Ricoeur, *Oneself and Another*, transl. K. Blamey, Chicago 1992; idem, *The Course of Recognition*, transl. D. Pellauer, Cambridge, MA 2005.

[20] See S. T. Gardner, "Taking Selves Seriously," in B. Weber, K. Herb, E. Marsal, T. Dobashi, P. Schweitzer (eds.), *Cultural Politics and Identity*..., op. cit., pp. 179–189.

[21] S. Overgaard, *Wittgenstein and Other Minds*..., op. cit., p. 140.

Still, do not "completion" and "substitution" of expression by speech mean at the same time suppression and by the more rational and universal language customs? Does it not happen from time to time to the deception of mental states, by colonizing, standardizing, conformist, and depleting rhetoric that becomes the access card to language games? The verbal medium expands the expression only when an individual creates his or her own narratives. Of necessity, however, one makes them not only about him or herself but also about someone else. One assigns other features, intentions, and characters in the image and likeness of those whose construct his own mind, in particular, through experience, memory, imagination, and language. Sometimes the estimating, unsolicited assessments and generalizations draw as many triumphant as false conclusions, considering the elements of narrative as a prerequisite for further steps to entering more deeply into the realm of the Other, arousing suspicion and fear by multiplying the stereotypes and forcing another "alleged integration."[22]

The escalation of asymmetric rhetoric sets the stage for polarization, domination and subordination, discrimination, and exclusion in human relationships. Foucault and Lévinas saw in rhetoric the source of indelible violence against defenceless human inner life and its expressivity. Even the most modest, the most fleeting expression is an expression of life and the respect for it is expressed in discrete thrifty glances, gestures, judgments, and a refraining from greedy selfishness. Tact and respect in question, however, is not the explaining of the other, that he is invisible, transparent, anonymous, or *faceless*. How is it possible to coexist with the other "and still leave his otherness intact?"[23]

This question above is an important question at a time when digital readers track, scan, and decode almost every human step, gesture, and eye flicker using the fact that human life exhibits itself as tangible and visible through the face – which is no longer ethics. Ethics exists only where the human being is revealed as both fragile and intelligent while calling the other for responsibility. Its face "brings the first signification of...," showing its presence as such, completely independent of mine and at the same time given together with it: marking pluralism and inviting the other to a conversation. In this basic face to face contact with the Other arises a basis for a dialogue between equal and free beings. The human life does not in fact present itself as "arousing fear and trembling [...]"[24] or as equipped in the features that would divide or

[22] E. Lévinas, *Totality and Infinity*..., op. cit., p. 42; see M. O'Connor Drury, *The Danger of Words*..., op. cit.

[23] Ibidem, p. 13, Introduction.

[24] Ibidem, p. 215.

antagonize. There is no reality of existence "somewhere, from something;"[25] for a split second it seems to someone else's eyes, as if shrouded in an "ignorance veil." It was in this meeting that the other manifests him or herself only as a merely subjective being who "presents himself in the face." When "I am facing another I," I am facing an intelligible being (so to speak, and in Arendt's words: I identify his or her ability to think because there are affinities between us, "we are what men always have been – thinking beings." The notion of an *ability* has a crucial meaning in this context because humans do not think all the time. "Absence of thoughts is not stupidity, it can be found in highly intelligent people"[26]). We are both able to read what another human face expresses. And it expresses an invitation, an introduction into the meaningful world that I am unable to ignore as an intelligible being. We are both ready to discover personal otherness. "*Orientation* of being 'starting from oneself' toward 'the Other'"[27] is an inevitable orientation but not necessarily a destination: because in making room for the other ethics reveals. The orientation of one toward another is the appropriate area of ethics, in particular of responsibility for own personal activity. "That is, a response to the being who in a face speaks to the subject and tolerates only a personal response, that is, an ethical act,"[28] as Lévinas says. It might be a risky act containing "constitutional uncertainties"[29] when people trust only in the rules of "the game of experiencing others *as others*."[30] But it is a very human act.

From the face, quite differently than from the surface of things, "its own light" emanates (Wittgenstein's and Lévinas' idiom), translucent "in the play of the features."[31] The expression, on the one hand, encourages us to penetrate the mystery of someone else's psyche and personality, while on the other hand, it protects and hides them against the insight of other people, and today also against psycho-political techniques as neuro-enhancement,[32] that do an outstanding business due to neuro-marketing. Therefore, the face with its expressions that allow us to look inside the human mind should be the subject of more ethical care. The face considered by Wittgenstein "in its own light" has become "the epiphany of the face" to Lévinas, which is, at the same time, the ethical expression of the self. Psyche, personality, and self are in fact

[25] Ibidem, p. 216.

[26] H. Arendt, *The Life of the Mind*, part I: *Thinking*, New York 1978, pp. 11–13.

[27] E. Lévinas, *Totality and Infinity...*, op. cit., p. 215.

[28] Ibidem, p. 219.

[29] L. Wittgenstein, *Culture and Value*, op. cit., § 35.

[30] S. Overgaard, *Wittgenstein and Other Minds...*, op. cit., p. 136.

[31] L. Wittgenstein, *Culture and Value*, op. cit., § 657.

[32] B. Schöne-Seifert, D. Talbot, U. Opolka, J.S. Ach (eds.), *Neuro-Enhancement. Ethik vor neuen Herausforderungen*, Paderborn 2009.

quite peculiar, sovereign, and radical existential events; but although epiphany gives a glimpse and invites one to explore the infinite, the infinity of nature defies inquisitive actions and concepts of other people, carrying on a no less strange and mysterious inner life. Personality transcends different personality, which is why "the facing position" is also the "opposition par excellence," which – as an epistemic problem – constitutes a vast field of ethical issues, fundamentally practical and social. Since it is impossible to know the infinite (transcendent for us) personality of the other, it is not possible either to know the totality that could include all personalities and be representative of them. "The objective totality *remains exclusionary or every other*"[33] and this is why it lacks an ethical character. The opposite is true: infinity that exceeds totality is of ethical character. We cannot tell when, or how often the creating – and even more so: usage – of universal norms is accompanied by reflection, *totality* and *infinity*, *disclosure,* and *inclusion*, which are concepts making up a framework for democracy. Their dialectic is replaced by dialogics. "Where being does not only manifest itself, but effectuates itself, or exerts itself, or holds sway, or reigns,"[34] Lévinas claims.

There is nothing negative in the unavailability or excluding; on the contrary, the identity and sovereignty of social experience does not allow one to forget, for even a moment, about interpersonality, freedom and related limitations (which also have nothing negative in themselves), individualism and pluralism, and dialogue and reason, which Lévinas' ethics strengthens, in a way, equally as well as did Fichte's ethics over 200 years ago. The fact that a person is endowed with an inner life turns out to be the only condition for the existence of plurality instead of a totality (or totalising collectivism. An encounter invites one to participate in a language game, and founds the field of conversation that revives reason as the fundamentally human activity (not only scientific and bookish). "Reason lives in language, the first rationality gleams forth in the opposition of the face to face."[35] Dialogue presupposes the presence of at least two interlocutors, but it is not dyadic but open to many. This multiplicity from the very beginning is meant, to Lévinas, as a multitude of sentient and thinking beings whose inner lives are something more than an activity ruled by "universal" principles. The inner life of an individual equipped with sensitivity and mental capacity in the face of many other individuals primarily need to talk, engage in understanding, dialogue, and participate – but at a different level than would generate asymmetry and an appropriation of *talking to*, *talking at* someone. It is, as P. Freire points out, about placing the other exactly

[33] E. Lévinas, *Totality and Infinity*..., op. cit., p. 221.

[34] Ibidem, p. 220.

[35] Ibidem, p. 208.

at the height of my eyes, about *talking with*[36]: an inclusive dialogue. Only such a language and dialogue are universal. "Language is universal because it is the very passage from the individual to the general"[37] and this passage establishes ethics as a significant and just relationship between I and Other.

Revealing pre-linguistic ethical relationships as constitutive of linguistic relations among people, Lévinas avoids – as he himself admits in interviews published in the volume *Ethics and Infinity* – constructing rules[38] that are of an impersonal dimension ("universality presents itself as impersonal and this is another inhumanity"[39]). Ethics is to him identical with morality, live action, and tension between closure, disclosure, openness, the personal, and the interpersonal. He says that participation is a way of relating to the other such that we can maintain and develop our own existence, provided that we do not lose contact with the other for any moment.[40] The dialogic nature of the participation involves language (possibly open, inclusive, and free from rhetoric), and in turn the language requires – as Lévinas emphasizes – speakers, many speakers. Their mutual contact is not the creation of reciprocal representation or participation in what is universal. In the first place their contact is ethics.[41] If the "talking is to make the world common, to create a common space,"[42] then Lévinas creates parallel individualistic and communitarian ethics, and none can be separated from another. Only recognition of mutual obligations from the individualist and community perspectives allows one to move beyond appropriating speech to accepting the infinite transcendence hidden behind the physical expression of the other, and to invite him or her to an open, endless conversation. Part of the infinite otherness will be revealed to me when I give up all domination, the desire of appropriation, of control and understanding of the other in my own image, and after my likeness. Accepting his or her expression and accepting the Other beyond one's own very limited skills of understanding the other Self, I deprive myself of nothing, "The ethical relationship is beyond knowledge," Nemo, a character from *Ethics and Infinity*, says.

---

[36] P. Freire, *Pedagogy of Freedom...*, op. cit., p. 108. In the Foreword to this book, D. Macedo refers to a number of examples of such assymetry, such as discrimination, domination, and paternalistic relationships: "no need to hear your voice when I can talk about you better than you can speak about yourself," as he claims D. Macedo in *Pedagogy of Freedom.* Ibidem, p. xxvi.

[37] E. Lévinas, *Totality and Infinity...*, op. cit., p. 79.

[38] E. Lévinas, *Ethics and Infinity. Conversations with Philippe Nemo*, transl. R. Cohen, Pittsburg 1985, p. 90.

[39] E. Lévinas, *Totality and Infinity...*, op. cit., p. 46.

[40] Ibidem.

[41] Ibidem, p. 75.

[42] Ibidem, p. 76.

The ethical relationship is beyond investigations, it is in experience, O'Connor Drury would agree with Nemo.

Acceptance is personal and comes from the self, from the inside – because only from the inside does a person see, experience, feel, reflect, and take responsibility: Self is emphasized once again (initially for another).[43] Therefore, moral phenomenology will never be studied academically, codified, and indoctrinated: it will only be experienced in vivo. Lévinas, but also Merleau-Ponty and Ricoeur, outlined visible space, the horizon, in which a person experiences an encounter, relationships, and bonds. The game of expression involves manifestation and manifestation implies spatiality. So to see the silent appeal emanating from someone else's anxious face,[44] and to answer it, we should look more carefully, recognizing the right of the Other to the *personal*[45] treatment without overwhelming it with an excess of our own self-expression. Then there is another shining of "its own light" and not "reflected light" that is typical of objects as secondary beings to subjects, as expressed by Wittgenstein and Lévinas.

The right of Self to a separate identity, expression, and respect in the face of another self was repeatedly noted in philosophy. Fichte, in his *Theory of Wissenschaftslehre* (1794), made interpersonality spatial by quantifying the freedom between selves in the overlapping unlimited expanding power of original agility. Hegel's *Phenomenology of Spirit* from 1806 took us through the history of institutionalized domination of some subjects over others, and in a still-yet-unrealized ethics, indicated an ideal of widespread recognition of self-knowledge as the mutually-recognizing expressed in the universal principle of law. However, the law belongs to impersonal, abstract order. Abstract law precedes here – both as an ideal and as a basic rule – true recognition and it cannot ensure mutual recognition among all persons because the recognition, as well as respect, are psychological acts. The social world is thus still filled with physical and direct, or alternatively: symbolic and indirect, i.e., semantic, structural, and procedural disrespect. Lévinas (as well as Ricoeur) unveiled a sense of what might be called the primacy of spiritual supra-éthique. Ethics repeals all the disordered structure and semantics of these relationships that do not comply with ethical requirements and calls for building them entirely from scratch, starting from a careful look into the face of a stranger that "has turned to me [...] [in] its very nudity,"[46] in its bare existence. For Ricoeur, in a similar way love repeals the difference

---

[43] E. Lévinas, *Ethics and Infinity...*, op. cit., p. 96. "All I can do is to step forth as an individual and speak in the first person," as Wittgenstein had confessed in *Culture and Value.*

[44] L. Wittgenstein, *Culture and Value*, op. cit., p. 52.

[45] S. Overgaard, *Wittgenstein and Other Minds...*, op. cit., p. 149.

[46] E. Lévinas, *Totality and Infinity...*, op. cit., p. 43.

between friends and enemies; in Lévinas, this repealing universal element is a discourse that is not the same as either with love or with "pathetic conversation." As for love, he warns against the tendency to full mental or spiritual fusion with another person because it would put an end to the responsibility, dialogue, the mutual responding to calls sent to another person, and the mutual respect for the personal sovereignty of a human being. That ground of ethics – as soon as it appears – inspires so much hope that it is immediately occupied by objectivising and regulating discourses and institutions. Meanwhile, it is about the fundamentally ontological irreducibility of the otherness, a situation in which each person tells the other: "you do exist for me and I express this fact; I respect you."[47]

The voice of ethics can and should be regarded as predominant within interpersonal relationships. Perhaps ethics begins with the very ordinary, inconspicuous ways of associating with another person, from everyday courtesy, rituals, intuitions, and giving.[48] The voice of ethics is still one of the leading voices in the culture. It is a very silent voice, but is predominant insofar as the personal "I" seems to be its source.

5. Facing otherness in the arts: Emotions in Michał Sobeski

The perception, identification, and understanding of emotional states, as well as the ability to empathize may also develop through contact with art. Many creative processes are based on that abilities from painting and sculpture to art performances. The primacy of feelings in the experiencing of art, aesthetic experience, and the interpretation of works was described by Polish aesthetician M. Sobeski at a time when James' discoveries had already been recognized. James argued not only that "the bodily changes follow directly the perception of the exciting fact, and that our feeling of the same changes as they occur is the emotion. [...] A purely disembodied human emotion is a nonentity."[49] These findings also show that emotions largely organize human consciousness and intra-objective states of affairs, those perceived, reproduced by memory, or designed by the imagination. Emotions affecting consciousness is not just a simple reflection, a simple registration of states of affairs. It becomes an orientation in the case of the diversity and importance of these states of affairs

---

[47] M. Hénaff, "On the Norm of Reciprocity," *Teoria e Critica della Regolazione Sociale*, 2010, Centro Studi TCRS, p. 2.

[48] N. Malcolm, *Ludwig Wittgenstein. A Memoir*, Oxford 1958, p. 61.

[49] W. James, "What is an Emotion," op. cit., pp. 189–190.

and their properties. That is, "practical orientation structures all experience and conceptualization. [...] Emotions are thus a constituent of intentionality, which is constructed in practical terms rather than as the disinterested representation of things external to us,"[50] Ratcliffe points out in his excellent analysis of James' conception.

For an artist who creates a completely new representation or expression of the deeply subjective and often sub-conscious design of things, "most vital roots grow out of the realm of the irrational feelings: this is also the case with the work of an artist,"[51] Sobeski assumes.

For Sobeski, the terms "irrational" and "sub-conscious" are synonyms. He explains, for example, that the cheerful and snappy mood in which I woke up in the morning can survive the day, provided it is from time to time fuelled by memories of the events that led to it, though the memories do not have to come to the surface of consciousness. To this extent they can be considered irrational, but they can also catalyze a number of mental activities. However, the same creative process is not based on a simple experiencing of feelings that the artist after all shares with any relatively sensitive person; not every sensitive person becomes a creator. To start the creative process, complex cognitive processes are needed, leading to a full, practical and motor expression of something that has already been inspired by impressions and emotional experiences; but it goes far beyond these impressions and experiences.

> The creative ability is ultimately not about that the artist is capable of individual experience – because such experiences are typical to every man – but about the fact that he can find a balanced expression for his individual emotional experiences.[52]

However, a work of art bears traces of experiences that allow us to conclude that the "painter loves and hates the colours and the musicians the sounds of music,"[53] but also that, on the other hand, the art is certainly a different world than the real world, relatively uniformly perceived by its residents. Art, having its origin in the inner life of a creative-demiurge, is "a world in itself, autonomous immersed in regulations. Separation of these two worlds"[54] takes us as consumers of art. We rely on the oscillation between what art covers

---

[50] M. Ratcliffe, *Feelings of Being. Phenomenology, Psychiatry, and the Sense of Reality*, New York 2007, p. 236.

[51] M. Sobeski, *Wybór pism estetycznych* [Selected Writings on Aesthetics], Cracow 2010, p. 119.

[52] M. Sobeski, *Myśl a marmur* [Thought vs. Marble], Warsaw 1959, p. 112.

[53] Ibidem, p. 113.

[54] Ibidem, p. 112.

and, only for a moment, reveals as its meaning: interpretation, or hermeneutics. In his psychology of creativity, Sobeski is restrained by generalizations. However, when discussing the role of emotions in arts in the subjective and specific context (the "matrix" of feelings, whose "seeds" each person has), he anticipates later discoveries, such as Damasio's conclusion that the emotional relationship with art covers a number of areas: being emotionally marked by events allows artists to create their works and trigger emotions. In recent years, one of the artistic experiences known worldwide that would not have occurred without a constitutive part of an expressed mental state from both the artist and participant (not just "customers") is Marina Abramovic's performance, *The Artist is Present* (MoMA 2010). This performance was an open-ended series of interpersonal events. Participants can experience their own mental states as stimulated face-to-face by another unknown person's mental state through eye contact, and facial and bodily expressions only. The time invested in that experience and stimulation allowed participants (and the artist) to also start reflected emotional experiences, which takes highly energy absorbing mental effort, as both Abramovic and the participants of performance reported.

In the history of arts, certain genres such as painting, sculpture, and contemporary visual arts assume a more complex creative process and less contingent effects than does performance. "Analysis of the creative process developing in the artist's soul, poses considerable difficulties [...]," notes Sobeski. On the other hand, "psychological raw material bears paramount relevance"[55] for understanding how the creative process leads to a "brighter and clearer" conceptualization and composition of the work, and finally also to embodiment in the "material entering the [...] creative work."[56] The creative mood includes transition between what is internal (creative, imaginative, and narrative) and what is external (ambient, already-existing, and experienced, and as such at least partially determining the content and structure of ideas). "Well, in the realm of sensation and imagination there is no way to create something completely new. Our sensations and imaginations are highly dependent on the reality outside us. We can only make new groupings of sensational elements."[57] Individual creative processes are always peculiar, but "creative essence" is taken by Sobeski to mean that an "artist's action is in a word searching for sensual ways of expressions for experience [...] but a truly creative moment is only just the *finding* of this very sensual form, which only matching with corresponds to a particular emotional content."[58]

[55] M. Sobeski, *Wybór pism estetycznych* [Selected Writings on Aesthetics], op. cit., p. 97.

[56] M. Sobeski, *Myśl a marmur* [Thought vs. Marble], op. cit., p. 112.

[57] Ibidem, p. 111.

[58] Ibidem.

In a natural way "everyone can easily express his feelings in face or body gestures," while an artistic way of expressing feelings and experiences has yet to be invented, or carefully selected from an infinite number of available forms. The possibly adequate sensual form only approximately "equals" the emotional content, the content may be fully experienced and recognized by the creator and yet remain unexpressed. Equally, Plato's ideas can be cognitively accessible to a person, and yet remain formally unrealized[59] (similarly, according to Kant a perfectly straight line is never perfectly realized in the empirical world). For the artist, however, a sensory form is a sine qua non, "a form is entitled for an equally outstanding significance along the feelings,"[60] Sobeski says. When "melting our feelings into marble, colour, sound, or a word" by means of a formal plan, an artist somehow "triggers" his or her hitherto blind and sub-conscious feelings to sight; a silent but powerful voice gains a sensual form; inner creative forces get some external expression. Out of this creative mood, which is inherently ephemeral,[61] beauty is born, and it is born "when the form is actually an expression of emotional content, i.e., when the emotional content is a principle, shaping the form."[62]

When a spectator of a piece of art wants to know more about the role and power of emotion in the creative process and about the final shape of the work, he can only rely on himself. He cannot trust "the testimonies of the artists themselves," and must be quite "suspicious of [...] their judgments of their own creation."[63] This is because an artist has no self-awareness. When he is heavily preoccupied with something, he "truly plunges into himself. [...] he does not see or hear what's going on around him. Somewhat he does the day-dreaming. He remains insensitive to external impressions, the more he subjects himself to internal sensations."[64] The spontaneous activity of the artist engages affective and cognitive processes, however, it consists in "transferring some special products of the imagination to sensual material: colour, marble, sound, word, etc.,"[65] at a rate incomparably faster than a fully conscious and carefully considered actions requires it. A creative action must keep up with the idea

[59] Ibidem, p. 114.

[60] Ibidem, p. 110.

[61] Ibidem, p. 127.

[62] Ibidem, p. 110. Compare M. Ratcliffe: "The view that we impose patterns upon a pre-given world or 'carve the marble into a statue' is a partial return to the subjective-objective or internal-external perspective that James himself tries to escape from when he emphasizes the world of the feeling organism over that of the disembodied theorist." M. Ratcliffe, *Feelings of Being...*, op. cit., p. 232.

[63] Ibidem, p. 96.

[64] Ibidem, pp. 101–102.

[65] Ibidem, p. 98.

because it can arise "in the artist's mind sometimes suddenly, unexpectedly," growing out of the experience and the feelings that "could have already been gone from memory, but their subconscious existence did not need to expire"[66] and may still influence the mental processes.

However, when the creative idea takes on sensual shapes, the creator stands in front of it as the first judge. But will he argue by referring to the experience that accompanied his creative effort? After all, "a feeling does not explain anything, but it just wants to be explained and legitimated,"[67] as Sobeski puts it in his *Selected Writings on Aesthetics*. Feelings regulate "the process and configuration of ideas. Feelings always serve his regulatory action,"[68] but little can be said about how exactly such a regulation occurs. An artist can not coldly explain why a form does or does not correspond to his plan. His perception is capable, however, of correctly recognizing that correspondence or its lack, prompting him to seek more adequate formal solutions.

A piece of art is a challenge for the spectator not only at the level of interpretation, but also – or even primarily – at the level of perception, intuition, and experience, which are only precursors to the launch of senso-creative processes. There are psychologically and culturally specific patterns of emotions, but most of the basic emotions seem to be universal to the human species. There may be many ways of integrating the individual psyche and the environment, and so different people might be more or less sensitive to different stimuli and, thus, possess a different ability to perceive and extract themes that attract attention at the sub-conscious level. Individualism and culturally diversity will also be expressed in works of art. Because of this diversity, Polish esthetician and author of *The Primitive Art*,[69] Michał Sobeski, has been recognized throughout the world.

Wittgenstein, spoke about the forms of life and cultures in which human individuals are included: we take over ways of expressing feelings and emotions from them, essentially we do not create our own templates of expression from scratch. Partial replacement of emotional expression and communication by verbal expression and communication is regarded as a sign of social maturity, but the latter should accompany the former rather than eliminate it completely. Accurate identification of one's own emotional states and those of the others, despite a possible discrepancy between verbalization and interpretation, on the one hand, and the experience at the visual and emotional level, on the other

---

66 Ibidem, p. 99.

67 M. Sobeski, *Wybór pism estetycznych* [Selected Writings on Aesthetics], op. cit., p. 117.

68 Ibidem, p. 119.

69 I. Piotrowska, M. Sobeski, "The Primitive," *Journal of Aesthetics and Art Criticism*, 1942, vol. 1 (4), pp. 12–21.

hand, is a valuable social ability. This ability, which makes us sensitive to the subtle and personal signals from the eyes, facial expressions, the play of facial features, gestures, motor actions, and intonation. This is crucial for an artist who skillfully memorizes such experiences so to "intuitively" create an expressive piece of work, which is then able to pull a spectator into the mood emanating from it. Not surprisingly, Michelangelo and Rodin are paradigmatic examples of artists with such an ability.[70]

6. Auguste Rodin and Kees Hageman: "I materialize. The Thinker thinks again"

Auguste Rodin's *Thinker* is such an expressive figurative sculpture that a viewer can enter the "most personal, most individual, the least sharable with others emotional relation,"[71] Sobeski says. His facial and bodily expressions, and fixed and characteristically structured figure truly embody the invisible life of the mind, the activity of thinking, drawing the attention and inspiring a one-of-a-kind atmosphere of concentrated thinking of something deeply, of "being lost in thought."[72] Through the artistically sublime signs of this condition, the spectator receives guided insight into the inner life of a thoughtful man and even feels the gravity and tone of the thoughts, giving this act a weight requiring the support of the head with the hand. Confrontation with the *Thinker* allows one to possibly experience more than a confrontation with a living, thoughtful man whom one would not disturb, and who emanates inaccessible distance evoking respect and even fear in the observer who comes at the wrong time. When the viewer is sensitive to the mental, hidden depth of the *Thinker's* mental state and the mood flowing out of it, for a while he or she will become closer to the act of thinking as the most secret element of someone else's psyche because he cannot yet penetrate the true subject and the cause of this thoughtfulness; he or she can, however, experience the meaningfulness of the subject that is thinking. Here empathy and even expertise ends. Observation and practice do not develop cognition and an understanding of

[70] Following Lévinas' conviction that artists produce silence and do not contribute to ethics as being a live experience, Brenda Hofmeyr collected arguments that may pose questions for my essay. In her paper "Isn't Art an Activity That Gives Things a Face?" published in *Image & Narrative*, 2007, no. 18: *Thinking Pictures*, she claimes that "for Lévinas, that which introduces true time and significance is the relation with the other person – a relation which is no longer limited to artistic or aesthetic categories but that constitutes ethics." Retrieved from http://www.imageandnarrative.be/inarchive/thinking_pictures/hofmeyr. htm [29.06.2013].

[71] M. Sobeski, *Wybór pism estetycznych* [Selected Writings on Aesthetics], op. cit., p. 117.

[72] S. Overgaard, *Wittgenstein and Other Minds*..., op. cit., p. 129.

someone else's mental states any further.[73] We are, however, certain of one thing with absolute evidence:

> Look into someone else's face, and see the consciousness in it, and a particular *shade* of consciousness [...]. Do you look into *yourself* in order to recognize the *fury* in his face? It is there as clearly as in your own breast.[74]

The viewer can stop at the experience of co-feeling and the reflective contemplation of melancholy moulded in bronze. He or she may also reach for historical knowledge and "learn [...] the conditions in which such and such artists created – but simply nothing more," Sobeski says, to interpret the spiritual state of the *Thinker* more fully. The figure of the *Thinker* appears as if it is "cut out" of the huge portal posing the gates of hell described in Dante's *Divine Comedy* and leading to one of the Paris cemeteries. The *Thinker* was originally intended to represent Dante himself as an integral part of the construction of the portal itself. In accordance with Sobeski's notion that "feelings demand an explanation," the expression of the *Thinker*, thanks to critical information, becomes more significant and much more meaningful to us than when we are deprived of the knowledge and watch the work with an eye of a layman. Both the figure and the experience of it become deeper: the *Thinker* in fact "incorporates" genius and the powerlessness in his face as being confronted with the human secret of unimaginable evil and sin. The genius here is so powerless both in the fight against evil and in the attempt for a reasonable explanation of its own failure. At the same time this feeling of helplessness remains in stark contrast with the athletic vigour of the *Thinker*, which again is explained by the knowledge of the conditions of its production: A well-known early 1880s boxer is said to have posed for Rodin.

The artist pictured the feelings of the *Thinker* in such a way that he experiences them subjectively, and the spectator familiarizes himself. "It consists in recreating the objective conditions, which are associated with experiences of emotional states,"[75] yet while interpreting the sculpture – quite different than in the case of a literary form or a film – one must be equipped with additional knowledge of history of these objective conditions, Sobeski argues. When it comes to recognizing and identifying the external expression of internal human life, "you can [...] only empathize with the feelings of others, which you yourself possess at least in the bud."[76]

---

[73] M. S. Gazzaniga, *The Ethical Brain*, New York 2005, p. 61.

[74] L. Wittgenstein, *Culture and Value*, op. cit., § 220.

[75] M. Sobeski, *Wybór pism estetycznych* [Selected Writings on Aesthetics], op. cit., s. 115.

[76] Ibidem, p. 116.

Picture 1.
© Kees Hageman

Picture 2.
© Harry Cutting

Picture 3. *The Thinker* is "breaking his head"
© Kees Hageman

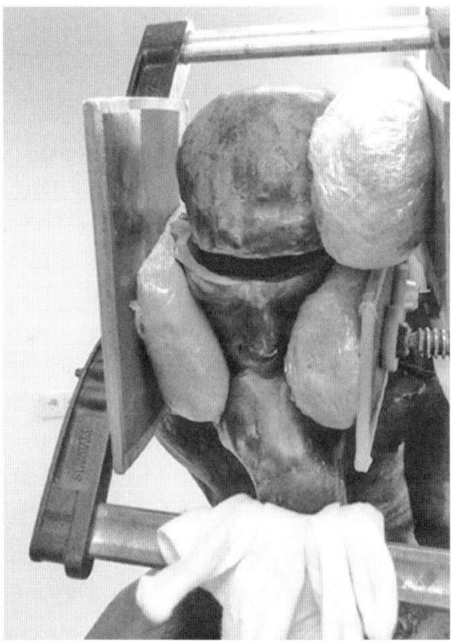

Picture 4. Ambulant treatement
© Kees Hageman

Picture 5. Surgery
© Kees Hageman

Picture 6. Operating *The Thinker*
© Kees Hageman

In 2007, from the garden surrounding the Singer Museum in Singer Laren (Netherlands), seven sculptures were stolen, including a valuable reproduction of the *Thinker* cast in bronze. The thief intended to scrap them, at the price of 5 Euros per kilogram. To do this, he cut the thinker into pieces. The stolen statue was then regained and subjected to arduous (quasi-clinical) "operations" and "therapy" in the Rijk Museum. Famous photographer Kees Hageman[1] has documented the work and entitled it "I Materialize. The Thinker Thinks Again."

The project emphasizes an aesthetic way of associating a man with a piece of art representing a genuine human, very subtle mental state in a unique, interactive way.

[1] Retrieved from http://old.materialise.com/materialise/view/de/3840344-Materialise+helps+The+Thinker+think+again.html [20.03.2013]. The author is grateful for permission to reproduce Harry Cutting's picture representing a Thinkful Boy.

Chapter IV

The concepts of respect revisited

> The great difficulty in philosophy is to say no more than we really know.
>
> Ludwig Wittgenstein

1. Introducing respect with Aristotle

Regardless of its long tradition as an issue of philosophical investigation, the notion of respect seems still to be underdefined. It is one of the most intuitively applied notions and the most demanding of an explanation. Following the implicit usage of the term that societal norms and philosophical systems articulate, respect can be a foundation for social relationships if it is practiced and experienced by individual subjects, but this must occur reciprocally. That is, respectful conduct bridges the gap between two or more interacting subjects forming an interpersonal relationship.

Respect is a personal attitude, too ("we judge a man's character from his actions"[1]) and it belongs to the "good attributes" together with "constructive or practical thought,"[2] all rooted in moral cognition. Today one tends to understand respectful conduct as an intentional act. Living beings are viewed as valuable and worthy of respect for life; human beings are viewed as valuable and worthy of respect for their humanity (this specific value will be considered below in the context of Kant and Dworkin); and the property and products of humans are viewed as valuable and worthy of respect for their individualistic authorship and legal ownership. We conduct ourselves gently with respect

---

[1] Aristotle, *The Eudemian Ethics*, transl. H. Rackham, London – Cambridge, MA 1935, 1219b11–12.

[2] Ibidem, 1214b4–5.

to sleeping people, strangers, individuals suffering from mental disorders, and those with disabilities of perception and deliberation. We feel affected by intrinsic values incorporated in someone or something, or in contrast, we exhibit respect without actual feeling or affection exchanged with the other (this case will be considered below within Smith's conception). In place of affection, we sometimes follow a rational "purpose," or an idea of respect, in order to protect equality, fairness, and justice, which is again with respect to values that are universally recognized. "For affection is measured by the worth of the friends and by one sort of equality,"[3] Aristotle teaches. In this chapter, selected philosophical, psychological, and sociological aspects of respect will be revisited, including respect as an ability to conduct oneself in a specific way that means something more to others than just toleration – i.e., letting be or letting go things.

Respect as a moral skill has been known to ancient Greek thinkers. Aristotle implicitly conceptualized the genuine psychological interiority of respect and discovered that respectful performance and responsibility belong together. In Aristotle, respect is not a private right because it occurs within interpersonal relations. "Our private rights in relation to our friends depend only on ourselves, whereas our rights in relation to the rest of men are established by law and do not depend on us."[4] As we know from historical sources, Greek social structures have been cultivated as communities and "voluntary associations"[5] (genuine rooted in house-holding) rather than as today's atomic societies. So to Aristotle it was natural to consider *homonoia* and *politiké philia* (civic friendship including like-mindedness and attention paying[6]: "People make their way together, on the basis that they will get some advantage from it [...] for it has to do with what is advantageous, and what affects people's life"[7]). "To promote friendship is thought to be the special task of political science,"[8] he says. At the same time, to Aristotle "friendship [...] is a state of the moral character"[9] that is based on the intentionality to which a virtuous person is able. However, in the age of the Greek *poleis*, citizens cultivated a minimal degree of friendship one with another too: "[...] useful friendship is of two kinds, the merely legal and the moral."[10] The first "is based on a definite agreement, which is a civic

---

[3] Ibidem, 1239a2.

[4] Ibidem, 1235a6.

[5] Ibidem, 1234b4.

[6] Aristotle, *Nicomachean Ethics*, transl. W. D. Ross, 1167b. Retrieved from http://classics.mit.edu/Aristotle/nicomachean.1.i.html [21.05.2009].

[7] Ibidem, 1160a, 1167b.

[8] Aristotle, *The Eudemian Ethics*, op. cit., 1234b2.

[9] Ibidem, 1234b3.

[10] Ibidem, 1242b15.

and legal friendship,"[11] Aristotle explains. In our considerations, we are following Aristotle's thinking as developed in his *Eudemian Ethics*, from the intimate interpersonal, through the utility and pleasure oriented, to the formal relationships, because we suggest that respect is a pre-condition for every kind of social relatedness. Aristotle describes step by step the friendships among relatives and unknown fellows living in the same polis (city): "Friendship of relatives, that of camrades, that of partners and what is termed civic friendship." The latter is still based on utility and not on neutrality as one might expect. The neutral and indifferent could be deductively derived from the following reasoning:

> Fellow-citizens are one another's friends in the same way as different cities are, and Athens no longer knoweth Megara... not similarly do citizens know one another, when they are not useful to one another.[12]

What might be surprising (and paradoxically: also not surprising) for Aristotle's contemporary reader is that he promotes a conditional utilitarian exchange that is reminiscent of Kohlberg's Stage 2 of moral reasoning – i.e., of "making fair deals in terms of concrete exchange and satisfying immediate needs."[13] This kind of reciprocity is a common characteristics of cooperation between "lower animals" and humans (we can compare historical definitions of zoon politicon in Aristotle, Darwin, Singer, and other researchers). In reality, as Aristotle shows in *Eudemian Ethics* and *Nicomachean Ethics*, here are many kinds of friendship. One of them presupposes sociability as a pleasure of being together, and trust and justice as the profound basis of friendship. But the pre-condition of such a social friendship is "to perceive and to know a friend, therefore, [it] is necessarily in a manner to perceive and in a manner to know oneself."[14] So friendship is a relationship reserved for closely related persons who affect one another reciprocally, and understanding and deliberating their "purposes" instead for unknown persons and strangers. This is, why an "active community of perception must of necessity be in a smaller circle."[15] By knowing another as one knows him or herself, one is able to trust other persons and to spend time with them. "It is not possible for people to spend their time with each other if they are not pleasent,"[16] as he claims in the *Nicomachean Ethics*

---

[11] Ibidem, 1242b17.

[12] Ibidem, 1242b14.

[13] G. Harman, J. J. Thomson, *Moral Relativism and Moral Objectivity*, Cambridge, MA 1996, p. 54. "But when they trust each other for repayment, it tends to be moral [...] because it founds at the intention [...] and friendly justice." Aristotle, *Eudemian Ethics*, op. cit., 1242b17, 1243a24, 1243b28.

[14] Ibidem, 1245a14.

[15] Ibidem, 1245b17–18.

[16] Aristotle, *Nicomachean Ethics*, op. cit., 1157a–b.

According to Aristotle, ignorance produces distance and exclusion; other is not only another person, he is a stranger, making initiating active interaction with him difficult. Are we able to trust without knowing the stranger? In this volume, otherness will be considered as transcending one's cognitive abilities and as a challenge for one's own morality because in social life epistemological problems and ethical problems are directly connected. To solve this difficulty, Aristotle applies his golden rule to demonstrate how dignity and respect can be reached at the philosophical level. Although his golden mean adresses *all* humans, one is able to apply his method of balance only in an intuitive way. Being respectful to others might be expressed in seeking for a mean with respect to them. Furthermore, behaving respectful to others is a mean between the excess of being ingratiating and the deficiency of being surly, Aristotle claims. On the other hand, respect for oneself ("the question whether one is one's own friend or not involves much consideration"[17]) is a mean between the excess of vanity and the deficiency of pusillanimity. He clearly considers respect and dignity in the *Eudemian Ethics*:

> A man who in his conduct pays no regard at all to another but is contemptuous is self-willed; he who regards another in everything and is inferior to everybody is obsequious; he who regards another in some things but not in others, and is regardful of persons worthy of regard, is dignified.[18]

Two thousands years later some quite different, Zeitgeist-related concepts of respect were proposed by Adam Smith in *Theory of Moral Sentiments* (1759[1]) and by Immanuel Kant in *Groundwork for the Metaphysics of Morals* (1781[1]). Because of their work, this chapter considers psychological, moral, and sociological claims of respect. Following G. Lind's educational theory of morality qua *virtue*, which is founded on experimental research, a respectful performance is rooted both in affectivity and cognition, the latter understood as a cognitively-structured skill. Some of the arguments of Kant and Smith confirm Lind's claim. When individuals respect one another, this enables them to follow social rules that are impersonal and abstract much better. What is genuinely worthy and regarded as valuable at the personal and interpersonal levels, is protected by social rules and entire regulatory systems.

2. Adam Smith: Between affection and reflection

The Theory of Moral Sentiments (1759) of the "Professor of Moral Philosophy in the University of Glasgow" was the manifestation of English moral

[17] Aristotle, *The Eudemian Ethics*, op. cit., 1240a1.

[18] Ibidem, 1233b5.

philosophy as based on experience and using the experimental method. It was difficult to ignore even by the rationalists of the Enlightenment. Smith rejected Hutcheson's "sixth" sense hypothesis and considered emotions to be cultivated – i.e., reflected and deliberated passions by involving them in the personal moral life. Only the brute passions already mentioned in Aristotle cannot be part of morality because they are misleading and confusing insofar as they contribute to moral decisions and conduct:

> [...] of the two types of incontinent man the one does not abide by the conclusions of his deliberation, while the excitable man does not deliberate at all. [...] the incontinent man is unable to act.[19]

In Smith's conception, respect belongs to the "reflected passions." From the first passages of *The Theory of Moral Sentiments*, respect and sympathy seem to be personal skills: individuals actively experience empathy, sympathy (or antipathy) as being motivated by them. This indicates the cognitive nature of respect. At the same time, sensitivity and one's cognitive equipment enable a person to perceive others in their specifically *human* existential and social condition. They can also identify natural and social opportunities that have impact on the human condition: "We sympathise even with dead [...] we are chiefly affected by those circumstances [...]."[20] Being guided by social empathy or sympathy is being guided by social cognition, by taking an interpersonal perspective, and not only by compassion. Respectful behavior result from "our own consciousness [...], from our putting ourselves in [...] [a] situation, and from our lodging."[21] Moreover, respect and sympathy are reflected affects. Awareness and thinking do not replace occasional affective motivations but they might transform them in a cognitive skill to empathize with others just in the social situations. In his psychological conception, Smith is familiar with the rationalist (and cognitive) model of moral subjectivity as a social one. As social beings, human reflection accompanies and regulates affective processes that can be misleading.

> It is reason, principle, conscience, the inhabitant of the breast, the man within, the great judge and arbiter of our conduct. It is he who, whenever we are about to act so as to affect the happiness of others, calls to us, with a voice capable of astonishing the most presumptuous of our passions, that we are but one of the multitude, in no respect better than any other in it.[22]

---

[19] Aristotle, *Nicomachean Ethics*, op. cit., 1052a.

[20] A. Smith, *The Theory of Moral Sentiments*, Saõ Paulo 2006, p. 13.

[21] Ibidem, p. 13.

[22] Ibidem, p. 120.

Paying attention and behaving respectfully can be fully rationally stimulated in a case of the "conditional" hypothetical sympathy to strangers or to human beings who do not evoke the appropriate emotional states in their fellows that *should take place*. The usage of situational awareness, self-investigation, and applying the proper social norms are recommended instruments to construct a corrective – the idea of "my" socially expected behavior instead of the missing moral emotion that one's mind is unable to produce. In the situation described below, Smith portrays a realistic mental life of a human being – a sovereign agency that acts instead of only reacts. People are sometimes unable of feel the situation-appropriate emotional states. Aristotle and Augustine (and Smith, through his criticisms) collected examples of situation-unappropriate emotional states, such as enjoying tragedy, death, and the like. It is intelligence and memory that picture things, persons, and situations in one's mind. Those mental representations, images, and narratives are meaningful (they have been memorized as such) and they can move the whole mental life. By self-investigating his mind, the subject creates the proper scenario and starts to act as an actor performing, in his mind, the role of himself as he wishes to be like in the moment.[23] And he wishes to be an empathetic self. What Smith describes seems to be role playing by a self-construction of his own emotional performance:

> A stranger passes by us in the street with all the marks of the deepest affliction; and we are immediately told that he has just received the news of the death of his father. It is impossible that, in this case, we should not approve of his grief. Yet it may often happen, without any defect of humanity on our part, that, so far from entering into the violence of his sorrow, we should scarce conceive the first movements of concern upon his account. [...] It is upon the consciousness of this conditional sympathy, that our approbation of his sorrow is founded, even in those cases in which that sympathy does not actually take place; and the general rules derived from our preceding experience of what our sentiments would commonly correspond with, correct upon this, as upon many other occasions, the impropriety of our present emotions.[24]

Reflection without memory and imagination would be only an analytical skill. But reflection that collaborates with memory and imagination is a stronger power that can evoke and regulate emotions ("passions," as Smith expresses it) whose nature is contingent and irregular even in highly moral

[23] "Acting [...] is a deliberate association of thought or meaning with chosen behavior [...]. And acting is similarly parasiting on real behavior, real action, thought, and speech." G.L. Hagberg, *Describing Ourselves. Wittgenstein and Autobiographical Consciousness*, Oxford – New York 2008, p. 200.

[24] A. Smith, *The Theory of Moral Sentiments*, op. cit., pp. 21–22.

personalities. Reflection may bring emotions into balance to establish self-control and the self-governance which is crucial for one to be an authentic socio-moral agent instead of following conventions. Reflection also enables one to communicate with other persons in place of handling them. "It is to be observed accordingly, that we are still more anxious to communicate to our friends our disagreeable than our agreeable passions"[25] in a direct way, within rude emotions, from "my own" perspective only which cannot be a universal measure. From respect for other persons, a transition from emotions to reflection seems to be unavoidable. People need to learn verbal and non-verbal modi of expression if they want to share their emotional representations with others in a reflected and careful way. They learn respectful expressions from the culture and education. To Smith, there are some affinities between respect, care, and "the virtue of sensibility."[26] Upon interpersonal relationships, Smith continues, "I judge of your sight by my sight, of your ear by my ear, of your reason by my reason, of your resentment by my resentment, of your love by my love. I neither have, nor can have, any other way of judging about them." In the beginning of social situations, impartiality seems to be proof of respectful judgment behavior:

> Reflected passion, which he [or she] thus conceives, is much weaker than the original one, it necessarily abates the violence of what he felt before he came into their presence, before he began to recollect in what manner they would be affected by it, and to view his situation in this candid and impartial light.[27]

The expression "in impartial light" means that it is a perspective of distance to others' feelings and their mental representations that I identify through verbal and non-verbal communication, and interpret them in a way constructing meanings in *my mind*. After my mind (as an epistemological and judging agency) coordinates them, a new perspective, namely *my perspective*, is crystallized. In sum: at the beginning, the process of respectful social judgment making requires an affectively-based mutual compassion which facilitates judging in my mind. In the end, forming social judgments and decisions in a respectful way requires distance from another person's mental states and their representations in my mind because another person became a part of my mental life: I have constructed my own interpretation of him/her.

Furthermore, reflected judgment making and discourse can strengthen personal affective self-control: "Society and conversation, therefore, are the most powerful remedies for restoring the mind to its tranquillity, if, at any time, it has

[25] Ibidem.

[26] Ibidem, p. 20.

[27] Ibidem, pp. 17–18.

unfortunately lost it,"[28] Smith concludes. In his eyes, rational, self-governing,[29] and respectful behavior belong together. Respectful reactions to others' facial, bodily, and discoursively expressed emotions provides distance and a place for understanding, thinking, and making a right decision. We can perceive, feel, and value emotions ("the very affectation is a proof" of an engaged participant in the social life), but we should not follow them immediately. Immediate effects of emotionally-based conduct "are mischief to the person against whom they are directed."[30] Smith provides an additional argument against emotions as guidelines for decision making: it is the "irregularity in the human breast"[31] that strongly diverges from the repeatability of human behavior preestablished in regulations, norms, and rules because these are created to guarantee repetition and forward planning. Living in a society, one's decisions and actions also have consequences for others; thus, people awaiting reflected and principled behaviors from that they can anticipate somehow by recognizing articulated criteria (e.g., principles and rules) they share with others. If this were not so, a person could have problems with self-understanding and self-esteem, on the one hand, and have mutual understanding and mutual respect, on the other hand. There are parallels to be seen in Smith's and Ekman's (2003) claims on respect and self-control of anger:

> If we are *attentive* to our emotional state, not only conscious of how we are feeling but pausing to consider whether we want to act on our angry feelings, it will still be a struggle if we decide not to act on our anger. That struggle will be greater for some of us than others.[32]

The "stronger power" of rationality, in both Smith and Habermas, is predestinated to winner in the social decision elaborating process where processing changes due to proceduralism.

As social beings, people can respect attitudes, social rank, wealth, greatness, and other phenomena. "We frequently see the respectful attentions of the world more strongly directed towards the rich and the great, than towards the wise and the virtuous. We see frequently the vices and follies of the powerful much less despised than the poverty and weakness of the innocent,"[33] Smith notes. This kind of attention seldom relates to the proper moral respect that is free of interests and benefits. "The respect which we feel for wisdom

---

[28] Ibidem, p. 18.
[29] Ibidem, p. 20.
[30] Ibidem, p. 30.
[31] Ibidem, p. 95.
[32] P. Ekman, *Emotions Revealed. Recognizing Faces and Feelings*, New York 2003, p. 116.
[33] A. Smith, *The Theory of Moral Sentiments*, op. cit., p. 54.

and virtue is, no doubt, different from that which we conceive for wealth and greatness,"[34] because wisdom and virtue are typical attributes of a moral condition and moral agency. By contrast, wealth and greatness are attributes of the morally neutral condition. To Smith, respect for ambition and avidity are similar. It could be, however, that high moral legitimacy can be reached if one undertakes additional activities to be respected by political authorities and law-givers in a non-democratic society. Instead of deepening this topic, Smith describes mechanisms of self-esteem in the same way as the interpersonal psychological theory of the 20th century did. Every one incorporates an innate "love of praise-worthiness" or "desire of approbation."[35] Further, Smith advocates the self-distant objectivity in making judgments about oneself that is a precondition for rational self-reflection. Another's perspective i part of the social perspective, but it must be coordinated with one's own perspective: the fully social perspective contains our perspective, too.

> But, in order to attain this satisfaction, we must become the impartial spectators of our own character and conduct. We must endeavour to view them with the eyes of other people, or as other people are likely to view them. When seen in this light, if they appear to us as we wish, we are happy and contented.[36]

Thus, a Smithian interpersonal struggle for recognition might be interpreted as a struggle for "equitable justice,"[37] which can only be morally legitimized if one is able of keep distance from one's selfish interests. This new social awareness enables an individual "to desire it [equitable justice] where it [the approbation] is really due, [...] [and] to desire no more than that a most essential act of justice should be done to us."[38] By contrast, "ignorant and groundless praise can give no solid joy, no satisfaction."[39] According to Smith, self-esteem and reciprocal social respect belong together. Their evolution presupposes both affective stimulation and reflective construction, the work of memory and projection, and taking a social perspective.

3. Immanuel Kant: The human ability of to be moral

Kant apparently refutes moral sentiment theory in his moral philosophy, but at the same time defends the importance of respect. He implicitly supports

34 Ibidem.
35 Ibidem, pp. 101–105.
36 Ibidem, pp. 102–103.
37 Ibidem.
38 Ibidem, p. 105.
39 Ibidem, p. 104.

Smith's claim that "we desire both to be respectable and to be respected"[40] in his deontological theory of interpersonal relations and self-esteem.

Kant clearly distinguishes between, on the one hand, things and attitudes as being solely conditionally valued natural beings, and on the other hand, *persons* as autonomous beings with their own *intrinsic value*.

> In the realm of ends everything has either a price or an intrinsic value. Anything with a price can be replaced by something else as its equivalent, whereas anything that is above all price and therefore admits of no equivalent has intrinsic value.[41]

What does the *intrinsic value* of a human being mean for Kant? In means that the use of a human being as the means to any other end than a self-determined moral action is strongly limited. A human being must be respected as a personally autonomous law-giver and subject of moral action. To be this sort of subject creates a sense of personal dignity, which is the foundation for "inviolable and inalienable human rights." Both human dignity, as being the foundation of autonomous rights, and autonomous rights as being derivate of human dignity, are objects of respect. Dignity, autonomy, and respect cannot be "preferred," i.e., dislocated within a value hierarchy, so they have only unconditional value:

> There is such a thing! It is a human being! I maintain that man – and in general every rational being – exists as an end in himself and not merely as a means to be used by this or that will at its discretion [...] have only relative value as means, and are therefore called "things" [Sachen]; whereas rational beings are called "persons," because their nature already marks them out as ends in themselves (i.e. as not to be used merely as means) – which makes such a being an object of respect, and something that sets limits to what anyone can choose to do. Things that are preferred have only conditional value.[42]

Following Kant, beings "whose existence is an end in itself"[43] are *persons* insofar as they are gifted with autonomous moral lawgiving. The law-giving as "intrinsic" value is "unalienable" insofar as it is innate to individuals. So, if a human perceives one's and his or her fellows as autonomous moral law-givers, he or she must behave with (and is to treat others as possessing) independent moral agency (i.e., as a moral person). Furthermore, persons respect their intrinsic value in two ways: through individual self-esteem and mutual recognition.

---

[40] Ibidem, p. 53.

[41] I. Kant, *Groundwork for the Metaphysics of Morals*, transl. J. Benneth, 2008, Chapter 2. Retrieved from http://www.earlymoderntexts.com/pdf/kantgw.pdf [24.05.2013].

[42] Ibidem, p. 28.

[43] Ibidem.

In Kant, mutual recognition seems to be rooted in respect but it is more than respect only. Mutual recognition requires a "positive harmony with humanity" in every personal moral action as well as in every interpersonal moral interaction. "It isn't sufficient that the action not conflict with humanity in our person as an end in itself; it must also harmonize with it"[44] in a supportive way. In his universalistic social system of ends in themselves ("the Kingdom of Ends"), Kant presupposes that everyone's moral ends harmonize with others' moral ends. It means "that everyone positively tries to further the ends of others as far as he can"[45] by showing respect for others and for him or herself as an autonomous subject of moral activity.

In sum, a rational and autonomous being is "indeed an irreplaceable end," or "supreme end,"[46] of moral actions, dignity, the "supreme" moral principle (i.e., the categorical imperative), and virtue (ability), following the autonomous lawgiving of reason and being "the object of [...] immediate respect"[47] and recognition. Kant notes:

> So morality, and humanity so far as it is capable of morality, are the only things that have dignity [...] [or] intrinsic value which I have called dignity [...]. [It must] be recognized as dignity or intrinsic value [...]. And what is it, then, that justifies virtue, or a morally good frame of mind? [...] It is its enabling the rational being to have a share in the giving of universal laws and thus to become fit to be a member in a possible realm of [supreme] ends.[48]

One hundred years before the capitalization and reification of humans in the market, Kant promotes respect for them by putting their dignity "infinitely above any price."[49] He makes his readers aware of the gap between value and price, which mirrors the gap between being a moral person and being a material thing:

> [...] everything has either a price or an intrinsic value. Anything with a price can be replaced by something else as its equivalent, whereas anything that is above all price and therefore admits of no equivalent has intrinsic value [...]. Something that involves general human desires and needs has a market price.[50]

Because of his unswerving respect for humanity, Kant did not allow either prostitution or organ donation as human activities. "Humanity in our

---

44 Ibidem, p. 30.
45 Ibidem.
46 Ibidem.
47 Ibidem.
48 Ibidem.
49 Ibidem.
50 Ibidem.

person prevents us from owning ourselves in the way that we might own a material objects."[51] In his ethics, however, he finally assumes that it is not a law as such but the moral ability of autonomous lawgiving that is the true and unique object of moral respect. If this is so, moral maturity is reached within an acknowledgment of the social rules as being derivatives of rational and autonomous law-giving and human dignity. In contrast, immature moral judgment demonstrates respect for laws without having reflected on their origins (universal autonomy as legitimacy) and having justified them. In this way, human dignity can be disrespected or violated. To Kant, the primacy of moral duty expressed in the "Grundgesetz" is the proper object of respect as being a very human source of moral conduct. Piaget, in turn, reasoned that moral duties are objects of reverence (*Achtung*) and humanity, as the source of morality, is the genuine object of properly understood moral respect. This essential moral respect addresses humanity for its ability to be moral. Morality is a pre-dominant transcendental feature of the human condition. Thus, morality can (and ought to) be respected for its intrinsic goodness ("so pre-eminent good which we call 'moral', which is *already* present in the person himself who acts in accordance with it"[52]), a goodness in itself.[53] Respect is the most relevant duty of humanity as being (reason) capable of moral law-giving, which is, in the deontological tradition, a synonym of good. "The law-giving that confers all value must therefore have dignity (i.e., an unconditional and incomparable value); and the esteem that a rational being must have for this is best described as 'respect.'"[54]

In Section 1 of the *Groundwork*, Kant clarifies his concept of respect by partially referring to affectivity and partially to the processes of moral cognition. He defines respect as being affected by the supreme principle of reason – i.e., "a concept of reason," which is the categorical imperative. It is the will that experiences respect as an "effect."[55]

[51] M. Rosen, *Dignity. Its History and Meaning*, Cambridge, MA – London 2012, p. 149.

[52] To compare the translation proposed by A. Wood: I. Kant, *Groundwork for the Metaphysics of Morals*, ed. and transl. A. Wood, New Haven – London 2002, p. 17.

[53] I. Kant, *Groundwork for the Metaphysics...*, transl. J. Benneth, op. cit., p. 35.

[54] Ibidem.

[55] In the contemporary moral sciences, a gap between intelligence and affectivity, on the one hand, and the gap between the will and the reflected emotions of approval and disapproval, on the other hand, seems already to be bridged as shown in the next chapters of this volume. In Kant, however, the genuine cognitive construction of the supreme practical principle effects "the will" and the will's response is of an affective character. Today the notion of "will" is treated as a philosophical construct that does not have its own existence in the mind.

> It might be objected that I tried to take refuge in an obscure feeling behind the word "respect," instead of clearing things up through a concept of reason. Although respect is indeed a feeling, it doesn't come from outer influence; rather, it is a feeling that a rational concept creates unaided; so it is different in kind from all the feelings caused from outside, the ones that can come from desire or fear. When I directly recognize something as a law for myself I recognize it with respect, which merely means that I am conscious of submitting my will to a law without interference from any other influences on my mind. The will's being directly settled by law, and the consciousness of this happening, is called "respect;" so respect should be seen as an effect of the law's operation on the person's will, not as a cause of it. Really, respect is the thought of a value that breaks down my self-love. Thus it is not something to be either desired or feared, though it has something analogous to both desire and fear. The only thing that can be respected is law, and it has to be the law that we impose on ourselves yet recognize as necessary in itself. As a law it makes us subject to it, without consulting our self-love; which gives it some analogy to fear. As imposed on us by ourselves, it is a consequence of our will; which gives it some analogy to preference. This is really the only basic sense of the term "respect." Any respect for a person is only respect for the law (of righteousness, etc.) of which the person provides an example. Our respect for a person's talents, for instance, is our recognition that we ought to practice until we are as talented as he is; we see him as a kind of example of a law, because we regard it as our duty to improve our talents. So respect for persons is a disguised form of respect for law. All moral concern (as it is called) consists solely in respect for the law.[56]

In this spectacular passage, Kant advocates his radical deontological viewpoint by emphasizing that "any respect for a person is only respect for the law": every rational and autonomous person represents moral law in his or her judgments and decisions which are based on this ("the person provides an example" of his or her "righteousness"). On the other hand, Kant's concern that the "pre-eminent good" "is *already* present in the person" clearly indicates that human beings are worthy of (reciprocal) respect as potential authors of the moral good. At the same time, the potentiality of "pre-eminent good" can be actualized only by following the supreme moral low: by principled moral action that maximalizes good in the world.

After Kant, the anthropocentric ideal of moral dignity and respect have been modified. With Derrida's essay *The Animal that Therefore I Am*, and later research, moral philosophy came to think that human autonomy does not entail a human right to assert authority over all other living beings as strongly as in the past. How is the dominion of reason over the emotions shared with

[56] I. Kant, *Groundwork for the Metaphysics...*, transl. J. Benneth, op. cit., p. 11.

non-human living beings established when this seems to promote the development of moral cognition in humans, as is shown in the next chapters? Of course, the socialization and education that we call *culture* or *Bildung* supports that development stronger than did the natural environment over millions of years. Kant as a non-naturalist and Spinoza as a naturalist moral philosopher considered certain mental faculties as being properly human – for example, reason, among others, is "the strongest of affects," as d'Espinoza calls it in his *Ethics*. The question of what *ought* to be proper to human and non-human beings was answered in classical moral philosophy. The question of what is *really* proper to them is still open. Kant's explanation of humanity as the "supreme end" of moral action presupposes reciprocal recognition between humans. The "norm of reciprocity" and "reciprocal altruism"[57] are universal in nature, as P. Singer argues, following H. Becker's category of homo reciprocus. But can we reasonably assume that a universal norm is, at the same time, the highest moral norm?

4. Kant, Dworkin, and Darwall: Discussion

In his last book, *Justice for Hedgehogs*,[58] R. Dworkin addresses some criticisms to the Kantian principle of respect for life. Let us examine his reasoning:

> Do you value your life as objectively important in virtue of something [subjectively] special about your life, so that it would be perfectly consistent for you not to treat other human lives as having the same kind of importance? Or do you value your life in that way because you think all human life is objectively important? [...] You should focus further on the question whether the objective importance of your life reflects a universal importance – your life has that value only because it is a human life – or a special [subjective] importance because you have some property that some other people do not have.[59]

Following Kant, Dworkin asks why humans feel respect for their lives. He identifies the typical subjective properties and values that are used to grant human lives *special* or *particular* qualities. Such properties and values may be universalizable only if they have an impact on a person leading a good life, i.e., morally qualified life, as Dworkin claims. According to Kant and Aristotle: if they have an impact on a virtuous life's conduct. They are not universalizable in themselves:

---

[57] P. Singer, *The Expanding Circle. Ethics, Evolution and the Moral Progress*, Princeton 1981^1, 2011^2, p. 37.

[58] R. Dworkin, *Justice for Hedgehogs*, Cambridge, MA – London 2011.

[59] Ibidem, p. 255.

> Subjective value is in its nature special [...]. Of course there is much that does distinguish you from other people [...]. Some of these properties, at least, might be important to you in considering *how* do you live [...]. But we are considering a different claim: not whether personal properties should affect how you live, but whether they account for the objective importance of your living well.[60]

Further, Dworkin demonstrates why overly simple reasoning (from "special importance" to "special objective importance"[61]) can lead to fanaticism if people who aspire to be law-givers for the whole community do not show respect for other people, which is a preliminary condition for collective and just law-giving. Such persons, on the contrary, pay respect to abstract values – e.g., to life-in-itself instead of to the life subjects and their autonomous dignity:

> Much of slaughter inspired by religion has presupposed, or at least not denied, the equal importance of the lives of those slaughtered: their death has been thought necessary to save their immortal souls or to spread the true faith and the true laws among their people [...].[62]

Dworkin assumes "that dignity requires recognition" (i.e., awareness, self-awareness, formal operations, and advanced social cognition) rather than a naive "appraisal, respect [...], because thinking your life important is a presupposition of thinking that it matters how you live."[63] Our life is one of many different lives: mutual respect among living persons is the only moral guarantee of coexistence. In all social circumstances, including democracies, there are individuals who misuse their autonomy to give moral directives that would be valid for everyone, in every situation, whereas "moral norm is linked to a feeling of autonomy."[64] They derive respect from pressured agreements on their directives and mix feeling of obedience and fear (the "obscure feeling" in Kant!) with the reflected feeling of respect.

But the feeling of obedience, as Piaget clarifies things, "has to do with what is necessary and not just what is desirable or preferable to do."[65] That is, obedience means the "unilateral respect" that "was present in the morality of obedience. It is the respect of the lower for the higher, for authority. Mutual respect differs from this in that it occurs between equals and appears

---

[60] Ibidem, pp. 256–257.

[61] Ibidem, p. 257.

[62] Ibidem, pp. 257–258.

[63] Ibidem.

[64] J. Piaget, "Intelligence and Affectivity," transl. T. A. Brown, C. E. Kaegi, *Annual Reviews*, Palo Alto, CA 1981, p. 55.

[65] Ibidem.

only with autonomy."[66] Full social respect takes place if persons perceive one another at eye level.

In his paper *Two Kinds of Respect*,[67] S. L. Darwall addresses the problem: "various ways of regarding and behaving toward others, and social arrangements which encourage those ways, are inconsistent with the respect to which all persons are entitled."[68] He asks several epistemological questions, such as: "How could respect be something which is due to all persons? [...] Is respect a single kind of attitude? Is it primarily, or even solely, a moral attitude? Are persons the only sort of thing to which respect is appropriate?"[69] He distinguishes different ways in which people can be respected[70] and categorizes the following facts as respect objects: 1. persons, 2. persons' features, roles, and products, and 3. social institutions.

As Darwall explains, people can be respected 1. as persons, 2. for their features or achievements (ideas, visions, works), and 3. for their institutional roles, positions, professions, etc. "Law [...] and social institutions with their positions and roles"[71] are objects of the same kind of respect: "this kind of respect consists in giving appropriate consideration or recognition to some feature of its object in deliberating about what to do, I shall call it *recognition respect*."[72] To Darwall, the meaning of recognition is that one is reasoning and making justified judgments about his or her behavior and its social context before performing it. Recognition of respect presupposes judgmental cognitive operations. "Indeed, it is just this sort of respect which is said to be owed to all persons"[73] by other persons as rational beings. If we say that persons are entitled to respect, we mean that "they are entitled to have other persons take seriously and weight appropriately the fact that they are persons in deliberating about what to do. Such respect is recognition respect"[74] accompanied by rational operations, situation awareness, and self-awareness. "What it requires as appropriate is not a matter of general agreement"[75] or official conventions. To take another "present self" in its otherness seems to be a highly relevant social skill, but it is, at the same time, a conceptualization of abstract otherness.

---

66 Ibidem, p. 67.
67 S. L. Darwall, "Two Kinds of Respect," *Ethics*, 1977, vol. 88, no. 1, pp. 36–49.
68 Ibidem, p. 36.
69 Ibidem.
70 Ibidem, p. 37.
71 Ibidem, p. 38.
72 Ibidem.
73 Ibidem.
74 Ibidem.
75 Ibidem.

By contrast, in everyday situations one can respect a given person for his or her concrete individual characteristics. One's feeling of respect may vary between strong, soft, very soft, and disrespect. Such a person, in my opinion, needs to be educationally strengthened in his or her respect experience. Philosophical considerations and open-ended discussions about social issues involving respect can open minds to otherness and human status both at the affective level and at the level of cognition and awareness, regardless of sympathizing with others' attitudes, bodily expressions, ideas, etc.

The second kind of respect (which seems to be more genuine and spontanous) might engage affects, intuitions, believes, and evaluations:

> Because this sort of respect consists in a positive appraisal of a person, or his [or her] qualities, I shall call it *appraisal respect.* Unlike recognition respect, one may have appraisal respect for someone without having any particular conception of just what behavior from *oneself* would be required [...]. Appraisal respect is the positive appraisal itself.[76]

In making his distinctions, Darwall is giving no important role to the feeling of respect in social experience.[77] Admiration and respect do not have the same weight, so they have different meaning, he claims. "The feeling of respect for a person is the one which is occasioned by the positive appraisal which constitutes appraisal respect for the person."[78] Darwall, however, considers the unidirectional oriented impact of feelings on the cognitive processes. Numerous feelings, emotional moods, evaluations, etc., are produced through the cognitive processes, information, experiences, recollections, and unconscious processes. They can strongly contribute to "recognition respect." Again, recognition makes facts relevant; recognized facts gain importance in beholder's eyes. It is much better for the stability of respect if one is reflecting on that relevance, sharing his or her reflection with other, evaluating, and making judgments on the deliberative and rational level. And this is, why "recognition respect" – following Darwall – "consists in giving it proper weight in deliberation. Thus, to have recognition respect for others is to give proper weight to the fact that they are persons"[79] and "to act accordingly."[80] To summarize, appraisal respect and recognition respect seem to be intimately linked in human minds as feeling and thinking.

76 Ibidem, p. 39.
77 Ibidem.
78 Ibidem.
79 Ibidem.
80 Ibidem, p. 40.

Is recognition respect an attitude? Darwall's reasoning speaks for recognition as a cognitive skill. If it would be an attitude only, people would follow social conventions exclusively to avoid sanctions; in such a case one might "regard it as requiring restrictions on the moral acceptability of actions connected with it. And, crucially, it is to regard such a restriction as not incidental, but as arising because of the feature or the fact itself."[81] But this kind of respect seems to be highly superficial because "it is true [...] that one can be 'respectful' of something without having any respect for it."[82] In ethics, we cannot agree with Darwall's conceptualization of respect as an attitude. It needs to be deepened by Smith's claim that "affectation is a proof." However, to protect one's own behavior against the deficiencies of "appraisal respect" and disrespect, Darwall recommends the use of "recognition respect":

> If one judges that someone is not worthy of (appraisal) respect because he is dishonest, one is commited to recognition respect for considerations of honesty. [...] The only beings who are appropriate objects of appraisal respect are those who are capable of acting for reasons and hence capable of conceiving of various facts as meriting more or less consideration in deliberation.[83]

Darwall follows the deontological criteria of intentional and rational self-determination as the main features of moral personality. Furthermore, "the only beings who are appropriate objects of appraisal respect are those who are themselves capable of recognition respect, this is, of acting deliberately."[84] For Darwall, humanity must be actualized as autonomous, and rational personal judgmental activity must be acknowledged, recognized, and respected by others as, similarly, autonomous and rational humans. His arguments might have important consequences for the status of persons having mental disorders and are dissocial; Darwall implicitly qualifies persons who are themselves incapable of being subjects of "recognition respect" as objects of "recognition respect" (instead of appraisal respect) in others' eyes. The reason is that their judgmental abilities cannot be actual.

5. The ways of respectful conduct: Conclusion

"Free beings alone can be stranger[s] to one another. Their freedom which is 'common' to them is precisely what separates them,"[85] E. Lévinas states. From

[81] Ibidem.

[82] Ibidem.

[83] Ibidem, p. 47.

[84] Ibidem, p. 48.

[85] E. Lévinas, *Totality and Infinity. An Essay of Exteriority An Essay on Exteriority*, transl. A. Lingis, The Hague – Boston – London 1979, pp. 73–74.

a sociological viewpoint, mutual respect is the unique remedy that protects individuals within their interpersonal relationships against "all imperialism of the same [...]. The collectivity in which I say 'you' or 'we' is not a plural of the 'I.'"[86] To Lévinas, respect is a mental withdrawal that enables strange persons to coexist. By being distant they can proceed "from the I to the Other" and, consequently, promote plurality instead of totality. This is why respect is so fundamental for democratic relationships as shown in one of Lévinas most impressive books, *Totality and Infinity*. Democratic relationships are not established forever, they cannot be institutionalized. They need to be cultivated by individuals themselves. Furthermore, in cultivating interpersonality we are not in one-sided relations with things, either mechanically or practically. We are in reciprocal, dialogical, and communicative relations with other persons (as Buber distinguished them in *I and Thou*). "The Other [...] is respected,"[87] that is, protected, against his or her de-individualization and is recognized in his or her otherness. He or she may become familiar to me without being dominated or represented by me. He or she is present him or herself. The sociological meaning of respect is connected with ontological individuality, irreplaceability, and sovereignty within the interpersonal and should never become intrapersonal. But a pure "let him be," "the pure disclosure," is not enough to be granted with respect and to gleam with one's own light, as Lévinas says. To him, a "face to face approach, a conversation,"[88] is the most proper interpersonal relationship. Exclusively in the face to face situation, "Justice is the recognition of his [others'] privilege qua Other [...]"[89] Lévinas' conversation, Darwall's deliberation, Smith's empathy, Kant's idea of self-lawgiving humanity, Aristotle's friendship, and Socratic dialogues are ways of promoting reciprocal respect and self-esteem. In this volume, these ways are explored again and again.

[86] Ibidem, p. 39.
[87] Ibidem, p. 69.
[88] Ibidem, p. 71.
[89] Ibidem, p. 72.

Chapter V

What is universal? Between subjectivity and intersubjectivity

1. Life project as moral challenge for every one

Human beings conduct their lives across the "span of time each man has between birth and death."[1] To be a "newcomer" in the world is part of the human condition. "The newcomer possesses the capacity of beginning anew, that is, of acting"[2] intentionally, capable of changing the world around themselves. However, it is the world they share with others. Being thrown into the world, they are also thrown in relationships with other, already experienced "aging persons" (to speak as Erikson) who have the task of educating the newcomers, i.e., to enable them to live in interpersonal relationships and to involve them in the social world "where we exist primarily as acting and speaking beings."[3] At the same time, it is (or should be) clear, that the newcomers will live in their own individual, new way because they live for the future and not for the past. But they are educated to conserve the past, too. They need time to learn how to deal with the closed or ongoing life projects of others, and at the same time, how to deal with their own open life project. In this *conditio humana* it is the consciousness that bridges the past and the future; human biography exists between memory and projects. This is universal for human beings.

Human beings are under a permanent formation process as moral subjects and participants of interactions. How universal is the impact of intersubjective

---

[1] H. Arendt, *The Human Condition*, introduced by M. Canovan, Chicago 1998, p. 192.

[2] Ibidem, p. 7.

[3] Ibidem, p. 181.

experiences on subjects' moral cognition and consistency? Does it make sense to speak about universal moral judgments, demands, criteria, and structures as derived from the moral consistency of *everyone*? Following Kant, universal demands and judgments are the just demands and judgments of rationality, which is the same ability in all users of reason. On the one hand, universal laws of reason are *impersonal*; on the other hand, it is each person who can achieve the highest "degree to which any of an individual's judgments approximate the criteria of a moral judgment,"[4] for example, the post-conventional universal criteria. In addition to Kohlberg's universalist approach, moral philosophers have also pursued the notion that there is not a single true morality.[5] To discuss this issue is to refer to the subjective and intersubjective aspects of morality that support universal ethics. I see them in cognitive structures of moral judging in particular, and also in inter-individual commitments. There exists a third position between absolutism and relativism, which will be advocated in this chapter, drawing on the classic philosophical arguments, on findings in cognitive-developmental research, and, finally, on work in neurocognitivism.

Arendt's description of human cognitive equipment is rooted in the philosophy of *bios* as a source of all human activities whose matured forms are *virtues*, as Aristotle said. In the early Enlightenment, d'Espinoza delivered the notion of *connatus* and affects, including the most subtle and potent of them: reason. To Kant, reason was the only faculty of universalization and the genuine source of the supreme moral law. With Kant, the moral semantics of reason become universal for every human being as a moral agent and the unique author of his or her own moral biography. Fichte radicalized Kantian "causality from the term" (*Kausalität aus dem Begriff*) and established the notion of a genuine *agility* which transcendentally presupposed a spontaneous activity in the Self: the ability to construct objects, other Selves, and even the moral Self itself. Nietzsche developed the construct of "will to live" as the autocreative power in an individual. In her description, Arendt refers to that tradition, and additionally to the moral logic of Piaget and the analogy between the law of nature and moral law (in Kant), both determining other and self with the similar strength.

In contrast to Kant, Arendt states:

> In the human faculties we are actually confronted with a sort of brain power [...]. The mental processes which feed on brain power we usually call intelligence

[4] L. Kohlberg, *The Development of Modes of Moral Thinking and Choice in the Years Ten to Sixteen*, unpublished PhD dissertation, University of Chicago, 1958, p. 7.

[5] For example Harman, in G. Harman, J. J. Thomson, *Moral Relativism and Moral Objectivity*, Cambridge, MA 1996; G. Harman, *Explaining Value and Other Essays in Moral Philosophy*, Oxford 2000.

> [...], their laws [...], the laws of logic, can be discovered like other laws of nature because they are ultimately rooted in the structure of the human brain, and they possesses [...] the same force of compulsion as the driving necessity which regulates the other functions of our bodies.[6]

When she speaks of laws that are rooted in cognitive structures, Arendt is implicitly referring to the Socratic conception of *anamnesis*, in which learning is stimulated by a midwife-teacher in dialogue and the learner becomes aware of his or her preconscious, intuitive knowledge. This the learner constructs by his or her own strength (*virtù*) by exploring the meaning of justice, good, truth, beauty, honesty, and so one. Thus, *virtù* is an internal, originally subjective source of strength available for everyone. Moreover, in Arendt's eyes, cognition refers to an intentional process that manifests itself in visible and measurable effects:

> [...] a process with the beginning and end, whose usefulness can be tested, and which, if it produces no results, has failed like a carpenter's workmanship has failed when he fabricates a two-legged table.[7]

Her judgment and performance-related understanding of cognitive ability is similar to Kohlberg's[8] and Lind's.[9] However, one cannot consider any cognitive ability without some repeatedly performed action that involves, at the same time, brain training.[10]

2. Coherent moral cognition, logics of freedom, moral coordinates

In Kohlberg, key moral competence is defined as the "capacity to make judgments and decisions that are moral (i.e., based on internal principles) and to act in accordance with such judgments."[11] So "practical considerations,"[12] moral

---

[6] H. Arendt, *The Human Condition*, introduced by M. Canovan, Chicago 1982, p. 190.

[7] Ibidem, p. 191.

[8] L. Kohlberg, "Development of Moral Character and Moral Ideology," in M. L. Hoffman, L. W. Hoffman (eds.), *Review of child development research*, vol. I, New York 1964, pp. 383–431; L. Kohlberg, *Essays on Moral Development*, vol. I: *The Philosophy of Moral Development*; vol. II: *The Psychology of Moral Development*, San Francisco 1984.

[9] G. Lind, *Moral ist lehrbar. Handbuch zur Theorie und Praxis moralischer und demokratischer Bildung*, Oldenburg – München 2009²; G. Lind, H. A. Hartman, R. Wakenhut (eds.), *Moral Judgment and Social Education*, New Brunswick – London 1982¹, 2010².

[10] See M. S. Gazzaniga, *The Ethical Brain*, New York 2005, p. 61.

[11] L. Kohlberg, "Development of Moral Character...," op. cit., p. 425.

[12] H. Arendt, *The Human Condition*, op. cit., p. 190.

deliberation, and judgment are proceeded in the individual mind. An individual is responsible for the use of his or her practical freedom in a principled way. Not only philosophers and moralists, but also laypeople are interested in their moral consistency. Let us compare the philosophical (idealistic) personal moral consistency approach and its developmental equivalent in moral psychology. The first one is most clearly illustrated in M. J. Siemek:

> Practical freedom, together with its ethical competence to self-determination and autonomous law-giving (*autonomy*) is subordinated to the same transcendental condition of the "original synthetic unity of apperception" which is [a] precondition of the logical and theoretical relevance, and truth of knowledge. Ethics is nothing more than a transcendental logics of freedom, and a canon of universally relevant rules of meaningful, so responsible action.[13]

It is typical of philosophical idealism that it requires an absolute (constant and not instant) cognitive coherence of individual judgment and agency, but varying cultural, historical, and situational contents (in Kant: maxims) of application are limited through several universal principles, such as the categorical imperative, benevolence, utility, etc. I think that more parallel cognitive structures can arise in an individual's moral mind under today's circumstances, where multiculturalism and relativism are widespread beliefs. Cognitive consistency is more typical of a more stable and coherent world and different but individually well-processed socialization impulses. Today, several opposite socializations can occur at the same time, across the different life spheres that we share with others, as we are confronted with a diversity of quickly changing experiences, to follow Z. Bauman. Are our minds still able to apply the universal logics of freedom? Are we still able to undertake commitments as rational and responsible agencies? I think, we are, but the "moral system of coordinates"[14] (values, principles, and ideals) strongly vary from person to person.

The second developmental approach requires, in contrast, the psychodynamic cognitive organization of judgment behavior – i.e., competence to make principled moral judgments that, although they might be quite various, *the most universal of them* can be identified with the orientations defined by Kohlberg as pre-conventional, conventional, and post-conventional. This is in agreement with the conventionalist G. Harman, who says concerning content: "the system of moral coordinates that is determined by a given person's values cannot be *identified* with all and only exactly those very values"[15] because false or wrong

---

[13] M. J. Siemek, "Freiheit, Recht, Gerechtigkeit," in idem (ed.), *Natur, Kunst, Freiheit*, Fichte-Studien Supplementa, vol. 10, Amsterdam – Atlanta 1998, p. 7.

[14] G. Harman, J. J. Thomson, *Moral Relativism and Moral Objectivity*, op. cit., p. 13.

[15] "Otherwise a person could never be mistaken about moral issues (in relation to the relevant system of coordinates) except being mistaken about his or her own values." Ibidem.

values do not exist. Consistency does not concern values and behavior: it only concerns cognitive structures (from the perspective of moral psychology), transcendental logics (from the perspective of philosophy), and the system of coordinates (from the perspective of meta-ethics). According to Lind, "it is only by referring to content that one speaks meaningfully of behavioral *consistency*. There is no consistency of behavior as such."[16] At once, cognitive structures are organized "moral coordinates" (Harman), but they can be re-organized too.[17] As a result, the inconsistency of personal judgmental behavior is thoroughly possible, both in its historical aspect (one can change his or her behavior with reference to differential moral challenges, contexts, etc.) and in its synchronic aspect – e.g., one can change between opposing values or reasons in one and the same dilemmatic situation.

Kohlberg followed the ancient Greek ideal of integral individuality and, at the same time, an ideal of integral community (polis). The question of how a just community is possible can be answered only if we know how a virtuous citizenship is to be promoted (but knowledge, *theoria*, and *virtù* are not the same). "Not only in the Heinz dilemma, but in real life, virtues or norms conflict and moral integrity requires consistent organization of these virtues and norms. Like Plato, we have called the integration of these virtues or norms justice."[18] All ideals fail on the direct and vertical connection between monadic subjects and political organization. A well-functioning government could result from such a way of thinking, but a just, fair, democratic self-governance could not.

There is continuity between consistent (integral) personality, self-consciousness, self-identification, and self-esteem. As the first moral philosopher Socrates postulated, the internal consistency of the Self needs to be continually questioned. As long as we ask *why do I do this...*, *what is right/just...*, *who am I*?, we follow the Socratic self-examination postulate. We are experiencing and founding ethics.

3. Classical ideals of intersubjectivity

As Fichte requires in his *Foundations of the Entire Wissenschaftslehre* and *Foundations of Natural Right*, a real Self (an empirical "I") cannot think of him or herself

[16] G. Lind, *Inhalt und Struktur des moralischen Urteilens. Theoretische, methodologische und empirische Untersuchungen zur Urteils- und Demokratiekompetenz bei Studierenden*, Universität Konstanz 1985, p. 30.

[17] R. L. Selman, "Taking Another's Perspective: Role-Taking Development in Early Childhood," *Child Development*, 1971, no. 42, pp. 721–734; idem, *The Growth of Interpersonal Understanding*, New York – London – Toronto – Sydney – San Francisco 1980.

[18] L. Kohlberg, *Essays on Moral Development*, vol. II: *The Psychology of Moral Development*, San Francisco 1984, p. 509.

without thinking of another Self (the "not-I"). This universal relationship is essential for the modern theory of intersubjectivity and the philosophical concept of self-awareness; indeed each internal development is co-related to others. The same for psychology: "personality is [...not] a purely internal category; rather it is that which is characteristic of the *relationship* between the individual and the social environment."[19] The quality of the social environment has a strong impact on the constitution if the individual personality, in particular on cognitive development. Furthermore, as Lind specifies:

> This relationship is twofold. On the one hand, moral behavior presupposes a cognitive structure: moral principles, norms, and values have to be balanced off against each other and in light of the specific circumstances of a decision situation. On the other hand, competence in moral judgment, that is, the ability to integrate and differentiated moral principles and apply them to everyday decisions, has a developmental character and so must be placed in reference to the individual's life experience.[20]

In its essential meaning, the theory of intersubjectivity presupposes a reciprocal universal recognition structure of humanity in individuals and in the active relationships between autonomous and intelligible moral agents.[21] These relationships are spatial (see the discussion of *distance* below) because a large number of agents must share one and the same finite life space – i.e., they must establish a social life space. The quantification of space (the Fichtean term *quantum*; see also D. Bachmann-Medick[22]) between subjects takes place in the following way: one's free activity creates a border for others' free activity. Otherness is mutually respected. The reciprocal determination through *freedom* requires, however, that the agents are able to recognize freedom. The meaning of recognition is ambiguous here, because agents must understand freedom in one's external expressions like physical and verbal action, property, right, etc. Human freedom is a reflected self-determination in accordance with principles: to recognize it requires understanding it (and differentiating it from other "freedoms") and accepting it as a limitation on one's own reflected freedom. In sum, with his "limitative synthesis," Fichte constructed a transcendental scheme of fully reciprocal interpersonal relationships among absolute Selves. The real Selves (moral subjects) must follow that scheme and recognize freedom and rationality in others, especially at the level of communication. It can be said

---

[19] G. Lind, *Inhalt und Struktur des moralischen Urteilens...*, op. cit., p. 27.

[20] Ibidem.

[21] J. G. Fichte, *The Science of Knowledge 1794*, transl. P. Heath, J. Lachs, Oxford 1982.

[22] D. Bachmann-Medick, *Cultural Turns*, Reinbeck bei Hamburg 2006 (in particular Chapter IV: *Spatial Turn*).

that there are transcendental affinities between reasonable and free beings, which Fichte describes in his later works.

When interacting in everyday relationships with others, individuals generate and experience unavoidable differences, incompatibilities, controversies, and conflicts with others. This experience confronts them frequently with the objective and institutional limitations of human freedom, and sometimes with penal sanctions. This is why the advanced (inter)personal, socio-moral competencies are required in the social life, as are rules for how to construct right or just maxims for everyday interactions. One such universal rule is the categorical imperative. As Kant emphasized in *Groundwork for the Metaphysics of Morals*: "So act that you use humanity, whether in your own person or in the person of any other, always at the same time as an end, never merely as a means." This requires three crucial abilities: respect, principled moral judgment, and taking an interpersonal perspective.

Kohlberg further develops the philosophical conception of intersubjectivity by including the placing of an individual in the middle of intersubjective relations in his notion of the subjective "capacity to make judgments." The competencies of respect, moral judgment, discourse, and taking the social perspective belong together; however, each of these is a "necessary but insufficient" pre-condition for being an integral moral agent and participant in social cooperation. The latter implies that we are involved in an interchange with other moral agents, and are confronted with different and changing value contexts, preferences, and interests. We mostly wish to live in an ideal community in order to cultivate our personal consistency and conformity to others. But the opposite happens: values and aims collide and conflict, and we are confronted with social controversies or dilemmas with which we must deal. Nicholson defines interpersonal conflicts as affect-loaded situations in which "two or more people or groups endeavor to pursue goals which are mutually inconsistent." Thus, the ability to resolve conflicts is needed in all persons in order to proximate reciprocal and harmonious relationships. Together with discursive ability, it is the crucial political skill.

The ancient Greeks promoted political competencies in the majority of citizens in their *poleis*. As a result, *demos* was able to create *democratic* institutions based on free discourse and participation. In today's democracies we still need "this revelatory quality of speech and action [that] comes to the fore where people are with others and neither for nor against them – that is, in sheer human togetherness."[23] Contemporary moral educational psychologists also developed settings of professional democratic education. In the 20th century

---

[23] H. Arendt, *The Human Condition*, op. cit., p. 200.

it was Kohlberg who established the most efficient of them: a discussion of dilemmas of justice that is open to "free and equal" participants, as Aristotle would have express it. Of course, today we still cultivate *agon* as a discursive form of conflict. Even mature democracies are not immunized to the asymmetries and dissensus of interpersonal relations when citizens declare the ideals of universal mutual respect, recognition, equality, and justice. A gap between democratic ideals and the ability to follow them seems to be a timeless phenomena. This ability needs to be strengthened.

Confronting Kohlberg's moral reasoning theory with philosophical conceptions of intersubjectivity, can reveal that both the affective and cognitive aspects of moral reasoning is closely connected with intersubjective relationships. In the ideal models reciprocal recognition is emphasized. But everyday democracy is not immunized to direct and indirect forms of social asymmetries like submission, dependence, control, exclusion, exception, pathology, etc., in every area of life and social institution. Other philosophers of intersubjectivity – such as Habermas, Gadamer, and Ricoeur – are searching for truth, rightness, truthfulness of practical judgments, and validity claims of argumentation. "Who are identifiable persons able to respond to the question: Who is speaking? Who is acting? [...] Who is a moral subject of imputation?;"[24] such questions (instead of the abstract ideals of intersubjectivity) can help identify a lived experience of validity that enables us "to encounter the other and to reach a mutual understanding that can serve as a base for a creative *Mit-einander*."[25]

Thus, what encourages people most efficiently to learn to reflect on the social validity of others in order to make just and fair decisions are opportunities that provide a maximum of reciprocity in effective democratic education, and in particular through "direct and repeated experience with socio-moral conflict."[26] In accordance with Piaget's affective-cognitive parallelism theory, there is a connection between social cognitive development and the development of interpersonal, social, and "seminormative" affects. As Piaget shows, "the ability to conserve feelings makes interpersonal and moral feelings possible and allows the latter to be organized into normative scales of values,"[27] which are relevant to consistent structures of moral cognition ("moral system coordinates" according to Harman, or "transcendental logics" according to Siemek).

[24] P. Ricoeur, *Oneself as Another*, transl. K. Blamey, Chicago 1992; A. Wierciński, *Hermeneutics between Philosophy and Theology. The Imperative to Think the Incommensurable*, Münster 2010, p. 300.

[25] A. Wierciński, *Hermeneutics between Philosophy and Theology...*, op. cit., p. 301.

[26] Ch. Armond, T.L. Dawson, "Developmental Trajectories in Moral Reasoning across the Life-Span," *Journal of Moral Education*, 1997, vol. 26 (4), p. 437; L. Kohlberg, *The Psychology of Moral Development*, op. cit., p. 171.

[27] J. Piaget, "Intelligence and Affectivity," transl. T.A. Brown, C.E. Kaegi, *Annual Reviews*, Palo Alto, CA 1981, p. 44.

In his *Essays on Moral Development*, Kohlberg assumes that "first, individuals attain a logical stage [...]. Next they attain a level of social perception or role-taking [...]. The development of a stage's social perception proceeds, or is easier than, development of the parallel stage of moral judgment."[28] According to Kohlberg, persons are involved in the interpersonal relations from the very beginning of their lives, a long time before they learn to reflect, verbalize, and discuss their beliefs, and to argue and justify them in morally demanding social contexts. For example, dilemmatic situations contain opposing normative premises and evoke normative dissonance in human minds. Regardless of the sequence of stages from the particular to the universal level, normative dissonance can occur even "prior-to-society."[29] The universal principles, such as the Kantian categorical imperative and the principle of utility, prescribe how to form just or fair practical judgments (e.g., maxims); however, it is not easy to make such judgments in today's growing pluralistic and multicultural moral contexts. The higher the reasoning level, the greater is the room for adequate interpersonal understanding and social cognition.[30] The social perspective is the foundation for each of Kohlberg's stages, including the asymmetric relationship of the first stage of power and authority (which is similar to the master-and-slave dialectic, as analyzed in the next chapter). I do not reconstruct the whole Six-Stages Theory here, but let us reflect on its "first component" – the "social perspective level:"[31]

"Stage 1 includes an undifferentiated or egocentric perspective" (commentary: asymmetric, strongly personalized, one-sided intersubjective relationships are done; punishment, authority). "Stage 2 takes the perspective of two actors aware of the individual needs of the other, coordinated through acts of concrete reciprocity" (commentary: in that case, the Aristotelian utility-based cooperation and Hegelian economical "system of needs" are related to justice as exchange). "Stage 3 understands the other in the context of shared role expectations in personalized relationships" (commentary: living in accordance to what is expected by others, imitation, conformity. Approval relates to recognition from others). "Stage 4 understands the other in the context of a less personalized social system of norms and roles" (commentary: intersubjective relationships become more abstract and some individuals respect conventions more than do others).

"Stage 5 has a 'prior-to-society' perspective" (commentary: this is a strict interpersonal relationship; reciprocal agreement, consensus, and contracts are

---

[28] L. Kohlberg, *The Psychology of Moral Development*, op. cit., p. 171.

[29] Ibidem.

[30] R.L. Selman, *The Growth of Interpersonal Understanding*, op. cit., p. 33.

[31] L. Kohlberg, *Essays on Moral Development*, vol. II, op. cit., p. 251.

reached, and interpersonality becomes more relevant than social conventions as people can justify and change them). "Hypothetical Stage 6: one engages in autonomous reasoning that is based in the universalistic principles, duties, and values such as mutual respect, justice, dignity, and the categorical imperative. Application of principles to all others and 'theoretical postulations'"[32] are take place here.

At the post-conventional level, contractual reasoning (Stage 5) and autonomous moral reasoning (Stage 6) are sources of legitimation of criticisms against unfair rules or unjust institutions. At this level, Kant's and Bovet's question of what comes first – obedience and moral law, or respect for other people – is answered. As Piaget highlights, reciprocal respect is the foundation for cooperative relationships. "Respect for other people was not the consequence, therefore, but the preliminary condition of moral law."[33] In a democratic society, respect for other persons and for oneself seem to be the preliminary conditions for making the social rules just and the procedures fair. In Kohlberg and most legal theories, conventional stages (conventions) are derived from interpersonal relationships; these relationships were one-sided and based on authority (*auctoritas*) earlier, but in democracy they are based on equal participation in practical discourse (in sensu Habermas).

4. Evolving to the conflicts solving

Let us continue this chapter with Nicholson's conflict definition quoted above that refers to the incompatible goals, preferences, or values as concern for desirability (of the radical disagreement of conflict actors) of a minimum of two persons. This definition is based on simple mutual exclusion. But certain social conflicts seem to be constrained in a more complex way,[34] as in, for example, dialectical conflicts. They can contain integrated social perspectives, needs, and demands. In his masterpiece *The Phenomenology of Spirit*, the German philosopher G. W. F. Hegel describes an original proto-social Master-and-Slave conflict between two simple "consciousnesses," i.e., subjects who are learning to make use of the socially-mediated self-consciousness and social cognition. Their interests are the same: self-consciousness as an independent subjectivity through the mutual recognition they are struggling for with each other. To became conscious of oneself, a person has to think of him or herself as an

[32] Quotations Stage 1 – Stage 6: ibidem, p. 271.

[33] J. Piaget, "Intelligence and Affectivity," op. cit., p. 53.

[34] M. W. Berkowitz, "Four Perspectives on Moral Argumentation," in C. Gibb Harding (ed.), *Moral Dilemmas. Philosophical and Psychological Issues in the Development of Moral Reasoning*, Chicago 1985, p. 4.

autonomous agent of action. According to Hegel, contemporary intersubjectivity psychologists R.L. Selman shows experimentally that humans have not only the strong need but also the cognitive capacity for self-awareness (self-consciousness).

Let me continue the Hegelian Master-and-Slave dialectic story that illustrates the kind of evolution of the Self ("consciousness" in Hegel's terms) in which there occurs a solving of conflicts with another Self ("consciousness"): both consciousnesses, in their 'first' confrontation, must prove their simple and selfish for-itself-existences, which is why they start to fight for recognition so radically that they are ready to risk their lives. They fight for their absolute independence, but the opposite occurs. The dramatic fight of the two antagonists' "reciprocal" interdependence results in a determination of social positions. The interdependence can be asymmetric or symmetric, or result in a hybrid. The consciousness that puts his or her life at risk will be "victorious," while the other, who experiences fear of the Master (in fact: absolute Master – the fear of death which is of a natural origin), will surrender. Thus, the first forces the second to recognize him or her as an independent subject. The recognizing consciousness becomes the Slave-consciousness, and the recognized becomes the master-consciousness. Despite the situation in which the Slave is "working" on his or her Master account, the Slave becomes the Master of nature he or she is modifying (but not consuming) by practicing and so developing his rationality and cognition.

The problem is that a truly free subject can be "satisfied" solely by being recognized by another truly free subject. A truly free subject incorporates both parties and is capable of self-recognition. As long as *two* consciousnesses exist, in their relationship the Master is not free because his or her (passive) existence fully depends on the Slave's will and self-activity, while his or her own activity is "estranged." The Master's Self, his identity, is elsewhere, not in him or herself. This activity is a pre-condition of freeing the Self, but it is the Slave only who is an active agent in this relationship. He does not receive recognition from the Master. The Slave needs only to open his or her "spiritual" eyes to see freedom in objective beings (*Dasein*) and the phenomenal manifestations that express and actualize his self-activity. In the forms of artificial things – in culture – the Slave recognizes his spiritual provenance: the Slave sees his own ideas, goals, aims, values, and meanings – in short, the products of his own mind.

The Master, in contrast, never reaches true self-consciousness. He or she "goes stupid because of do-nothing, excessive consumption and pleasure use," as A. Kojève, with bitter satisfaction, puts it. As a result, the Slave-consciousness will be the winner of the dialectic duel. He or she reaches self-confirmation as an active and minded subject. To this point, *The Phenomenology of Spirit* is reporting on the Slave's evolution of emancipatory activity. The reader meets him again in Hegel's *Philosophy of Right.* Here, the free and self-conscious subjects must establish a universal, reasonable legal order. This order should not be just conventional (positive). It should be based on the reciprocal recognition between subjects. For Hegel, universal recognition is the essential "objective right principle," and right is the objective being of universalized personal freedom (*äusseres Dasein der Freiheit*). *Everyone's* freedom gives legitimacy to the universal right's guilt. From Hegel's viewpoint, the relationships between Self and others – in particular their struggle for recognition – are pre-conditions of both moral Self-formation and bourgeois-citizen formation. In *The Phenomenology of Spirit,* both consciousnesses still behave intuitively (i.e., without having interpreted, and having agreed upon an "objective" sense of their decisions and relationships). Their conflict has been resolved in a one-sided way – they did not cooperated in any discursive way, and did not established social agreements, common rules, etc. They only established a pre-modern institution of submission and servitude that always results from power or authority, and are in this sense are irrational.

For a modern type of intersubjective relationship, discursiveness and dialogical interaction is crucial. Fichte was the first thinker who developed the model of discursive and dialogic intersubjectivity. But among real participants of intersubjective relations, different types of conflicts can occur. Berkowitz characterized two types of discursive moral conflict: the competitive and the cooperative. Both correspond to the classical conceptions of intersubjectivity in philosophy. According to Berkowitz, Pruitt, and Lewis, "the theory of integrative bargaining is based largely upon the assumption that many apparently competitive situations can be reconstructed to allow for resolutions that fulfill the goals of each side of the conflict."[35] The "reorienting of the opponents may be all that is necessary to transform a competitive conflict into a cooperative enterprise,"[36] as Berkowitz says. In the cooperative conflict, "discussants share the same goal."[37] The Master-and-Slave interaction seems to be a competitive conflict, which cannot transform into a cooperative conflict because of the lack of communication. Thus, the Master-and-Slave conflict can be called a mediating but pre-discourse conflict, or a pseudo-mediation conflict between submission and service. Mediation means that finally submission and service have to be cancelled (*aufgehoben*) at the level of knowing, understanding, thinking and deliberating and other interactive forms of "the movement of the

[35] Ibidem, p. 4.

[36] Ibidem.

[37] Ibidem.

Notion," which, from Hegel's viewpoint, "[...] involves mediation" (*Encyclopedia of Philosophical Sciences*, § 161–166).

Why did Master and Slave not seek a cooperative conflict resolution as shown in Hegel's model? Their intuitive decisions are rather typical of Kohlberg's pre-conventional level of egocentrism, authority, punishment, and fear. One could add that in the pre-institutional and pre-communicational level, unsocialized, immature subjects mostly solve their conflicts by producing, institutionalizing, and reproducing power-based, submissive relationships. Within the strongly asymmetric relationship between the Master and Slave's monologues, the initial distance and submissive and serving behaviors are preserved. Such one-sided intersubjectivity does not create a favorable opportunity for socialization – i.e., for development of a free, and intersubjectively mediated (*vermittelt*) subjectivity (self-identity). It is representing a natural ego-oriented and in-itself-being state of human existence. According to G. Lind, one comes to the point where one depends on the other, and one is no longer an individual. This independence, which is based partially on acceptance and partially on the rejection of conformity, will be related to the belief that total independence is meaningless, as is total dependence.[38] Moral decision making requires inner cognitive structure that enable autonomous, differentiated, and reflective consideration of principles, norms, and situational factors that are integrated in the decision. An individual achieves this level of independence by dealing with the situation and by developing socially-mediated strategies of conflict solving.[39]

In Hegel, the philosophical staging of socialization evolves from individualistic to intersubjectively-mediated conflict solving, from dependence through interdependence to independence. Hegel reports on this evolution in *The Phenomenology of Spirit* (1806[1])[40] and *Philosophy of Right* (1830–1831). The Master-and-Slave dialectic is understood as a social learning process. Its historical order corresponds to (inter)personal developmental order. A self-consciousness recognizes itself in the other, and the other recognizes it as well. Communicative actions are performed and mutually exchanged. Both self-conscious subjects found the first fully inclusive – i.e., reciprocal – relationship. Their mutual recognition creates a principle of the new, interpersonal order, objectively expressed in the universal rules, citizenship, and social institutions. Subjects will reflect on all these objective institutions and justify them. Reading the 4th Chapter of *The Phenomenology of Spirit* and, then, *Philosophy of Right*,

[38] G. Lind, *Inhalt und Struktur des moralischen Urteilens...*, op. cit.

[39] Ibidem.

[40] G. W. F. Hegel, *Phenomenology of Spirit*, transl. A.V. Miller, Oxford 1977.

we can observe the development of social cognition in modern subjectivity from intuition to reason, from monologue to dialogue, and from asymmetry to equality. The construction of a "socialized" individual occurs under changing social (and historical) circumstances as a reciprocal construction. Furthermore, from this construction, larger durable institutions result. The individuals produce them in order to guarantee their social integration. Finally the ethical (*sittlich*) principle of interpersonal recognition is expressed in the following way: *Be a person and recognize others as persons.* "Man must be accounted a universal being, not because he is a Jew, Catholic, Protestant, German, or Italian, but because he is a man. This thinking or reflective consciousness, is of infinite importance."[41] As Honneth believes, the individual is recognized in the room created by reasonable participants of a reciprocal relationship:

> As a *rational being*, as free, as a person; and the individual, on his side, makes himself worthy of this recognition by overcoming the natural state of his self-consciousness and obeying a universal, the will that is in essence actuality will, the *law*; he behaves, therefore, towards others in a manner that is universally valid, recognizing them – as he wishes others to recognize him – as free, as persons.[42]

Let me explain the dynamic rational-dialogical socialization process by connecting it to Kohlberg's cognitive-developmental theory.

> The just community's schools that Kohlberg created in 1970s appear to do just that. By making high school students create their own rules, enforce their own discipline, and vote on numerous policies, Kohlberg created an environment where students enacted democracy. By putting students and teachers on an equal footing (all had just one vote; all used first names only; all sat in a circle on the floor at community meetings), Kohlberg created an environment where students and teachers enacted equality.[43]

As a defender of the intuitionist approach, J. Haidt proposed a somehow reduced interpretation of Kohlberg's cognitive-developmental theory. Kohlberg did not educate particular "intuitions," but he trained rational and principle-legitimizing reasoning as a legitimation of moral judgments during his community meetings regarding just discourse and participation:

> A more intuitionist approach is to treat moral judgment style as an aspect of culture and to try to create a culture that fosters a more balanced, reflective and

[41] G.W.F. Hegel, *Philosophy of Law*, transl. F.W. Dyde, Kitchener 2001, § 209.

[42] A. Honneth, *The Struggle for Recognition. The Moral Grammar of Social Conflicts*, transl. J. Anderson, Cambridge 1995, p. 108.

[43] J. Haidt, "The Emotional Dog and its Rational Tail: A Social Intuitionist Approach to Moral Judgment," *Psychological Review*, 2001, vol. 108 (4), pp. 828–829.

> free-minded style of judgment. [...] Years of such an implicit learning, coupled with explicit discussion, should gradually tune up intuitions [...] about justice, rights, and fairness, leading perhaps to a automatic tendency to look at problems from multiple perspectives [...].[44]

Before learning to live in a cooperative way, people often experience conflicts; therefore, it might be reasonable to continue the education initiated by Kohlberg in its most efficient forms – in particular, with the Konstanz Method of Dilemma Discussion.[45] Students learn to seek resolutions while experiencing conflicting cognitions, intuitions, and affects through, for example, educational moral dilemmas.

Let me reflect on the question of what is essential in the distance between two or more persons. The distance between persons is always a social distance that can either disconnect or connect them. It is an empty space that can be filled with hostility and conflict, or in contrast, with communication and cooperation. If communication is initiated, a meaningful rational dialogue replaces former irrational violence and fears. Dialogue is the negation of violence. It builds a bridge across the distance through, for example, the construction of relationships with others. As long as one speaks and listens to others, a person cannot be directly touched or injured.[46] Nevertheless, the verbal and rhetorical instrumentalization of violence and dominance is an important object of critical poststructuralist research. Communication changes "my" world into "ours," as Lévinas suggests. Speaking and listening would never arise in an indifferent, abstract environment. It is only possible in a world in which cooperation and helping behavior are needed.[47] Following Lévinas and Habermas,[48] we can conclude that the nature of speech is moral. "Hence, one has certain ethical obligations when interacting with other person[s]"[49] in the most efficient medium of communication – i.e., through conversation.

When it is time to approximate the coherence of the self, as well as the sources of the subjective self-narrative, we need to be self-aware agents of our performance (including the formation of moral judgments) in the area of neuroscientific theories of morality. As M. S. Gazzaniga nowadays claims,

---

[44] Ibidem.

[45] G. Lind, *Moral ist lehrbar*, op. cit.

[46] E. Lévinas, *Totality and Infinity. An Essay on Exteriority*, transl. A. Lingis, The Hague – Boston – London 1979.

[47] Ibidem.

[48] J. Habermas, *Communication and the Evolution of Society*, transl. T. McCarthy, Boston 1979; idem, *Moral Consciousness and Communicative Action*, transl. Ch. Lenhardt, S. W. Nicholsen, introduced by T. McCarthy, Cambridge, MA 1990.

[49] M. W. Berkowitz, "Four Perspectives on Moral Argumentation," op. cit., p. 17.

> We feel like one, coherent self with intentions and reasons for what we feel are our unified actions. How can this be? [...] [human brain] includes a special region that interprets the inputs we receive every moment and weaves them into stories to form the ongoing narrative of our self-image and our beliefs.[50]

In classical philosophy we can find symbolic figures of self-perception and self-awareness corresponding to this, such as Minerva's owl in the Introduction to Hegel's *Lectures on the Philosophy of Right.* Minerva's owl "spreads his wings only in the falling of the dusk" and flies in order to take in the light of consciousness, to understand, to reflect, and create a narrative about everything that happened in past days.

---

[50] M. S. Gazzaniga, *The Ethical Brain*, op. cit., p. 148.

Chapter VI

Experimenting with values in legal contexts: Hegel and Radbruch[1]

What can two thinkers: Georg Wilhelm Friedrich Hegel – the most influent idealist of the 19th century – and Gustav Radbruch – witness of the pathologies of the legislature and jurisprudence of the Third Reich – have in common? Both of them criticized legal positivism and looked for validity of legal rules. Radbruch's warning not to trust the rule that a law is a law and an order is an order[2] is one of the most notable achievements in the philosophy of law. Since the 1930s, however, legal positivism in its radically Kelsenian, neo-Kelsenian, semi-Kelsenian, soft-Kelsenian[3] or "inclusive" varieties has been predominant in legal theory. It has also guaranteed the autonomy of statutory law. Modern

[1] The author is grateful for permission to publish this paper in extended and updated version by K. Guczalska and J. Hartman. The paper first appeared in K. Guczalska (ed.), *Zrozumieć Hegla* [Understanding Hegel], Cracow 2009, pp. 163–184 (in Polish) and in M. Wischke, A. Przyłębski (eds.), *Recht ohne Gerechtikeit? Hegel und die Grundlagen des Rechtsstaates*, Würzburg 2009, pp. 243–253 (in German).

[2] G. Radbruch, "Gesetzliches Unrecht und übergesetzliches Recht," in idem, *Rechtsphilosophie*, eds. R. Dreier, S. Paulson, 2nd edition, Heidelberg 2003, p. 211; in English: "Statutory Lawlessness and Supra-Statutory Law" (1946), *Oxford Journal of Legal Studies*, 2006, vol. 26, 1/1; G. Radbruch, "Fünf Minuten Rechtsphilosophie," in idem, *Rechtsphilosophie*, op. cit., pp. 209–210; in English: "Five Minutes of Legal Philosophy" (1945), *Oxford Journal of Legal Studies*, 2006, vol. 26, 13/13. See also R. Alexy, *The Argument from Injustice: A Reply to Legal Positivism*, transl. B. Litschewski-Paulson, S.L. Paulson, Oxford 2002.

[3] H. Kelsen, *Reine Rechtslehre. Einleitung in die rechtswissenschaftliche Problematik*, Studienausgabe der 1. Auflage 1934[1], ed. M. Jestaedt, Tübingen 2008; M. Zirk-Sadowski, "Soft Kelsenism Versus Multicentrism: Some Remarks on Theoretical Foundations of European Law," in M. Zirk-Sadowski, M. Golecki, B. Wojciechowski (eds.), *Multicentrism as an Emerging Paradigm in Legal Theory*, Frankfurt am Main 2009, pp. 51–68.

Western legal systems do not incorporate moral values. Employees become legal subjects instead of people and citizens. However, people from all eras would wish that their laws were right and just. Therefore, the ideal of justice should at least be considered to be a value to be realized by law, as postulated by Radbruch. Following Radbruch, it is impossible to refuse legal subjects their moral voice – i.e., the right to an independent evaluation of legal rules. Law is the most efficient regulatory system in society and its efficiency must result from consensualised social values (a constitution) or from intrinsic legal values (which might be indicated, for example, by human rights). Social discourses, however, are primarily not based on values, but on reasons. The same is true in legal and philosophy of law discourses. Thinkers have purposed a number of intrinsic legal values by formulating reasons and reasonings: we can find samples in Hegel, Radbruch, Fuller, Hart, Waldron, and others. In this chapter, the need for these kinds of values and their role will be considered by a comparison of Hegel and Radbruch in the context of contemporary legal philosophy.

In order to evaluate law with respect to value one has to differentiate between cultural and moral values and legal values. Although the philosophy of law proposed by Hegel belongs to the pre-Kelsenian era and may seem somewhat old-fashioned now, the problem it expresses is as important as is that voiced by Radbruch in the 20th century. It can be stated as follows: Which values, and in what way, should society include in its statutory laws as *legal values*, and which values should be relegated to the cultural and moral categories, which are increasingly diverse and pluralistic. Because from the social point of view the creation and application of law are still imperfect, citizens need the knowledge and criteria that would enable them to evaluate law with respect to justice. The theory of legal positivism after Kelsen requires a minimal set of intrinsic legal values that are, at the same time, socially based. However, legal reality can be frequently value-deficient; we still observe inequalities, social exclusion, discrimination, and other phenomena of unjust legal rules. Connections between legal rules and the supreme legal norm (or the basic norm, German: *Grundnorm*) are sometimes weak or nonexistent. Of course, an act of statutory law can be challenged as unconstitutional in the European Court of Human Rights, but if it is bad it ought to be changed regardless of such findings and should be based on appropriate criteria.

In previous centuries, when public opinion was not reckoned with and social communication was vertical (i.e., with the ruler dictating the rules and subjects obeying), natural laws of supernatural or divine origin were considered to be supreme legal norms. After two world wars in the 20th century international commitees proclaimed human rights which entail universally shared values, starting from innate personal dignity. There is no clear hierarchy of those values and they can collide, just like moral values. Nowadays, human rights are the most important criteria referred to in criticisms of the application of positive law by institutions, their employees, and other individuals. Previously, though, at the time Hegel and Radbruch developed their theories critical of legal positivism, values were such criteria; the aim was to achieve a relative balance between legal and moral validity. This is also the case today in cultures with little knowledge or acceptance of human rights. Individuals have their own inner values and when statutory law contradicts them, human rights turn out to be a distant and still too weak tool. I have in mind here especially the Polish context and societies which still live in conditions of political dictatorship.

In contemporary discourse on values, the question of how we learn values is not of great importance.[4] People do not so much learn as *experience*, share, and – most of all – use values. The key issue for us is the question of the application of values to a legal context. "For us" is not limited to legal philosophers, however, because citizens' opinion and social dialog are a far more effective tool for improving legal conventions than is the philosophy of law. Still, it was philosophy of law that asked, through Hegel, Radbruch, and other thinkers wheter a legal system can be a career of area-specific values – so-called legal values – and how they relate to social expectations.

According to Hegel and Radbruch, the legislator should also consider these questions. Only then can the legislator enjoy social trust. In Radbruch's view, law is not only capable but should strive to realize a certain set of legal values (several years later that postulate would be commented upon by Kelsen in his pure theory of law). Over one hundred years ago, Hegel indicated that the modern principle of recognition requires that what is perceived as a value must also be viewed as legally authorized.[5] This refers to a set of values, the realization of which or the participation in which is secured by a legal system; i.e., there is an institutionalized framework or room to practice chosen values or worthy activities. In a liberal system, the legislators protect citizens' free choice concerning values. A value choice depends on their self-obligation and not on external obligation. In an ethically (*sittlich*) mature, late modern society one could expect law to protect chosen values, such as freedom in its various manifestations, justice, property, etc., in a special, priviledged way. A set of values comprising freedom, property, and justice is, however, not representative of legal values. Only justice is a social value governed by law in the full positive and negative meaning. Property, freedom, and especially life cannot be fully governed – given or taken away, distributed, or redistributed – by law.

[4] G. Radbruch, *Rechtsphilosophie*, op. cit., p. 74.

[5] G.W.F. Hegel, *Philosophie of Right*, transl. S.W. Dyde, Kitchener, Ontario 2001, § 317.

It would be even more difficult for a legal system to govern life (that issue will be discussed below). Law cannot force individuals to realize such values as freedom, property, or life;[6] the legislator who uses force in regard to these must be prepared for morally justified resistance against a value grounded in force. Besides, if law forced people to realize a number of values it would have to introduce a false hierarchy for them so as to not drive individuals into a conflict of values.

When we speak about proper legal values (i.e., intrinsic values of right) the list of such values will, therefore, be limited. The list of extrinsic values will be infinitely longer and will also include grievances against the legislator by individuals, minorities, and even social or cultural majorities (the arithmetic criterion is not here considered to be a self-sufficient ethical criterion nor a criterion useful for infusing law with values). From the point of view of the psychology of values, a latent similarity exists between intrinsic and extrisic values that allows a layperson to correctly evaluate whether a given regulation is just. In Hegel's words, we do not need to be shoemakers to know if our shoes fit. It is a greater intellectual challenge to provide sufficient argumentation for such an evaluation. The goal of reflections such as this is to support citizens' judgment and decision making competence in legal ethics. Modern citizens' judgment needs to be informed judgment.

In Hegel's, Radbruch's, Kelsen's, Dworkin's, and, in particular, Habermas' works we find encouragement to evaluate the legal and moral validity of law. Before Kelsen's and his followers' achievements, evaluation of the legitimacy of law looked different than it does today. An evaluation, after all, can involve two things: the constitution of a statutory law and its application (issuance). Already at the moment of its creation, a legal system presupposes a set of values. From the perspective of legal positivism, the intrinsic axiological pool of a legal system is as it is: it has been formed by certain facts or social practices that gave rise to that system. Within the framework of jurisprudence and judges' discretion there may appear valuations; however, these valuations, or the law-immanent sphere of legal normativism, are not accessible to moral or ethical judgments.[7] Generally, it is extremely difficult for a layperson to directly address the reasons for the injustices in a legal system and in its application because the system is dynamic and the application changeable. A layperson will eagerly examine the content and substance of a single regulation or sentence. However, such a person operates with tools and criteria that are incompatible with a positive legal system; following the theory of legal positivism, there is

[6] Despite modern "biocratic" tendencies, see R. Esposito, *Bíos. Biopolitics and Philosophy*, Minneapolis – London 2004, p. 54.

[7] M. Zirk-Sadowski, "Soft Kelsenism Versus Multicentrism...," op. cit., p. 53.

nothing that would have normative or ruling force except the letter of the law. A legal system, then, is sovereign with respect to moral judgments, authorities, and external pressure. By a "layperson" we would also include philosophers of law insofar as they are not at the same time lawyers and use criteria other than the formal criteria of evaluation. On the ground of the theory of legal positivism, the hands of a philosopher of law who would attempt to form valuational judgments are tied. For the defenders of legal positivism such a thinker is not so much a challenge as a foreign body. Legal positivism protects itself against external judgment by, on the one hand, its own gradual construction and, on the other hand, the dynamic connections between legal principles. This kind of construction marginalizes the role of the content of legal norms and of moral judgments regarding it. A normative issue just stems from another normative issue, regardless of its merit. M. Zirk-Sadowski reasons that "[t]he substance of legal norms does not have any influence on their binding nature, but the fact of their establishment. Moving up this hierarchy we justify the binding of the lower norm competence to its issuing included in the higher norm. Therefore, the question arises: how should one justify the binding of the highest norm [...]?"[8] A formal transcendental argument would here suffice for a legal positivist, and, as already mentioned above, the broad field of judges' discretionary competence in law is highly indeterminate. But this is not enough for other traditions within legal philosophy, represented for example by Hegel and Radbruch. In Radbruch's view, the central task of philosophy of law is to evaluate law. "The philosophy of right, then, would reflect on and evaluate the law, the 'theory of the right law.'"[9]

Existent values seem to be legal, regardless of cultural, historical, and moral relativisms. The intersection between legal and moral validity is also timeless. It is discussed in all kinds of social communication. Public debates on social facts create discursive social facts such as a compromise or consensus. In a democracy, they have an impact on the lawmaking process, which is still open. In a democracy it is not the political authority who enforces legal solutions; citizens' conceptions compete and contribute to the making of law. Law is not an isolated phenomenon in such a context. It is a sociocultural and historical one, as Hegel and Radbruch emphasize. Cultural and civic participation presupposes free and open judgment as well as identifying, evaluating, and justifying those legal principles or sentences that promote social injustice, exclusion, or cruelty, or that generate future legal practices that produce unjust consequences. By considering the substance of legal rules and by making judg-

8 Ibidem, p. 55.

9 G. Radbruch, *Rechtsphilosophie*, op. cit., p. 13.

ments regarding justice and rightness, citizens draw on a huge set of particular values as they check whether those values can be protected – and to what extent – within the current legal framework. These values do not have to be literally mentioned in legal acts. The opposite is recommended: citizens expect law to be formulated in such a manner that the precious values are inscribed in the legal system, with law creating only room for citizens' free axiological choices (since this is what social justice demands as an intrinsic legal value: liberty of moral choice).

Distinguishing between intrinsic and extrinsic legal values will be the proper task of the next two chapters. There still are people – the so-called fundamentalists – who try to force their particular values literally into the legal system. People who have not discovered their own rights yet and are oriented toward the purely positive law interpret human rights as particular ideas "forced" by Western culture because they can only be ratified by a politically sovereign (state). An irrevocable legitimacy for ratification is granted by a referendum because in a democracy all voters are the sovereign. In societies in which pre-democratic consciousness prevails and high political authority is looked up to, an instance which is higher than the state awakens patriotic resentiment that evokes an irrational fear of losing sovereignty. Actually, "civil rights and human rights included in positive law are not granted directly by the sovereign, the acceptation of a concrete conception of these rights is based on the international commitments accepted by the sovereign."[10] When we look back to the values Hegel and Radbruch considered to be the intrinsic values of law, we will see they anticipated human rights. These are individual rights which could not be secured by individuals themselves, often against institutions treating them unjustly. International commitments fulfill a formal role here, whereas the substantial role of the source of those laws belongs to individuals, and the importance of the laws is derived from values cherished by those individuals. Although Hegel was against supranational legal instances, his *Philosophy of Right* adequately describes the nature of human rights and the role of education in their application:

> It is the essence of education and of thought, which is the consciousness of the individual in universal form, that the I should be apprehended as a universal person, in whom all are identical. Man must be accounted a universal being, not because he is a Jew, Catholic, Protestant, German, or Italian, but because he is a man. This thinking or reflective consciousness, is of infinite importance.[11]

---

[10] Ibidem, p. 57.

[11] G.W.F. Hegel, *Philosophy of Right*, op. cit., § 209.

1. The idea of right and its intrinsic values in Hegel's thought

Because Hegel's approach to law was partially historical, he could locate the legitimacy of the positive law ("statutory law") outside of the domain of classic natural law that was, in fact, frequently considered to be supranatural or divine law. By doing this he initiated a definition of the legitimacy of law for the purposes of a post-secular state. At the same time, Hegel provided a counterweight to pure legal positivism because that position, in very simple words, presupposes that a legislative act (in fact, a social construction) is enough to make a law legitimate. A legal positivist reasons in the following fashion: "because the legislature decided so and so with respect to X, the decision is valid and binding." The inference ("the legislature decided") is here taken to imply full validity of a legal rule, whereas, in fact, there are no real reasons here, i.e., there are no valuational arguments that would explain how certain social facts had determined a legislative act. The content and its merit or demerit (in J. Austin's words) do not determine the existence of law. What is more, the legal validity of a rule does not entail its moral validity, and vice versa. Law is indeterminate on the ethical-normative level. That implies judicial discretion and the problem of law-immanent interpretation. One hundred years later Radbruch summarized it as follows:

> The positiveness of law here becomes the condition of its own rightness – in the most suspicious manner. However, there are two tasks which are equally vital for the term "the right law": it must be a positive law and its content must be right.[12]

So, Radbruch represents a positivist theory of law insofar as he does not pay attention to the *content* of law in his theory of validity. His theory is of a philosophical, not ideological character. He represents Western democracy in which the authoritarian role of a national legislature is restricted by citizens' judgmental and voting competencies. He believes that citizens should participate in justifying the validity of law in an axiological, proceduralist, or hybrid way (i.e., in comparison with ahistorical natural law, or through social discourse), regarding the content of law and its changes. A citizen's right to evaluate law is an inevitable result of such long-term processes as the historicization, cul-

[12] In original: "Die Positivität des Rechts wird damit in höchst merkwürdiger Weise selbst zur Voraussetzung seiner Richtigkeit: es gehört ebensosehr zum Begründund des richtigen Rechts, positiv zu sein, wie es Aufgabe der positiven Rechts ist, inhaltlich richtig zu sein." G. Radbruch, *Rechtsphilosophie*, op. cit., § 9, pp. 73–75.

turization, relativization, and democratization of law. The processes begin in the emancipation of legal culture with respect to natural law. The lawmaking process becomes increasingly immanent, lay, and rational. "It is self-caused and self-realized reason,"[13] as Hegel puts it. Radbruch is right when he points to Hegel as the thinker who described most of these processes:

> As a matter of fact, Hegel shares the dislike of natural law with the historical school. In contrast to the science of natural law he does not juxtapose the individual lawgiving reason with the reality of law. Rather, he reveals natural law in the very matrix of law, that is in its historical reality: "what is rational is real, and what is real is rational." Despite the solidary objections there is a chasm between Hegel's philosophy and the historical school. For the historical school the identification of values and reality is based on the conviction that history is ruled by God's inscrutable will. For Hegel the identification is grounded in the dialectic reconstruction of reason which manifests itself in the historical process: "only what is rational is real." Hegel's reason opposes the national spirit and his rationalism contradicts irrationalism and romantic myths. That fundamental difference was reflected in the radical, personal polemic between Hegelians and the representatives of the historical school.[14]

In § 209 of his *Philosophy of Right*, Hegel assumes that the source of the idea of right is thought that has reached maturity, virtue, and appropriate intellectual scope. The thought does not pretend to discover universal truths and values "within the limits of reason alone" (in Kant's words). As Hegel claims,

> Right must be known in thought. It must be a system in itself, and only as a system can it be valid for civilized peoples [...]. To have the thought of right, one must be educated to the stage of thinking, and not linger in the region of the merely sensible [...]. Justice and virtue [...] have in the sphere of conscious reality their definite meaning and value, and find in that sphere judgment and their due.[15]

"This due is, however, as yet incomplete" from Hegel's perspective of the progressive realization of the world-spirit. Ordinary people are frequently "the unconscious tools and organs of the world-spirit,"[16] so at first they must *learn about* what is right, as Hegel says, and moreover, understand that what is right needs to be constituted as a *law* because it is only binding if it becomes a law, i.e., a legal rule.[17] Making laws that are based on the idea of what is right, and

[13] G.W.F. Hegel, *Philosophy of Right*, op. cit., § 341.

[14] G. Radbruch, *Rechtsphilosophie*, op. cit., p. 24.

[15] G.W.F. Hegel, *Philosophy of Right*, op. cit., § 209.

[16] Ibidem, § 345.

[17] Ibidem, § 212.

being ruled by such laws is a manifestation of culture, which[18] in modern times is being created by more and more rational citizens. Citizens' culture, with its specific, grass-roots, critical, and founding rationality, also has an impact on the ways of justifying law and its validity. "In the civic society what is intrinsically right becomes law."[19] For Hegel the ideal of right and rightness is an intrinsic and, at the same time, an extrinsic value of law. Citizens must first recognize what is right before they can participate in the lawmaking process. They are the rational carriers (*vehiculum*) of rightness. "The sun and the planets have laws, but they do not know them. Barbarians are ruled by impulses, customs, and feelings but have no consciousness of them. When right is established as law and known, all random intuitions and opinions, revenge, compassion, and self-interest, fall away,"[20] and rational institutions are established instead.

When we look at the lawmaking process from the point of view of citizens' interests, they all presuppose freedom as their condition. For Hegel freedom is the second substantial intrinsic legal value. According to the idea of progressive socialization described in Hegel's *Phenomenology of the Spirit* (1806), at the beginning of social history only one individual is free as a dominating consciousness (in Hegel's nomenclature: *a Master*) over the others (*Slaves*). With time, more and more individuals gain freedom. Finally, when the time comes for the republican civic community, freedom becomes the experience of all individuals, and the master-slave relationship is replaced by mutual recognition. By mutually recognizing their value they undertake a mutual obligation for such recognition when they give freedom the form of general law which is "no-one's" because it belongs to everyone. Their freedom obtains its objective Dasein and *validity* in the formal principle of right. "This right, being abstract, must be formal also. Its mandate is: Be a person and respect others as persons,"[21] as Hegel puts it. Freedom accepted in a universal and reciprocal manner invests a law with validity. And again, the right of freedom returns validity to freedom in case a crime is committed against freedom.[22]

According to such a finale of social history, ending in the recognition of freedom as a principle of citizenship, individuals experience that "right concerns freedom, the worthiest and holiest thing in man, the thing which

[18] G. Radbruch, *Rechtsphilosophie*, op. cit., § 1.

[19] G.W.F. Hegel, *Philosophy of Right*, op. cit., § 217.

[20] Ibidem, § 211, Note.

[21] G.W.F. Hegel, *Philosophy of Right*, op. cit., § 37.

[22] In the corresponding passage of his book *The Struggle for Recognition*, A. Honneth described the right of fredom (already quoted in this book, p. 121); idem, *The Struggle for Recognition, The Moral Grammar of Social Conflicts*, transl. J. Andreson, Frankfurt am Main 1995, p. 108.

he [a citizen] must know in so far as he is answerable to it."[23] Therefore, it is certain that for Hegel freedom, or the idea of freedom, is a legal value too. All subjects capable of rational management of their freedom in cooperation with others (embodying, as Hegel puts it, the "full manhood of free ethical self-consciousness"[24]) are internally entitled, that is, entitled without the need for additional legitimacy, to create statutory law. In this way the lawmaking process stops being the sole domain of professional legislators and lawyers, although, as has been said at the beginning, it would become such a domain again in the 20th and 21st century. Such an egalitarian approach, based on the recognition of the universality of the right to freedom, is clearly visible in the following excerpt:

> Jurists, who have a detailed knowledge of the law, often look on it as their monopoly. He who is not of their profession, they say, shall not be heard. [...] But we do not need the services of a shoemaker to find out if the shoe fits, nor do we need to belong to a particular trade in order to have a knowledge of the objects which are of universal interest in it. Right concerns freedom, the worthiest and holiest thing [...].[25]

In their reasonings, argumentations, and judgments concerning the validity of law, citizens should refer to freedom only if they mean "the unity of objective freedom with subjective freedom."[26] Thus, in Hegel's conception, the idea of freedom is a leading legal value and is to be discovered by the philosophy of right, similarly to Radbruch's conception.

> The idea of right is freedom, which, if it is to be apprehended truly, must be known both in its conception and in the embodiment of the conception [...]. The science of right is a part of philosophy. Hence it must develop the idea, which is the reason of an object, out of the conception.[27]

By contrast, freedom, in its "infinite subjectivity," belongs to the principle of morality.[28]

When considering values such as material and intellectual property, Hegel says: "Value is the true essence or substance of the object, and the object by possessing value becomes an object for consciousness"[29] – i.e., objects have no

[23] G. W. F. Hegel, *Philosophy of Right*, op. cit., § 215, Addition.
[24] Ibidem, § 347.
[25] Ibidem, § 215, Addition.
[26] Ibidem, § 258.
[27] Ibidem, Introduction, pp. 21–22.
[28] Ibidem, § 104.
[29] Ibidem, § 63.

independent legal value in themselves but only in connection with persons as conscious subjects having things at their disposal. By contrast, human life constitutes an indivisible, integral, infinite, and total value to Hegel – a value which transcends finite legal relations: "Life is the total context of one's existence, and cannot be measured by value [...]. Thus the disposal or sacrifice of life is not the manifestation of one's personality so much as the very opposite."[30] Life belongs to a different order than the order of legality. Admittedly, a murderer pays with his own life for taking someone else's life, because that is required by the measure of infinity ascribed by Hegel to life. Still, although life belongs to the realm of morality, it has a natural dimension over which morality does not exercise full power:

> As *this* individual, I am not master of my life, for the comprehensive totality of activity, i.e. life, is not something external to subjectivity, which is itself immediately *this*. Thus, it is a contradiction. To speak of the right of a person over his life is a contradiction, since it implies a right of a person over himself. But no one can stand above and execute himself.[31]

Life, then, is not a legal value, nor is it merely a moral value; it cannot be measured in such terms and the concept of value does not apply to it. Likewise, in Hegel's opinion risking one's life does not have any value in itself.

> To risk one's life is indeed something more than fear of death, but it is yet a mere negative, having no independent character and value. Only the positive element, the aim and content of the act, gives significance to the feeling of fearlessness [...].

A legal system is not interested in regulations within the natural life bios or individual existence. It is only interested in regulations concerning interpersonal relationships, social life, their key forms and values.[32] "In right, taken strictly, nothing depends upon my purpose or intention [...]. The subjectivity which is its own object is infinite, and freedom in its infinite subjectivity constitutes the principle of morality."[33] Morality seems to be the most approppriate place for subjective values. By justifying legal rules citizens sometimes invoke moral values and norms, but they mean (consideration-based) the application of law rather than the letter of statutory law. I think that, on the one hand, people's moral argumentation will never cease because its concrete *infinity* will never

[30] Ibidem, § 101.
[31] Ibidem, § 209.
[32] G. Radbruch, *Rechtsphilosphie*, op. cit., § 8, p. 65.
[33] G. W. F. Hegel, *Philosophy of Right*, op. cit., § 104–106.

match the abstract *infinity* of legal rules. On the other hand, "it is essential to understand that, owing to the nature of finite material, any application to it of principles, absolutely reasonable and in themselves universal, must be an infinite process."[34]

Hegel differentiates between the idea of rightness (*das Rechte*) elaborated in philosophical thought and in statutory law (positive law, *Gesetz*). Yet, we know that they should meet and become one. Statutory law must aim at a union with what is right. That is the way the development of law should function: as the realization, by statutory law, of what is rational, and overpowering the irrational. "Hence, the actual law may be different from what is in itself right."[35] Right itself (*das an sich Rechte*), or right in its idea, becomes positive law at the moment an act of statutory law is passed.[36] "Right is realized in the first instance in the form of constituted law," as Hegel claims in § 213. In § 212 he explains the constitution of law as the existence of an essential right:

> What is in essence right becomes in its objective concrete existence constituted [*Gesetzt*], that is, made definite for consciousness through thought. It, having right and validity, is so recognized, and becomes law [*Gesetz*]. Right in this characterization of it is positive right in general.

And although human moral judgment can subjectively deprive positive law of its legitimacy, it is not a sufficient counterweight for it until it assumes the form of rational reflection, the example of which is Hegel's philosophy of right. Philosophy of right "at least cannot recognize the authority of feeling, inclination and caprice" just "when they are set in opposition to positive right and the laws."[37] The legitimacy of law must be considered in all aspects or rightness, not "in an isolated and abstract way," as Hegel adds. He indicates Montesquieu as his master. "In this interrelation the various elements [of right] receive their meaning and justification. – The purely historical treatment of the phases of right, as they develop in time, and a comparison of their results with existing relations of right have their own value; but they are out of place in a philosophic treatise."[38] The full idea of right is only accessible from the perspective of the philosophy of right. Hegel, however, ascribes a self-originating, autonomous, social genesis to positive law, just like the doctrine

[34] Ibidem, § 216, Note.

[35] Ibidem, § 212.

[36] G.W.F. Hegel, *Philosophie des Rechts. Die Vorlesung von 1819/20 in einer Nachschrift*, ed. D. Henrich, Frankfurt am Main 1983, p. 169 (quote in German version only).

[37] G.W.F. Hegel, *Philosophy of Right*, op. cit., p. 23.

[38] Ibidem, p. 24.

of legal positivism. "Hence the origin of the conception of right falls outside of the science of right."[39]

2. Statutory law and legal values according to Radbruch

"Law is the reality the meaning of which is to serve justice,"[40] Radbruch states. As a cultural creation and unlike natural objects, law is not blind to values, and since "what is just, similarly to goodness, truth, and beauty, is an absolute value which cannot be derived from any other value [then] an absolute value is absolutely binding."[41] The question arises about the way in which law realizes the legal value of justice, which becomes an axiological contribution to the social criticism of law in a situation of such a spectacular violation of the value as "statutory lawlessness." Another question is what is the message of Radbruch's "theory of the right law" (*Lehre vom richtigen Recht*)?

As a subject of the law, a layperson would be interested in the idea of justice while a professional lawyer would be interested in legal certainty, says Radbruch.[42] Nowadays professional circles also seem to sidestep axiological discussions. The discussions are most often engaged in by ordinary people leading everyday lives in the varied, increasingly multicultural world. This is because it is those people who experience the direct pressure of cultures being born and reborn who are convinced, as the representatives of those cultures, that at a minimum legal regulations should somehow secure space for the realization of their values, and who sometimes behave in a very fundamentalist manner, claiming a privileged place for the values specific to their culture. If those culture-specific values clash with others, they pose a huge challenge for the legislator who must somehow cool the multi-cultural, multi-valued crucible. In such cases, Radbruch's postulate that it is the task of law to guarantee space for the realization of values appears to be very up-to-date.

Nevertheless, at this point there arises the difficult question about the way in which law should provide for such a guarantee and, indirectly, a question about the way in which it should be oriented toward values even as it remains fair and universal. On the one hand, we have to agree with Hegel that "law is a manifestation of the existence of culture,"[43] and that culture, especially as social practice, is the proper context for creating positive law (another problem is

[39] Ibidem, Introduction, p. 22.

[40] G. Radbruch, *Rechtsphilosophie*, op. cit., § 4.

[41] Ibidem.

[42] Ibidem, § 13.

[43] Ibidem, § 1.

how culture is self-defined). On the other hand, culture means the development, differentiation, and growth of forms of life. In his *Rechtsphilosophie*, Radbruch notes that forms of life are ahead of law already at the moment a legislative act is passed, and not the other way around. The capacity for rational law-making is, then, limited in comparison to the pace of development of social relationships. Law is not capable of fully securing all those relationships and, therefore, it cannot guard all the values created in those relationships. As we refer to Hegel's notion regarding the advantage of law over weakly developed rationality and culture, then, we can also assume, following Radbruch, that the reverse situation can take place: it may happen that even a person with high culture and standards of reasoning "must be obedient to acts of statutory law like a slave" and meet the legislator's demands "with clenched teeth," that is, with a feeling of external pressure and actual injustice.[44] Such a person will be the author of judgments which can constitute a significant contribution to the legitimization and delegitimization of law, creating a social counterweight to radical legal positivism. But what is so wrong with legal positivism?

The legal-positivist turn has established a fully new conception of law expressed in the so-called *separation thesis*. Legal rules can simply be posited and understood in a legal-order immanent way (in Kelsen: *Eigengesetzlichkeit des Rechts* and *der Rechtswissenschaft*), by sovereign legislatory bodies, "without the mediation of interpretation"[45] (or translation) in terms transcending the domain of law, such as the concepts of moral theories, natural and supra-natural laws, ideals, values, ideologies, political authorities' intentions, etc. In 1933, E. Voegelin wrote about H. Kelsen, the creator of modern pure legal science:

> The Kelsenian theory of statutory legal forms lacks a theory of ideas [...]. As it cleansed the theory of law of all that is not its positive content he elevated positive legal theory to the very top. However, heretofore not much has been gained from that purification.[46]

That was to change already in 1933, the year Hitler came to power and the Nuremberg laws began to be passed. At this time, Voegelin was postulating a revival of the "prepositivist" political framework for people, which would include ideals that offer "more than the positive rules that govern their behavior and actions."[47] But let us consider the crucial point of Kelsen's stance toward values for Radbruch and us. In the initial passages of *Reine Rechtslehre*

---

[44] Ibidem, pp. 226–227.

[45] A. Marmor, *Positive Law and Objective Values*, Oxford 2001, p. 78.

[46] E. Voegelin, *Rasse und Staat*, Tübingen 1933, pp. 6–7.

[47] T.W. Heilke, *Voegelin on the Idea of Race. An Analysis of Modern European Racism*, Baton Rouge – London 1990, p. 55.

(1934), Kelsen says: "As a moral category, right means exactly as much as justice does."[48] This means, the unity of right and justice calls any additional idea of justice into question. Furthermore, the therm justice expresses an eternal. The term justice expresses an eternal social yearning for happiness, he claims. To be just in the legal sense means to be right (*recht*) in accordance to the general norm's value. According to Kelsen,

> In its proper, non-legal sense, justice is an absolute value. Its content cannot be determined by the Pure Theory of Law. It is not available for rational knowledge [...] it is a metaphysical Platonic idea, outside of all appearance. A dualism of justice and right is of the same metaphysical character. [...] Societies may affirm themselves as being or not being just. [...] If justice would be done as existent, the existence of positive law would be unecessary and inscrutable. [...] Justice is an irrational ideal, inaccessible for our mind. Only positive law is given, or more exactly: given as a task of recognizing.[49]

Radbruch opposes legal positivism because it has been massively abused by the National Socialism authorities that promoted harmful values and the principle "law is law" within their legal orders. In consequence of that abuse, Kelsen had to defend himself by emigrating as far as the United States. Radbruch was deprived of his professor's position at the University of Heidelberg. In 1932 he defined the idea of law in the following way: "The idea of law is a value because law is a reality directed at values, and a cultural phenomenon."[50] Ergo, the same social culture which is developed by a given society also creates law and, following H. L. A. Hart, the axiological and normative foundation for critical morality. In Radbruch, critical morality is distingushed from positive (subjective and objective) morality as a "morality actually accepted and shared by a given social group [...] Hence, each particular positive morality must be distinguished] from the general moral principles used in the criticism of actual social institutions, including positive morality. We may call such general principles 'critical morality,'"[51] according to Hart's distinction. Radbruch also proposed general principles, including the principle of justice. However, following him, those raising moral criticisms may autonomously formulate principles and judgments related to the principle of justice. In Radbruch the question is whether such judgments satisfy the two criteria of rationality and generality?[52]

[48] H. Kelsen, *Reine Rechtslehre...*, op. cit., p. 26 (free translation).

[49] Ibidem, pp. 26–28.

[50] G. Radbruch, *Rechtsphilosophie*, op. cit., § 3.

[51] H.L.A. Hart, *Law, Liberty, Morality*, London 1963, p. 20.

[52] H.L.A. Hart, *The Concept of Law*, Oxford 1961, p. 178; see also N. MacCormick, *H.L.A. Hart*, Stanford, CA 1981.

In Kelsen's eyes the answer is that they do not, while in Hart's eyes they do, although value-related principles are highly difficult to rationalize. Additionally, they contain potentially ideological claims. This is why modern authors discussing legal argumentation procedures frequently alternate between such terms as "legal values" (Radbruch), "general principles" (Hart), "socio-moral considerations,"[53] "evaluations,"[54] or "existing standards."[55]

However, similarly to Hegel (and Hart), Radbruch omits in his idea of law particular values derived from any individual or collective preferences or morals ("feeling, inclination and caprice when they are set in opposition to positive right and the laws,"[56] in Hegel's words). From the very beginning, Radbruch writes about legal values, the very first of which is justice. Many people, though, "are prone to seeing justice as only a kind of a manifestation of a moral good. It is such a manifestation, indeed, but only when we consider justice as a positive personal trait or a strength of character, called virtue."[57] The idea of justice toward which law should be oriented is a completely different matter. It is the basic legal value and law-immanent value that Radbruch juxtaposes with the formal *Grundnorm* (which, although it ought to be a transcendental value, can be arbitrarily, voluntarily, and decisionistically proposed by legal authorities) of law that had been proposed by the doctrine of "pure" legal positivism. It is only on the basis of the idea of justice as an idea of right and a legal value that one can make a binding statement that a given statutory law is unjust. Both in the conditions of the political dictatorship during the Third Reich and in the conditions of legal (and formal) positivism opposed to it after the period of the Third Reich, the argumentation which invokes moral or cultural, and thus varied and flexible, interpretations of justice had less rational power than the argument of justice considered as a legal value. Radbruch is interested in a tool which would be able to, in the situation of extreme legislated injustice (like the anti-Semitic Nuremberg Laws from the 1930s), prove the invalidity of such law, empower citizens to influence the legislature, encourage judges not to apply such unjustice law during a trial, and, last but not least, protect judges against the accusation of breaking current statutory law.[58]

---

[53] K. Larenz, *Methodenlehre der Rechtswissenschaft*, Heidelberg – Berlin 1975.

[54] R. Alexy, *A Theory of Legal Argumentation*, transl. R. Adler, N. MacCormick, Oxford 1989.

[55] N. MacCormick, *H. L. A. Hart*, op. cit., p. 128.

[56] G. W. F. Hegel, *The Philosophy of Right*, op. cit., p. 23.

[57] G. Radbruch, *Rechtsphilosophie*, op. cit., § 4.

[58] Justice understood in cultural or moral categories is another issue; it involves realizing law-extrinsic values by all individuals, in the possibly wide dimension of self-realization. According to Radbruch, the total content of a moral value is only exhausted by an infinite number of individuals. It is only then that the particular aspect of a moral value disappears. It becomes an ethical value (*sittlich*) but it is separate and independent from legal values. In that

Viewed in this light, justice would be a legal value to which law, including its legislation and application, aspires as a supreme value. Justice understood in this way opens or returns to a person access to a number of extrinsic values, including freedom, property, etc. Still, the legitimacy (validity) of law does not stem from non-legal axiology. In this respect, claims Radbruch, "law must remain law."[59] At the same time, he refers to Fichte and states that the content of legal rules may stem from objections to an act of legislation that has become outdated. Following Radbruch, "law may arise not only from law. A new law grows from wild shoots every moment."[60] In contrast to the "pure" theory of legal positivism, the formalist-normativist dominant is here juxtaposed with the more socially relevant dominant of the content of law. Radbruch himself never exhibited the temptation to revise the particular content of legal rules when seeking criteria for law's validity. This is why he had already always spoken about intrinsically legal values and the autonomous room protected by them.[61]

> It cannot be here understood that justice is a proper material for building real law because the chief principle of distributive justice does not say who should be defined as an equal and who as an unequal [...]. Equality is never directly given [...]. Equality is always an abstract term derived from inequality, from a particular point of view.[62]

The idea of law suggested by Radbruch contains, apart from justice, two other intrinsic legal values: legal certainty and purposiveness. In the area of the spectacular injustices committed during the Third Reich period (but also in the Soviet Union, which is less studied in this respect), justice is the only one of the three values that retains a moral meaning; the other two values have a more technical character. Various cultures and eras "put a special emphasis on one of those elements."[63] Similarly, various cultures and eras are characterized by different emphases and borderlines between the fields of legal and moral values. Radbruch's view on this issue stands out as he claims that law and morality are strictly distinct but law – formally and informally – guarantees

---

respect Radbruch's concept does not diverge much from Hegel's ideas expressed in *Philosophy of Law*, op. cit., § 8.

[59] G. Radbruch, *Rechtsphilosophie*, op. cit., p. 90.

[60] Ibidem, pp. 90–91.

[61] See J. Zajadło, *Dziedzictwo przeszłości. Gustaw Radbruch: portret filozofa, prawnika, polityka i humanisty* [Heritage of the Past. Gustav Radbruch Portrayed as Philosopher, Lawyer, Politician and Humanist], Gdansk 2007, p. 122.

[62] Ibidem, p. 38.

[63] A. Kaufmann, *Gustav Radbruch – Leben und Werk*, Gustav Radbuch-Gesamtausgabe, vol. I, Heidelberg 1987, pp. 75–76.

axiological safety to individuals in the moral and, probably, also cultural sense. It is not in conflict with "pure" legal positivism, it avoids all fundamentalist solutions usually based on a literal proclamation of such and such values in the self-proclaimed name of *universalism*, it does not suggest any hierarchy of values, and it retains a tactful, distant, but respectful attitude toward all values carried and created by a given society. In regard to extrinsic moral values, this view is the most democratic we can imagine on the grounds of legal sciences. It is rooted in justice as an intrinsic legal value.

> [L]aw can serve morality not by imposing legal duties but by protecting certain rights. It is directed toward morality through rights and not duties. It guarantees an individual rights which allow a better fulfillment of moral duties.[64]

3. From natural law to human rights

Radbruch gave up legal doctrines based on natural law, being convinced that they subvert the validity of the constitution and that they introduce an anarchism[65] under the pretext of a deeper, transcendental foundation of legal rules. He also opined that it was:

> [...] not the historical school of law but critical philosophy, it was not von Savigny but Kant who dealt the fatal blow to natural law. Kant's criticism of reason showed that reason is not a treasury of ready-made theoretical cognitions or ethical norms waiting to be used [...]. It is not so much the source of answers as of questions born out of experience. Reason has at its disposal forms which are yet to be filled with content, it has categories which can lead to significant evaluations or judgments only when applied to specific materials. Such cognitive judgments defined with regard to content are never the creation of only "pure" reason but, at the most, the result of applying reason to a particular subject matter. They can never be important in general because their importance only refers to the given material [...]. Only the category of right and just law and not any effect of its application is common and general. Thus, if we wished to define "natural law" [...] as "the only proper law" we should [...] decidedly oppose the interpretation of natural law in the old style, as an absolute, a "natural law with changeable content," or [...] "law of cultural character."[66]

Radbruch cosidered *ius naturale* to be a construct of reason without superior, universal content. He implicitly used here the key argument formulated by legal positivism. The content of the category of just law as such is not

---

[64] G. Radbruch, *Rechtsphilosophie*, op. cit., p. 48f.

[65] See J. Zajadło, *Formuła Radbrucha* [Radbruch's Formula], Gdansk 2001, p. 175.

[66] G. Radbruch, *Rechtsphilosophie*, op. cit., p. 24.

available to human knowledge either in a deductive (transcendental deduction) or inductive manner, on the basis of data provided by experience. Following Radbruch, the process of law creation as well as its application should, then, consequently turn toward so-called relativism. If this is all true, there arises an inevitable demand to work out a potentially strong social legitimacy for those norms of statutory law that are associable with the idea of justice (the norms that are not derived only from dynamic connections within a legal system), especially in the case of basic law – the constitution. For the philosophy of law, this entails the requirement to observe the legitimacy of law on the basis of an already limited set of criteria: the intrinsic legal values. After Radbruch, due to the works of Habermas, Dworkin, and others, philosophy of law is interested in more than a legally-ordered society. Expressions such as "well-ordered" and "well-ordered society" best express the tradition.

In the face of the experiences related to the legislature (or legacy, rather) in the Third Reich and the Soviet Union, the legislator and citizens have the duty to contribute to a just legislature and to constantly monitor both lawmaking the application of law to guard against the iniquity and injustice inherent in the existing legal order. Radbruch strongly emphasizes legal education as an important element of civic education in response to the failures of institutional and administrative mechanisms, and the lack of social consciousness and civil courage of lawyers' and citizens' during the period of National Socialism to evaluate the pathologies of the legislature and legal order. He recommends developing a citizens' "sense of rightness" (*Rechtssinn*), starting as early as the school years. The idea of all citizens evaluating the way individuals are treated by crucial social and political institutions, from the perspective of injustice, exclusion, intolerance, and other blatant wrongs committed in agreement with primary and secondary legislation, became the impulse for creating the Convention on Human Rights. From the Weimar period, Radbruch showed in his works the genesis of and the need for critical moral judgment in legal subjects, directed at institutions, including the institution of statutory law, and the legitimacy of law. Citizens' contestation of the law, reflecting Radbruch's contestation of "pure" legal positivism during the National Socialism period, can be called ethical judgment in the post-conventional sense, with reference to universal criteria and to ethical procedures – as long as they invoke intrinsic legal values. Such judgment may seem unnecessary to the beneficiaries of a stable, just legislature, and by proponents of conventionalism it may even be considered to be an attack on the integrity and authority of law as the crucial political institution. From time to time, however, the gravity of circumstances makes such judgment crucial as the authority of law does not end but begins from the fact of the existence of legal order.

This is why the criteria that could justify such an evaluation cannot be contingent or accidental. They cannot be drawn from particular morals, although, as mentioned earlier in this chapter, moral and cultural regulatory systems have a strong impact on concrete legal systems. As a critic of natural law and, at the same time, of radical legal positivism, Radbruch did not have an easy task. As he justified the importance of legal certainty as a key legal value, Radbruch said that if one could not ultimately establish just law, then what law ought to be should at least be established. Nevertheless, the existence of a legal system (and minimal-legal certainty) is a necessary but insufficient criterion of law's validity. The first criterion is enough for a legislator to justify obliging citizens to abide by the law but it is not enough for a citizen to justify his or her self-obligation to observe the law. According to Radbruch, the validity of law should result in self-obligation. Its invalidity, on the other hand, can (and should) result in civil disobedience and administrative disobedience. Radbruch calls invalid law and the injustice represented by it "statutory lawlessness" – seeming justice (*scheinbare Gerechtigkeit*) that is in conflict with real justice (*wirkliche Gerechtigkeit*). In the work *Statutory Lawlessness* Radbruch claims:

> Where there is not even an attempt at justice, where equality, the core of justice, is deliberately betrayed in the issuance of positive law, then the statute is not merely "flawed law," it lacks completely the very nature of law. For law, including positive law, cannot be otherwise defined than as a system and an institution whose very meaning is to serve justice.[67]

Critical reflection on invalid law must go beyond the range of the procedures which invested it with its "invalid validity." It ought to include moral reflection, a "sense of truth" (*Wahrheitssinn*[68]), and a "sense of rightness" (*Rechtssinn*), because "only morality can justify the obligatoriness of law. Legal statements expressed in the imperative form can only result in coercion and never in obligation"[69] (Radbruch indicates that the ideal of justice is of moral provenience). Yet, if someone invokes the letter of the law, or is even professionally obliged to act by the law in the way judges are, he or she faces a serious dilemma (though not a real dilemma since we know that on the one side is only "seeming justice" and on the other "real justice." Giving the example of a judge's conscience when making a decision about the application of law, Radbruch claims that "a judge can never administer justice by appealing to

---

[67] G. Radbruch, "Statutory Lawlessness and Supra-Statutory Law" (1946), op. cit., supra note 6/7.

[68] To Kelsen and Radbruch, regardless of their different stances with respect to justice, recognizing justice and recognizing truth seem to be similar tasks for judicial thinking.

[69] G. Radbruch, *Rechtsphilosophie*, op. cit., § 5, p. 47.

a statute that is not merely unjust but criminal. We appeal to human rights that surpass all written laws, and we appeal to the inalienable, immemorial law that denies validity to the criminal dictates of inhuman tyrants." There were, and there still are, situations in which a statutory law entails injustice. Such a law makes it impossible to treat every person equally, with the same standard of justice, as explained by Radbruch in *Five Minutes of Legal Philosophy*. Consequently, legal equality should be included among key legal values. In the face of "statutory lawlessness" we cannot look for justice beside law, but above it in a sphere completely independent from positive law. Radbruch calls this sphere the "supra-statutory law." It comprises the idea of justice that could not always be defended in itself and therefore was incorporated in, for example, the human rights proclaimations after World War II.

Radbruchs' famous 1947 work, *Statutory Lawlessness and Supra-Statutory Law*, is probably the most important text on morality in the history of philosophy of law. The text constituted the moral significance of human rights, which is more universal than the significance of any particular moral rights. For centuries legal philosophers reflected in a more speculative fashion, which was restricted to the context of a nation state. In contrast, during the interwar era and after the wars, philosophical reflection assumed the appearance of political criticism and became the international voice in answer to both the supranational scale of the injustice of the internal legislature of the Third Reich, and painful international problems, starting with the Nuremberg Laws. As a minister of justice of the Weimar Republic (1920–23) and a distinguished lawyer, Radbruch suggested the following task for the philosophy of law: instead of indoctrinizing citizens and forcing a ready-made normative judgment on them (it is at this point that Radbruch writes his famous *ignorabimus*), it should provoke people to ask questions about the meaning of a *concrete* legal statement as an "objective meaning of an act of the will." More precisely, it should sensitize both lawyers and laypeople to the issue, being conscious of the fact that for some individuals values other than justice might be a priority, and for others justice and equality will remain a priority for as long as the blatant injustices committed in the name of the law are remembered – there is also no scarcity of such injustices in the contemporary world. In the period when the Nazi legal system[70] crystallized, justice as a paramount legal value became a priority and remains so to this day. In contemporary political formations, exclusion of particular groups (defined by ethnic, socio-economic, cultural, educational,

[70] If the Soviet legislature were more available for research, i.e., if it left more manifest traces – these were diligently hidden and destroyed by the Soviet regime – and if it could be subjected to objective critical reflection, Radbruch's formula could be easily applied to it. As it is, the regime remains a blank spot on the map of contemporary philosophy of law.

gender, and other criteria) on the legal level can be still experienced and must be permanently signaled.

The meaning of law should reflect the ideal of justice instead of an arbitrary political gesture, examples of which were copiously provided by the Third Reich and the Soviet Union. In order to be recognized by society, the ideal must be one of the socially authentic ideals. If the ideal of justice were biased or denied actually shared social ideals, citizens would have the right to reject it as merely "seeming." However, the "feeling of rightness" (*Rechtsgefühl*) and the "sense of rightness" (*Rechtssinn*) that should be promoted in the citizens of a democratic society:

> [...] does not take away from any individual the right to an independent choice of attitudes toward the law. That choice may contradict another person's choice but it should have sufficient systemic validity. The philosophy of law is restricted to presenting the possible points of view to an individual but leaves the final decision to the deep, personal reflection of that individual [...]. It is on purpose that the philosophy of law makes such a distinction, as its stance toward ultimate evaluating judgments is expressed in the immovable *ignorabimus*. [...] The presented method is called *relativism* because it aims to establish the rightness (*Richtigkeit*) of each judgment.[71]

Radbruch defined the aim of philosophy, from the perspective described above, as "reflection on the value of law" (*Wertphilosophie des Rechts*). In some measure, that aim should also be adopted by all citizens as users of a "sense of rightness," or even only a subjective "feeling of rightness," which is a non-institutionalized independent source of critical considerations on unjust or imperfectly just legal rules. Radbruch does not demand that they evaluate – like the philosophy of law – each legal statement. Their evaluation should prove, at least, that a specific legal rule is illegal or unjust to the degree that it has a severe negative effect on people (and not in the name of some subjective moral opinion). Radbruch proposes a scale of injustice that ranges from the so-called "intolerable degree of injustice, unbearable level of injustice" to "insufferable injustice" (*Unerträglichkeitssthese*), and is an elementary, egalitarian moral criterion, available to all people. One need not be an expert lawyer to identify lawlessness and injustice (and to know that the majesty of law is capable of promoting it), nor do we – let us repeat, following Hegel again – need to be shoemakers to know if our shoes fit. At first glance, the criterion of injustice may seem to be an imprecise, affective, rather than rational, measure. It is so, indeed. But the moment it is used it triggers a process of reflection, judgment, argumentation, justification, etc., which leads to a citizen's rational judgment.

[71] G. Radbruch, *Rechtsphilosophie*, op. cit., § 2.

As we have proved in another chapter, it is within the nature of moral judging that a judgment is born out of a feeling of approval or disapproval, triggering a series of rational reflections. Still, in spite of the fact that "Faith and trust belong to the beginning of reflection, presupposing picture thought and such discernment as is implied in the judgement that to believe in a heathen religion is different from being a heathen,"[72] feeling itself does not make a judgment rational and valid to the degree required by contemporary social life. "Inner inspiration and feeling [is] the very soul of particularity," warns Hegel as he draws the reader's attention to the fact that a mere feeling can be unreliable in situations as complex as an evaluation of the justice of a law. Radbruch also warns against relying on intuition. For example, he recommends that judges put themselves in the accused's shoes, but not by way of ordinary feeling and empathy.[73]

> From among all virtues, justice should be the least reliable on intuition, feeling, or untrained consciousness [...]. If the maxim of justice says that one should not do unto others as one does not wish to be done by them, then justice presupposes the ability of abstract reasoning of two types: the ability to put oneself in someone else's shoes and, as a consequence, the ability to generalize that position. That transference and generalization also require [...] a certain ability to evaluate theoretically.[74]

This is because right is "not only injustice but also decisions and conclusions."[75]

Radbruch also recommends such an exercise to laypeople so they can become more enlightened participants in the process of creating law. He treds in Hegel's footsteps, following the claim in *Philosophy of Right* that "there is no reason for supposing that the judge is the only one to decide upon matters of fact. For this not the legal mind alone but any man of ordinary intelligence is competent."[76] It is worthwhile to once more take a look at the function and meaning of Radbruch's "sense of rightness." This sense does not have to verify law with respect to justice. Rather, it should falsify and unmask "an intolerable degree" of injustice. Individual judgments should trigger a wave of social criticism. *Radbruch's formula* clearly states that both lawyers and citizens "must, in their consciousness, become deeply convinced that laws which transgress

[72] G.W.F. Hegel, *The Philosophy of Right*, op. cit., § 147.

[73] G. Radbruch, *Bildungs- und Religionspolitik*, Gustav Radbuch-Gesamtausgabe (RGA), vol. 13, Heidelberg 1987–2003, pp. 191–264.

[74] Ibidem.

[75] Ibidem, p. 264.

[76] G.W.F. Hegel, *Philosophy of Right*, op. cit., § 227.

any measure of injustice and social harmfulness, laws which should not only be denied binding force but also any legal character are *possible*."[77]

Both groups should be able to evaluate how "problematic law and justice can be"[78] and take a stance oriented toward justice as a value. "A layman's sense of rightness is measured by how strongly he is convinced that unjust laws and sentences should be binding, too, whereas a lawyer's sense of rightness is measured by how hard it is for him or her to accept the injustice of the existing statutory law or 'final and binding' sentences."[79] So far Radbruch's formula has been used on many occasions by the German Federal Constitutional Court and Federal Court of Justice. We are considering its application to everyday legal life, assuming that in a democracy all citizens are entitled to evaluate law. Some of them will remain unsatisfied forever because a concrete legal system can be only "approximately" just[80] and "only ideal social order can be the embodiment of the ideal of justice."[81] However, in contemporary times – sometimes compared to the period of the Weimar Republic (because of the economic crisis, educational crisis, unemployment, social frustration, young democracies, fundamentalist movements, and the revival of nationalisms, phobias, and other radicalisms) and not only in Central Europe, as many citizens as possible should actively react to injustice committed in the name of the law and in the face of various pressures exerted on the legislature. It is easier, after all, to prevent injustice by avoiding it (the so-called *Verleugnungsthese*) rather than dealing with fait accompli.

"Justice is not the total and only basis for creating law, however, it is a principle specific to law, a necessary measure for defining the concept of law. Law is a reality the significance of which consists in serving justice. Therefore, it is impossible to define the concept in a different way than as a reality the meaning of which is to realize the ideal of law. A law can be unjust (*summum ius – summa iniuria*) but it remains a law, at least because in its intention it is the stronghold of justice"[82] as the supreme intrinsic legal value. This conclusion does not change anything in the order proposed by R. Dworkin and N. MacCormick: legal principles such as justice are based on legal values. They "occupy an intermediary space between legal rules and moral principles. Legal rules are posited by recognized institutions and their validity derives from their

[77] G. Radbruch, "Five Minutes of Legal Philosophy," op. cit.

[78] G. Radbruch, *Bildungs- und Religionspolitik*, op. cit., p. 264.

[79] Ibidem, p. 265.

[80] A. Kaufmann, *Gustav Radbruch – Leben und Werk*, op. cit., p. 72; see also J. Zajadło, *Formuła Radbrucha* [Radbruch's Formula], op. cit.

[81] G. Radbruch, *Rechtsphilosophie*, op. cit., § 4.

[82] Ibidem, § 1.

enacted source. Moral principles are what they are due to their content, and their validity is purely content dependent [...]. The validity of a legal principle [...] derives from a combination of facts [including a set of socially shared general values] and moral considerations [including citizens' moral judgments and criticisms],"[83] as clearly demonstrated in Radbruch's writings.

[83] A. Marmor, *Positive Law and Objective Values*, op. cit., p. 82.

Chapter VII

Democracy begins in the mind. Developing democratic personality[1]

> Mother, remember what you said just now. You promised that I might state my opinion freely without fear.
>
> Euripides

1. A gap between democratic ideals and citizens' behavior

In both young and old democracies a gap between democratic ideals and behaviors exists. Civic activities are decreasing proportionally to increasing economical, social, and educational inequalities. It is not enough to produce high level theories of democracy while, at the same time, individuals stop speaking and listening to others, and "computer-mediated groups"[2] like, for example, the Anonymous, "make better quantitative judgments" (often with global consequences!) than do citizens. But the "face-to-face deliberation may be more appropriate in the political arena because of the nature of political decisions. Political involves complex issues, moral conflicts [...]. Just as complex tasks lend themselves to more democratic methods in group discussion."[3]

---

[1] This study would not have been possible without the two-years research grant from Alexander von Humboldt Foundation at the University of Konstanz (Germany, 2008–2010). The author is also grateful for permission to republish this paper by Łukasz Gałecki (Peter Lang Publishing). The paper first appeared in E. Nowak, D. Schrader, B. Zizek (eds.), *Educating Competencies for Democracy*, Frankfurt am Main 2013, pp. 399–416.

[2] J. Gastil, "Is Face-to-Face Citizen Deliberation a Luxury or a Necessity for Democracy?," *Political Communication*, 2000, no. 17, pp. 358–359. Retrieved from http://faculty.washington.edu/jgastil/pdfs/LuxuryOrNecessity.pdf [24.06.2013].

[3] Ibidem, p. 359.

Moral discourse and democratic competencies need to be fostered in order for citizens to more fully participate in the democratic cooperative process, and to empower their voices in democracy. First at all, democratic education must offer opportunities to exercise that competencies soon.[4]

Teaching university students in the discipline of practical philosophy and ethics, I observe that they discuss on democracy at a highly abstract level. Rosen calls this phenomena "overprofessionalization"[5] and Berkowitz emphasizes that democratic education should not be only "focused on the interpenetration of reasons and justifications."[6] At the same time, most of students have never been in the middle of a real democratic deliberation. They have never experienced how to discuss concrete social problems openly, beyond particular ideological sympathies or just in respect one for another. In Poland, official press- and television-mediated discourses do not strengthen democratic skills in citizens. Polish democracy still has posttotalitarian features. In my opinion, "posttotalitarian" means that the official constitution expresses democratic ideals and principles, but, at the same time, people are strongly accustomed to the very predemocratic (i.e., submissive/servile, anxious, misrespecting, misconducting, etc.) behaviors. Behaving in a nondemocratic way, people produce hierarchical and submissive interactions with others. These interactions have a strong impact on the social discourses, institutions (in particular on the schools and universities), democratic inclusion, and participation. In result, the Polish democratic life does not provide democratic experiences for anyone; but everyone must learn to live in a democratic way. Additionally, the Polish schooling system does not offer supportive opportunities in order to educate democratic skills in students.

In consequence, repeating nondemocratic behaviors seems to be cognitively structured and this is, why I consider that we cannot *live* democracy, untill we are not democratically minded enough. So, democracy begins in the minds and requires some kind of democratic personality, too.

In this paper I refer to the pre-conditions of democratic personality in Georg Lind's educational-developmental conception of democracy. According to Lind, Sandberger, and Bargel[7] we can consider integrated democratic personality to exist when "a person has developed consistent relations between

---

[4] A. Colby et al., *Educating for Democracy*, San Francisco 2009, p. 134.

[5] M. Rosen, *Dignity. Its History and Meaning*, Cambridge, MA – London 2012, p. XIII.

[6] M.W. Berkowitz et al., "Discourse, Development, and Education," in F. Oser, W. Veugelers (eds.), *Getting Involved*, Rotterdam – Taipei 2009, p. 194.

[7] G. Lind et al., "Moral Competence and Democratic Personality," in G. Lind, H.A. Hartmann, R. Wakenhut (eds.), *Moral Judgments and Social Education*, New Brunswick – London 1981[1], 2010[2], p. 61.

various orientations, values, and goals"[8] and when she or he developed "*mature* moral judgment both in its justificational function and when [she or he] applies norms," as Habermas[9] assumes. The developmental approach in both moral psychology and moral philosophy clearly harmonize one with another. This harmony provides a highly favorable atmosphere to implement moral and democratic education at the academic level.

The term "moral" means to me a set of personal cognitive competencies. Sociomoral cognition is based on the personal mind's strength (*virtue*), as Socrates and Aristotle already demonstrated it. Neither individual nor social flourishing could be possible without being *virtuous* so the main moral duty of humans against themselves is to develop their cognitive capacities by practicing judgmental behavior in socially demanding situations.[10] *Virtue* cannot be imparted by academic teaching culture. This is why Polish university students in the first or second semester start to reflect, argue, and make decisions after having participated in several dilemma discussions (KMDD) sessions and open discussions. They feel better understood by others and they understand others better by discussing whatever they experience and think. They become integral members of the first democratic community in their lives. This makes a highly important motivation for a university teacher like me, experiencing democratic transformation in persons and institutions since its beginning in the Middle Europe in the 1970s.

"A fully developed democratic personality"[11] presupposes more than "a particular configuration of unrelated drives, attitudes, or traits." It requires from an individual "the self commitment to one's *own* moral ideals"[12] while being confronted with others' moral beliefs in open discourse. Moreover, it requires from an individual that she or he will apply basic democratic values like personal dignity, respect and autonomy in an unconditional way. "Only if conflicts do not involve disagreement with regard to basic values can they be solved by means of rational discourse."[13] In democracy, basic competence means "the capacity to make judgments and decisions which are moral (e.g.,

[8] Ibidem, pp. 55–78.

[9] J. Habermas, "Philosophical Notes on Moral Judgment Theory," in G. Lind, H. A. Hartmann, R. Wakenhut (eds.), *Moral Judgments...*, op. cit., p. 13.

[10] Aristotle, *Nicomachean Ethics,* transl. W. D. Ross, 1130a–1130b. Retrieved from http://classics.mit.edu/Aristotle/nicomachean.1.i.html [21.05.2009].

[11] G. Lind et al., "Moral Competence...," op. cit., p. 75.

[12] G. Lind, *Moral ist lehrbar. Handbuch zur Theorie und Praxis moralischer und demokratischer Bildung*, München 2009, p. 31.

[13] G. Lind et al., "Moral Competence...," op. cit., p. 62.

based on internal principles) and to act in accordance with such judgments."[14] There are countless cognitive competencies like rationally-discursive construction of one's own feelings and preconscious beliefs, accountability, cooperation, representation, leadership, etc. which are crucial for democratic personality. It makes not sense to recall all of them, but it makes sense to emphasize that the opening of individual mind to others (in their otherness which constitutes democratic diversity) is only possible with a developed moral judgment competence because judging occurs in the medium of discourse. So in democracy, morality is already always "interpersonal morality,"[15] and

> [...] the key democratic competence is discourse competence... [and] democracy is essentially a moral institution [which] has to include the competence of confronting other people and other opinions, and the participants of such a confrontation must be oriented toward moral principles. This is what the competence of solving problems and social conflicts in a rational way demands.[16]

2. Measuring the quality of democratic education: the Polish Moral Judgment Test validation (2009)

Georg Lind and his colleagues started to develop the "Moral Judgment Test" in 1978.[17] It is a highly precise experimental measuring instrument. One can consider a test to be a "test" when it contains some tasks for participants. The MJT design consists of two moral tasks, i.e., the Workers' Dilemma and the Doctor's Dilemma that are challenges for personal judgment competence. At the same time, a test can be treated as valid only when it measures the cognitive (and affective) processes that researchers expect to measure, and when the set of scientific criteria is fulfilled. With the MJT personal moral judgment competence ($N=1$) is scored (C-score means: competence score), but only group scoring is allowed. The MJT is used to evaluate the impact of education (in particular at the academic level) on the development of moral judgment

[14] L. Kohlberg, "Development of Moral Character and Moral Ideology," in M.L. Hoffman, L.W. Hoffman (eds.), *Review of child development research*, vol. 1, New York 1964, p. 425.

[15] R. Döbert, G. Nunner-Winkler, "Value Change and Morality," in G. Lind, H.A. Hartmann, R. Wakenhut (eds.), *Moral Judgments...*, op. cit., p. 142.

[16] G. Lind, *Moral ist lehrbar...*, op. cit., pp. 19–31.

[17] G. Lind, "Wie misst man moralisches Urteil? Probleme und alternative Möglichkeiten der Messung eines komplexen Konstrukts," in G. Portele (ed.), *Sozialisation und Moral*, Weinheim 1978, pp. 171–201; G. Lind, "Moral Regression in Medical Students and Their Learning Environment," *Revista Brasileira de Educaçaõ Médica*, 2000, vol. 24 (3), pp. 24–33; idem, *Moral ist lehrbar...*, op. cit.; G. Lind et al., "Moral Competence...," op. cit., pp. 55–78.

competence among students. Until 2012 the MJT has already been validated for 39 languages. Since 2004 the electronic version of MJT has been in use. The table below shows the impact of my academic teaching course on participants with elements of the Konstanz Method of Dilemma Discussion on moral judgment competence (AMU Poznan, Poland 2011; *N* = 25; pretest and posttest *N* = 21). The electronic picture (Figure 1) shows scores for persons' preferences toward each of six levels of moral reasoning in the sense used by Kohlberg, for both dilemmas:

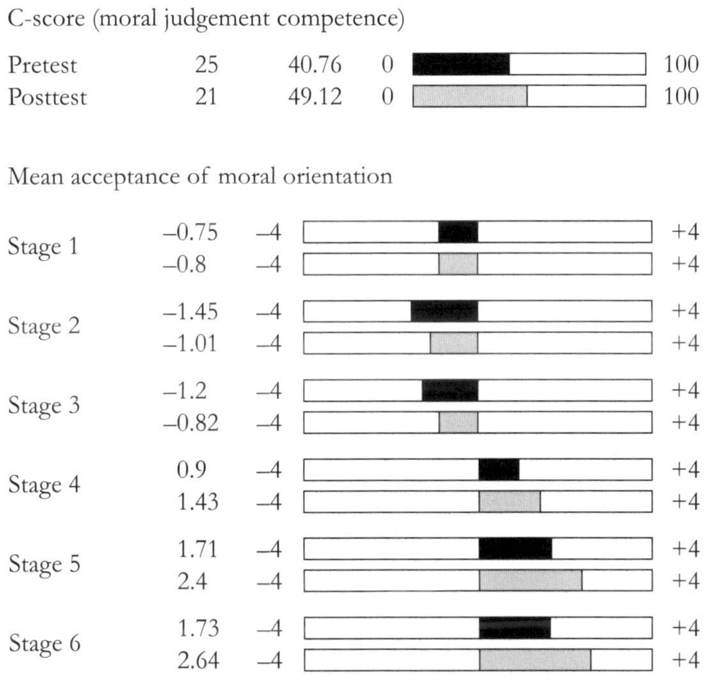

Figure 1. Scores for persons with complete data at each time (considering 25: Pretest, 21: Posttest records)

Source: E. Nowak, G. Lind, 2009, ITSE Archive 2010, University of Konstanz.

In 2009 the Polish version of MJT was validated. The sample consisted of 370 participants representing seven disciplines of study: medicine, law, philosophy, business, pedagogy, sociology, and polytechnic. The data were fully in line with the validity criterion "preference hierarchy." As the Figure 2 below demonstrates, the preferences increase monotonously with the level of moral orientation (stage of moral reasoning). The slight inversions between Stage 1

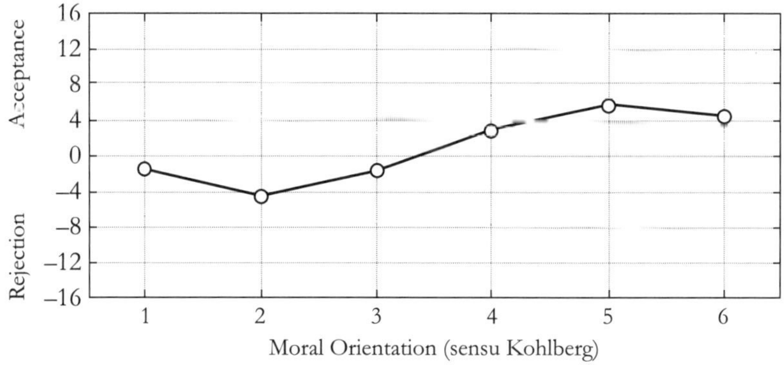

Figure 2. Preference hierarchy
Polish validation sample, N = 370 F (5,1845) = 409,82; p < 0,000

Source: E. Nowak, G. Lind, 2009, ITSE Archive 2010, University of Konstanz.

and 2 and between Stage 5 and 6 have been found in almost all studies and do not in any way invalidate this MJT version.

According to Lind's Dual-Aspect Theory of Morality, the affective aspect (i.e., internal ideals, norms, preferences that *affect* people to make judgments and decisions) and the cognitive aspect (i.e., the capacity to follow one's own ideals, norms etc. in a reflected and efficient way, in different, demanding and challenging social contexts) can be separately measured with the same measuring instrument, namely with the MJT (the cognitive aspect is always understood in its performative meaning, any competence is considered without having observed a given behavior – here: the personal judgment behavior – repeatedly). The hierarchically organized preference for the moral stages indicates to the affective aspect of moral judgment behavior which refers to the strength of MJT participant's acceptance of pros and cons in both dilemmas provided in the MJT design. The data collected in 2009 were almost perfectly in line with the validity criterion "affective-cognitive parallelism" operationalized as correlations between the six moral orientations, on the one hand, and the C-score, on the other. Again, there are only two slight deviations from this, again with Stages 1 and 2, and Stages 5 and 6. Additionally, the Polish translation of the Stage 4-arguments in both the Doctor and Workers' Dilemmas has been optimized through several pilot-validation tests. Polish students undervaluated conventional arguments of Stage 4 in the Workers' Dilemma, and overvaluated conventional arguments of Stage 3 in the Doctor's Dilemma. The first fact could be explained in the following way: after the democratic turn in 1989,

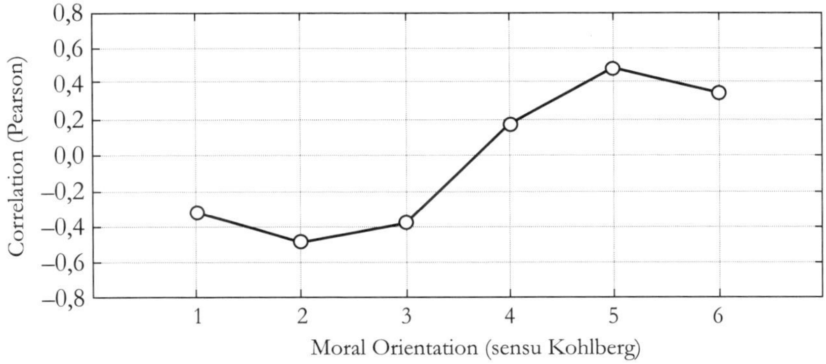

Figure 3. Affective-cognitive parallelism
Validation sample, Poznan, N = 370

Source: E. Nowak, G. Lind, 2009, ITSE Archive 2010, University of Konstanz.

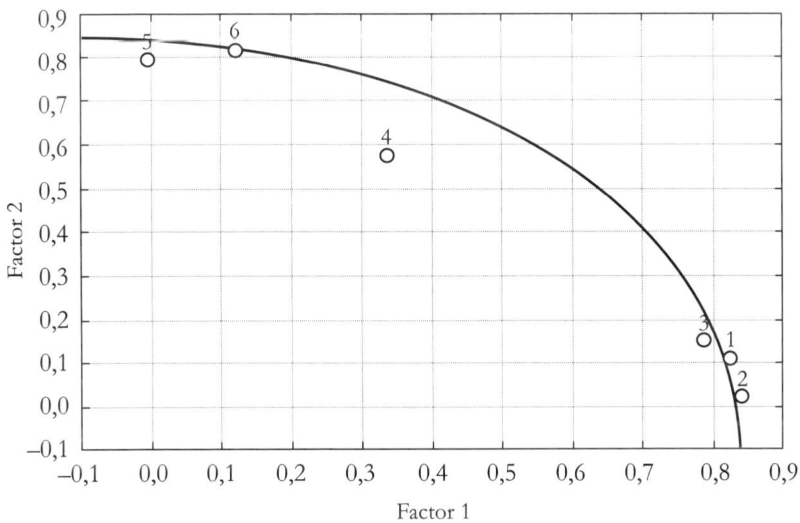

Figure 4. Quasi-simplex Moral Orientation
Rotation Varimax (simple), principled components, N = 370

Source: E. Nowak, G. Lind, 2009, ITSE Archive 2010, University of Konstanz.

people in Poland still mistrusted the legislative process. This process does not fully conform to EU guidelines and human rights and is strongly influenced by ideologies and parties. Countless politically based modifications of law make it implausible in the citizens' eyes. Additionally, the competence of people to interpret and apply law in institutions and in the private life is low. Second fact probably results from participants' mistrust against corrupted relationships in the medical institutions. The validation study clearly demonstrates that in Poland the level of education is positively related to moral judgment competence (C-score), but the correlation is rather low (no significant increasing of the moral judgment competence between 1st, 5th and 9/10th semester of studies). This correlation is not a criterion for MJT-validity anymore, because the strength of correlation can vary according to the democratic quality of education in various countries. It indicates, however, to the insufficient democratic quality of public education in Poland.

To complete this brief report on the MJT validation in Poland: the data were almost perfectly in line with the validity criterion "quasi-simplex" (varimax rotation) of inter-correlations of the six moral orientations that correlate more strongly with one another (e.g., Stage 3 and 4) than orientations that are more distant (e.g., Stage 2 and 6). There are only two slight deviations from this, again with Stages 1 and 2 and Stages 5 and 6. An over-valuated Stage 1 indicates to the fear-of-punishment orientation that seems to be relatively strong in Poland as being one of the young, posttolitarian democracies.

3. Developing democratic personality

What constitutes a human being, is not merely his having to think, but his thoughts, his beliefs, doubts, understandings, his awareness of his own ignorance, his wants, preferences, choices, sentiments, emotions, purposes and his expression of them in utterances or actions which have meanings; and the necessary condition of all or any of this is that he must have *learned* it. The prize of the intelligent activity which constitutes being human is learning.[18]

In its simplest meaning, democracy is just being together with others in a mutually respectful and cooperative way, which is ordered by a set of commonly established and individually followed rules. All of the involved processes require basic skills that have been described by democratic theorists from Aristotle (*zoon logon echon*) to Arendt, Habermas, Rawls, and others. We usually believe that democracy is based on the gift of speech and that it requires more speaking than listening. But listening to others is equally important. It means "being open to the word of the other [...], to differences of the other [...].

[18] M. Oakeshott, *The Voice of Liberal Learning*, New Haven – London 1989, p. 20.

Qualities that build up the practice of listening democratically [...]."[19] These qualities, as Freire puts it, "build up the practice of listening democratically."[20]

Furthermore, democratic society needs "intelligent activity" from citizens. Educational programs are focused on the strengthening of abstract and sophistic reflection. However, democratic education is still deficient in "helping students experience how the democratic process really works."[21] By offering students opportunities to take responsibility, to discuss and resolve social controversies, and creating didactic tasks which challenge their social cognition and personal skills, we can strengthen the democratic quality of education.[22] Not only knowledge and technology transfer, but also room for free discourse efficiently affects the democratic behavior of students.

I have observed how efficient free democratic discourse can be for strengthening moral-discourse and democratic competences in both Polish high schools and universities (2008–2012), as I arranged KMDD sessions among 16–19 years aged students when their moral judgment competence score were low ($N=23$, $C=16$). I refer to one of the most relevant experiences here. Standing in front of these students made me actually experience the relevance of learning moral judgment and moral discourse competencies for a young democracy. I began one of my first dilemma discussions by presenting a story of a ficticious girl who discovered that her boyfriend was a criminal. I let students clarify the dilemmas it contained. Then I was supposed to ask for a vote on the protagonist's decision. According to Lind's long-standing experience, all but a very few students feel free to vote on any issue presented in KMDD sessions, although they concern mostly "hot" issues like abortion, violence, etc. But in this class of Polish adolescents, one-third did not raise their hands. They refused to vote. They avoided eye contact with me. They bowed their heads. I tried to encourage them to vote but nothing helped. Apparently, this was the first time in school that someone asked them to express and discuss their moral opinion openly. They did not seem to trust teachers or to know how to handle this situation. We agreed that the non-voters would not participate in the plenary discussion but remain silent listeners during that phase. Perhaps these non-voters felt overwhelmed by the difficulty of the issue and needed more time to reflect on it and to work through arguments

[19] P. Freire, *Pedagogy of Freedom. Ethics, Democracy, and Civic Courage*, transl. P. Clarke, Lanham – Boulder – New York – Oxford 1998, p. 107.

[20] Ibidem.

[21] A. Colby et al., *Educating for Democracy*, op. cit., p. 117.

[22] G. Lind, *Moral ist lehrbar...*, op. cit.; M. Schillinger-Agati, *Learning Environment and Moral Development: How University Education Fosters Moral Judgment Competence in Brazil and two German-Speaking Countries*, Aachen 2006.

justifying their decision. Maybe as a teacher I representated some "higher authority," and hence was threatening to them. Even though this generation was born after the end of communist dictatorship in Poland in 1989, Polish students still seem not to feel comfortable in a democratic discussion in which they must expose their autonomous and true opinions. Another hypothesis is that the Polish catholic system (similar to the communist system before the democratic turn in 1989) and traditional family education do not tolerate doubts and hesitations in children's judgmental behavior. Both systems promoted the idea of single, absolutely correct judgments because they proposed single sets of absolutely correct criteria too (e.g., an acceptance of a particular ideology conflicts with plurality and the diversity of moral reasons typical in a democracy). In Polish schools, teachers expect clear and one-dimensional judgments from their students; they follow the 0–1 logic where "0" means *wrong*, and "1" means *right*. This results from the predemocratic, monological, authoritarian teaching discourse. High school students still are not acquainted with other teaching methods.

If the KMDD discussion starts in the classroom, it is, at the beginning, never free of authority and the monopoly of the "one" right solution. But only one hour later, after some lively discussion of the pros and cons, when the class was asked to vote a second time, the proportion of non-voters decreased from one-third to almost zero. Only two students still refused to vote in the end. I believe that the atmosphere of trust and mutual respect and the experience of each person as an equal and free discussant, which the Konstanz Method helped me create during the discussion phase, turned the tide.

In 2010, while leading another KMDD session for 22–26 years aged students of a private university, I experienced a similar situation: 11 of 50 participants refused to vote in both the first and second voting. Also in 2010, another Polish KMDD-Trainee led several KMDD sessions among girls living in a closed reform house that is similar to prison.[23] In this case, the girls (13–21 years aged) always voted for the same option because some of them control and dominate the others (power-plays are typical in prison communities). In this group fear exerts a stronger influence than does civic courage. The polarization of moral opinions that we make visible in KMDD sessions could evoke conflicts between the opposing groups that the girls belong to. But during a free discussion (without voting) we then began experimentally, the girls argued in an autonomous way and collected "pros" and "cons" on the black boards. In the third experiment, the girls voted with closed eyes, with-

[23] See E. Nowak, A. Urbańska, "Can the Konstanz Method of Dilemma Discussion Support an Emotional-Cognitive Balance in Aggressive Juveniles," *Journal of Strategy and Decision Making*, October 2011, pp. 77–85.

out being observed by their antagonists. In this way, freedom and democracy have been protected. Fully autonomous voting happened, regardless of the violence-polarized relationships.

Moral-discurse competence is a basic need in a democracy. As mentioned above, the social environment, public media, and public education in Poland does not foster it sufficiently. And this is why so many young people feel overwhelmed if they are confronted with social problems to solve. Supervising my dilemma discussion classes, teachers have some-times remarked that they did not know that their pupils could engage in discussion. This encouraged me to collect observations from other European countries. When I compare the judgment and discourse behavior of students between the ages of 10–20 years, living in Germany, Switzerland, and Poland (established as democracy in 1989), I see striking differences. Polish students avoid expressing their true moral judgments openly because social discourses are generally dominated by authorities, disrespect, verbal aggression, mistrust, and fear.[24] Later, as adults and citizens they might be unable to discuss social controversies at higher levels than the Kohlbergian stages of punishment and "good guy and nice girl" morality; this is an unfavorable framework for democratic discourse.

However, in students' eyes, discourse seems to be less relevant than other democratic activities. The Konstanz Method of Dilemma Discussion encourages students not only to discuss and cooperate. In 2010 I conducted a pilot study called "Democracy as Competence" with a small group of Polish university students ($N = 10$) in order to measure their preferences for free discourse teaching, and teaching that demands real democratic activities on the campus (in correlation with their C-scores) by using the MJT. The pilot study demonstrated that students with higher C-scores clearly preferred democratic activities on the campus, while students with lower C-scores preferred discussions on democratic issues. The active group got successfully involved in the decisions relevant to campus life. The conclusion seems clear: discussion is not everything in democratic education (Figure 5).

Additionaly, my pilot study demonstrates that students with higher C-scores participated in all seminars (nearly 100% frequency) while students with lower C-scores participated in only 70% of the seminars. As Figure 6 demonstrates, active participation clearly correlates with high moral-democractic competencies.

In my experiences with students of other countries, I observed that discursive behavior of German and Swiss students is quite different. They speak

[24] From Interview after dilemma-discussion in October 2007 at the University of Poznan (G. Lind), 80 discussants, 25 Interview-participants.

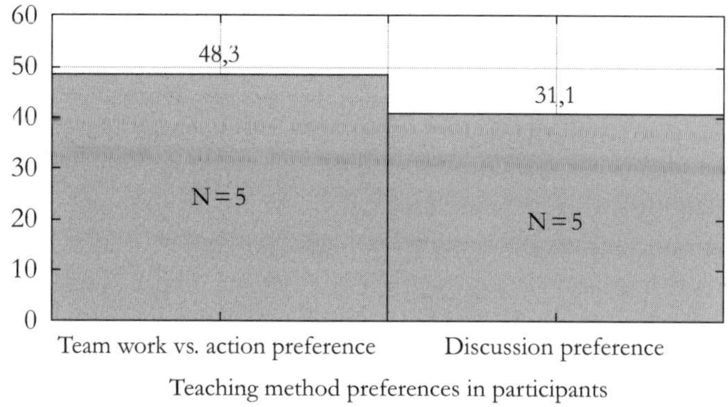

Figure 5. Teaching program: Democracy as competence.
Correlation between C-scores and learning method preferences in participants
F (1,8) = 2,22; p < 0,1749, abs. ES = –17,2 C-point, r_{xy} = 0,56

Source: E. Nowak, 2010, ITSE Archive 2010, University of Konstanz.

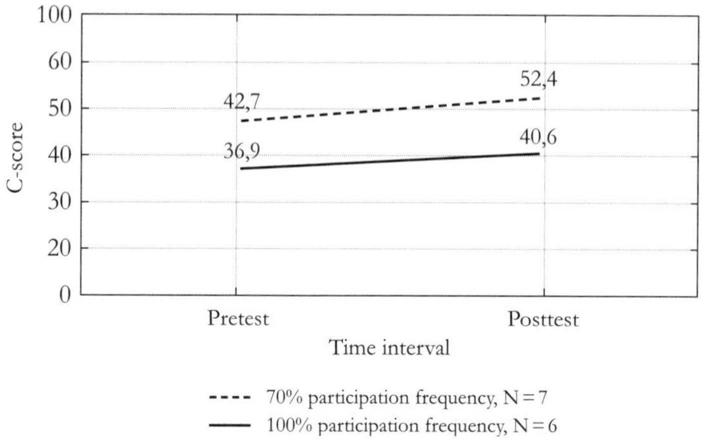

Figure 6. Interaction plot: Double interaction
F (1,11) = 0,01; p < 0,9093

Source: E. Nowak, 2010, ITSE Archive 2010, University of Konstanz.

freely and openly about social matters and their independent viewpoints. Direct democracy (in Switzerland) and, in general, matured democracies offer more favorable opportunities for autonomous judging, exchange, and responsibility taking than newer, or more limited, democracies. However, living in a democratic society today always confronts young people with countless conflicting values, decisions, and lifestyles. Young people are overwhelmed when making decisions and choices against demanding social and cultural contexts. The danger of being manipulated, controlled, marginalized, discriminized against, and, finally, excluded from democratic processes is very high.

The way to democratic inclusion should be primarily constructed in a bottom-up manner: it is the people, not institutions that engage in democracy. If citizens are to be enabled to more fully live in a democratic way, democratic quality in education must be supported through systemic educational policy.

4. Examining the "simple" voting competence

To demonstrate what a "simple" democratic competence like voting means, I would like to collect some external and internal conditions which are necessary to promote that competence. In fact, voting competence is the moral judgment competence performed in the social context we can define as a democratic one. In both young and old democracies voting competence (and participatory competences generally) seems to regress because the moral judgment competence regresses too. Regression is stimulated through (1) the "bottom" factor of deficient education of moral, discursive and democratic competences, and (2) the institutional participation system.

Participatory democratic systems heavily conventionalized space for interpersonal and public discourse. Hierarchical associations like parties evolve in order to strengthen the individual's influence on politics. But the opposite occurs: free discursive activity among citizens is weakened.[25] Leaders of political parties, economic lobbying, and last but not least, the oversized administrative machinery hamper the development of free access to the democratic decision making process.

Living in a representative democracy, people have only a few chances for direct action, discursive interaction with other citizens, and full democratic inclusion. But they still have elections and can vote to express their opinions and will. And this supplies another reason for exploring the complexities of voting competence and how it can be fostered.

Possessing a precise election (voting) competence requires some preliminary institutional and environmental preconditions:

1. The electoral law needs to exist and to be institutionally conventionalized (for example in a constitution). Some democratic countries introduced an obligation to vote in order to maintain a regularly sufficient voting turnout, for a negative turnout might hinder an important juridical or political decision. Still, there are legitimate reasons why a citizen might refrain from voting, such

[25] J. Habermas, *Kultur und Kritik*, Frankfurt am Main 1973.

as civil disobedience. This refers to a civil response to unfair politics of the state, political repression, or imminent danger of vote-rigging.

2. The political framework must be democratic, legally firm, and transparent. A sudden call for a vote in a dictatorship is not feasible, because it might evoke mistrust and feeling of political fiction among people. If the political framework is democratic, stable and supportive, the voter feels safe and familiar with the electoral process. He or she is convinced of the sense and importance of her or his vote and believes that it is not subject to manipulation or suspension.

3. Civic education must harmonize the basic regulatory systems: the legal, the moral, and the cultural one, at the more universal level. For example, the educational programs have to follow the human rights, the constitution, the citizens' rights, and not the particular moral ideologies (especially if that ideologies are incompatible with democracy).

4. Moral authorities (like the church) and other voters cannot sanction, discriminate, ridicule, or stigmatize a voter for her or his convictions, decision, participation, non-participation, voting boycott, etc.[26]

5. Voting competence, as is the case with other moral-discourse competencies, must be fostered within educational settings on each level. Students' voices and choices must be promoted in the classroom, and repeatedly experienced by students.

There are seven personal preconditions of voting competence:

1. Elementary cognitive skills (it is impossible to establish political democracy among illiterated and uninstructed people).

2. Political awareness (understanding what is democratic self-determination; knowing candidates and differences between them).

3. Motivation: a voter represents him or herself as a moral subject, along with the principles, aims, and interests that are important to her- or himself and her or his social surroundings (the personal affective aspect of voting as moral judgment behaviour). If one does not represent any personal interests, one votes for reasons of empathy or solidarity with other citizens.

4. Autonomy and civil courage: a voter needs to form and articulate judgements and opinions in an autonomous, non-conforming way and confronts the opinions of others. He openly stands by his opinion (cognitive aspect of person's morality).

5. Self-trust: a voter has faith in himself, and in other voters, to not discriminate, ridicule, punish, or outcast others in any way.

[26] J. Habermas, "Werte und Normen. Ein Kommentar zu Hilary Putnams Kantischem Pragmatismus," in M.-L. Raters, M. Willaschek (eds.), *Hilary Putnam und die Tradition des Pragmatismus*, Frankfurt am Main 2002, pp. 280–305.

6. Respect for people who hold opposing opinions.

7. Trust in the political power of one's own voice; voters feel an inner obligation to vote and to contribute to the democratic will-formation process. This moral self-obligation refers to a high moral competence. In particular, this competence includes the notion that the democratic principles of an individual are internalized and he or she applies them in her or his decisions; in short, these principles have become "internal principles" that the individual adheres to in respect to democratic decision making.

However, we cannot forget that the democratic process requires much more than voting competence only. It requires permanent face-to-face citizen deliberation (to call Gastil again) in front of everyday social challenges. We decided to live in democracy, so we have to learn and to teach how to live democratically.

Bibliography

Alexy R., *A Theory of Legal Argumentation*, transl. R. Adler, N. MacCormick, Oxford University Press, Oxford 1989.

Alexy R., *The Argument from Injustice: A Reply to Legal Positivism*, transl. B. Litschewski-Paulson, S. L. Paulson, Clarendon Press, Oxford 2002.

Apel K.-O., *Diskurs und Verantwortung*, Suhrkamp, Frankfurt am Main 1990.

Appiah K. A., *Experiments in Ethics*, Harvard University Press, Cambridge, MA – London 2008.

Arendt H., *The Human Condition*, introduced by M. Canovan, The University of Chicago Press, Chicago 1958[1], 1982[2].

Arendt H., *The Life of the Mind*, part I: *Thinking*, Harcourt Brace, New York 1978.

Aristotle, *Nicomachean Ethics*, transl. W. D. Ross, 1994. Retrieved from http://classics.mit.edu/Aristotle/nicomachean.1.i.html [21.05.2009].

Aristotle, *The Eudemian Ethics*, transl. H. Rackham, Harvard University Press, London – Cambridge, MA 1935.

Armond Ch., Dawson T. L., "Developmental Trajectories in Moral Reasoning across the Life-Span", *Journal of Moral Education*, 1997, vol. 26 (4), pp. 433–453.

Bachmann-Medick D., *Cultural Turns*, Rowohlts Taschenbuch Verlag, Reinbeck bei Hamburg 2006.

Bargel T., Markiewicz W., Peisert H., "University Graduates: Study Experience and Social Role – Empirical Findings of a Comparative Study in Five European Countries (FORM Project)," in M. Niessen, J. Peschar (eds.), *Comparative Research on Education*, Pergamon, Oxford 1982 pp. 55–78.

Baron-Cohen S. et al., *Mind Reading. Emotions Library*. Version 1.2., University of Cambridge, Jessica Kingsley Publishers, London – New York 20021 20032.

Beane J., Affect in the Curriculum: Towards Democracy, Dignity, and Diversity, Teachers College Press, New York 1990.

Ben-Ze'ev A., *The Subtlety of Emotions*, The MIT Press, Cambridge, MA 2000.

Berkowitz M. W., "Four Perspectives on Moral Argumentation," in C. Gibb Harding (ed.), *Moral Dilemmas. Philosophical and Psychological Issues in the Development of Moral Reasoning*, Precedent Publishing, Chicago 1985, pp. 1–24.

Berkowitz M. W. et al., "Discourse, Development and Education," in F. Oser, W. Veugelers (eds.), *Getting Involved*, Sense Publishers, Rotterdam – Taipei 2009, pp. 189–204.

Blatt M., Kohlberg L., "The Effect of Classroom Moral Discussion Upon Children's Level of Moral Judgment," *Journal of Moral Education*, 1975, no. 4, pp. 129–161.

Boler M., "Disciplined Emotions: Philosophies of Educational Feelings," *Educational Theory*, 2005, vol. 47 (2), pp. 203–227.

Brehm J.W., Cohen A. R., *Exploration in Cognitive Dissonance*, Wiley, New York 1962.

Breyer T., *Attentionalität und Intentionalität. Grundzüge einer phänomenologisch-kognitionswissenschaftlichen Theorie der Aufmerksamkeit*, Wilhelm Fink Verlag, München 2011.

Brugidou M., "Argumentation and Values: An Analysis of Ordinary Political Competence via an Open-Ended Question," *International Journal of Public Opinion Research*, 2003, vol. 15 (4), pp. 413–430.

Brünner G., Gülich E. (eds.), *Krankheit verstehen. Interdisziplinäre Beiträge zur Sprache in Krankheitsdarstellungen*, Bielefeld 2012.

Colby A. et al., *Educating for Democracy*, Jossey-Bass, San Francisco 2009.

Craig A. D., "How Do You Feel Now? The Anterior Insula and Human Awareness," *Nature Reviews in Neuroscience*, 2009, no. 10, pp. 59–70. Retrieved from doi: 10.1038/nrn2555 [7.09.2012].

Craig A. D., "Interoception: The Sense of the Physiological Condition of the Body," *Current Opinion in Neurobiology*, 2003, no. 13, pp. 500–505.

Cutting H., *Photographs*, 2013, http://www.harrycutting.com/; http://ruff-draft.tumblr.com/; http://harrycutting.blogspot.com/.

Damasio A., *Looking for Spinoza. Joy, Sorrow and the Feeling Brain*, Harcourt Brace, New York 2003.

Damasio A., *The Feeling of What Happens*, Harcourt Brace, New York 1999.

Darwall S., "Two Kinds of Respect," *Ethics*, 1977, vol. 88, no. 1, pp. 36–49.

Deigh J., *Emotions, Values, and the Law*, Oxford University Press, Oxford 2008.

Derrida J., "Animal Therefore I Am," *Critical Inquiry*, 2002, vol. 28, pp. 369–418.

Dewey J., *Democracy and Education. An Introduction to the Philosophy of Education*, The Free Press, New York 1966.

Dewey J., *Moral Principles in Education*, University of Southern Illinois Press, Cambridge 1975.

Döbert R., Nunner-Winkler G., "Value Change and Morality," in G. Lind, H. A. Hartmann, R. Wakenhut (eds.), *Moral Judgments and Social Education*, Transaction Publishers, New Brunswick – London 1981[1], 2010[2], pp. 125–154.

Dworkin R., *Justice for Hedgehogs*, The Belknap Press of Harvard University Press, Cambridge, MA – London 2011.

Dworschak M., "Die Macht des Mitgefühls," *Der Spiegel*, 2013, no. 29, pp. 118–121.

Eckensberger L. H., Gähde U. (eds.), *Ethische Norm und empirische Hypothese*, Suhrkamp, Frankfurt am Main 1993.

Ekman P., *Emotion in the Human Face – Guidelines for Research and An Integration of Findings*, Pergamon, New York 1972.

Ekman P., *Emotions Revealed. Recognizing Faces and Feelings*, Henry Holt & Co., New York 2003.

Ekman P., "Facial Expressions of Emotion: New Findings, New Questions," *Psychological Science*, 1992, no. 3, pp. 34–38.

Elster J., *Alchemies of the Mind: Rationality and the Emotions*, Cambridge University Press, Cambridge, MA 1999.

Elster J., *Reason and Rationality*, Princeton University Press, Princeton 2009.

Elster J., *Strong Feelings. Emotion, Addiction, and Human Behavior*, A Bradford Book, The MIT Press, Cambridge, MA – London 1997.

Esposito R., *Bíos. Biopolitics and Philosophy*, Minneapolis – London 2004

Fichte J. G., *The Science of Knowledge 1794*, transl. P. Heath, J. Lachs, Oxford University Press, Oxford 1982.

Fischman J., *Criminal Minds. The Chronicle of Higher Education*, 12.06.2001, http://chronicle.com/article/Can-This-Man-Predict-Whether/127792 [24.05.2013].

Freire P., *Pedagogy of Freedom. Ethics, Democracy, and Civic Courage*, transl. P. Clarke, Rowman Littlefield Publishers, Lanham – Boulder – New York – Oxford 1998.

Gadamer H. G., *Schmerz. Einschätzungen aus medizinischer, philosophischer und therapeutischer Sicht*, Universitätsverlag Winter, Heidelberg 2003.

Gastil J., "Is Face-to-Face Citizen Deliberation a Luxury or a Necessity for Democracy?," *Political Communication*, 2000, vol. 17, pp. 357–361. Retrieved from http://faculty.washington.edu/jgastil/pdfs/LuxuryOrNecessity.pdf [11.02.2011].

Gardner S. T., "Taking Selves Seriously," in B. Weber, K. Herb, E. Marsal, T. Dobashi, P. Schweitzer (eds.), *Cultural Politics and Identity. The Public Space of Recognition*, LIT Verlag, Wien – Berlin 2011, pp. 179–190.

Gazzaniga M. S., *The Ethical Brain*, Dana Press, New York 2005.

Gibbard A., *Wise Choices, Apt Feelings. A Theory of Normative Judgment*, Clarendon Press, Oxford 1990.

Goldman A. I., *Simulating Minds. The Philosophy, Psychology, and Neuroscience of Mindreading*, Oxford University Press, Oxford 2006.

Grahek N., *Feeling Pain and Being in Pain*, Verlag der Universität Oldenburg, Oldenburg 2001.

Greene J. D., "The Secret Joke of Kant's Soul," in W. Sinnott-Armstrong (ed.), *Moral Psychology*, The MIT Press, Cambridge, MA – London 2008.

Gutman A., *Democratic Education*, 2nd edition, Princeton University Press, Princeton 1999.

Habermas J., *Autonomy and Solidarity. Interviews with Jürgen Habermas*, introduced and ed. by P. Dews, Verso, London – New York 1985.

Habermas J., *Communication and the Evolution of Society*, transl. T. McCarthy, Beacon Press, Boston 1979.

Habermas J., *Kultur und Kritik*, Suhrkamp, Frankfurt am Main 1973.

Habermas J., *Moral Consciousness and Communicative Action*, transl. Ch. Lenhardt, S. W. Nicholsen, introduced by T. McCarthy, The MIT Press, Cambridge, MA 1990.

Habermas J., "Philosophical Notes on Moral Judgment Theory," in G. Lind, H. A. Hartman, R. Wakenhut (eds.), *Moral Judgments and Social Education*, Transaction Publishers, New Brunswick – London 2010, pp. 3–20.

Habermas J., *The Theory of Communicative Action*, vol. 1, transl. T. McCarthy, Beacon Press, Boston 1983.

Habermas J., *The Theory of Communicative Action*, vol. 2, transl. T. McCarthy, Beacon Press, Boston 1981.

Habermas J., "Werte und Normen. Ein Kommentar zu Hilary Putnams Kantischem Pragmatismus," in M. L. Raters, M. Willaschek (eds.), *Hilary Putnam und die Tradition des Pragmatismus*, Suhrkamp, Frankfurt am Main 2002, pp. 280-305.

Hagberg G. L., *Describing Ourselves. Wittgenstein and Autobiographical Consciousness*, Clarendon Press, Oxford – New York 2008.

Haidt J., "The Emotional Dog and its Rational Tail: A Social Intuitionist Approach to Moral Judgment," *Psychological Review*, 2000, vol. 108 (4), pp. 814–834.

Hamlin J. K., Wynn K., Bloom P., "Social Evaluation by Preverbal Infants," *Nature*, 2007, no. 450 (7169), pp. 557–559.

Harman G., *Explaining Value and Other Essays in Moral Philosophy*, Clarendon Press, Oxford 2000.

Harman G., Thomson J. J., *Moral Relativism and Moral Objectivity*, Blackwell Publishers, Cambridge, MA 1996.

Hart H. L. A., *Law, Liberty, Morality,* Oxford University Press, London 1963.

Hart H. L. A., *The Concept of Law*, Clarendon Press, Oxford 1961.

Hegel G. W. F., *Faith and Knowledge*, transl. W. Cerf, H. Harris, Sunny Press, Albany, NY 1977.

Hegel G. W. F., *Lectures on the Philosophy of Right*, transl. T. M. Knox, Oxford University Press, Oxford 1967.

Hegel G. W. F., *Phenomenology of Spirit*, transl. A. V. Miller, Oxford University Press, Oxford 1977.

Hegel G. W. F., *Philosophie des Rechts. Die Vorlesung von 1819/20 in einer Nachschrift*, ed. D. Henrich, Suhrkamp, Frankfurt am Main 1983.

Hegel G. W. F., *Philosophy of Right*, transl. S. W. Dyde, Batoche Book, Kitchener, Ontario 2001.

Heilke T. W., *Voegelin on the Idea of Race. An Analysis of Modern European Racism*, Louisiana State University Press, Baton Rouge – London 1990.

Helkama K., "Change in Moral Judgment in Medical School," in E. Nowak, D. Schrader, B. Zizek (eds.), *Educating Competencies for Democracy*, Peter Lang, Frankfurt am Main 2013.

Hénaff M., "On the Norm of Reciprocity," *Teoria e Critica della Regolazione Sociale*, 2010, Centro Studi TCRS.

Hofmeyr B., "Isn't Art an Activity That Gives Things a Face?," *Image & Narrative*, 2007, no. 18: *Thinking Pictures*. Retrieved from http://www.imageandnarrative.be/inarchive/thinking_pictures/hofmeyr.htm [12.05.2013].

Honneth A., *Das Ich im Wir. Studien zur Anerkennungstheorie*, Suhrkamp, Frankfurt am Main 2010.

Honneth A., *Das Recht der Freiheit*, Suhrkamp, Berlin 2011.

Honneth A., *The Struggle for Recognition, The Moral Grammar of Social Conflicts*, transl. J. Andreson, Suhrkamp, Frankfurt am Main 1995.

Honneth A., *Unsichtbarkeit. Stationen einer Theorie der Intersubjektivität*, Suhrkamp, Frankfurt am Main 2007.

James W., "What is an Emotion," *Mind*, 1884[1], vol. 9, no. 34, pp. 188–205.

Joas H., "Values versus Norms. A Pragmatist Account of Moral Objectivity," *The Hedgehog Review*, 2000, Fall 01. Retrieved from http://www.iasc-culture.org/THR/archives/Pragmatism/3.3EJoas.pdf [27.03.2013].

Kant I., *Groundwork for the Metaphysics of Morals*, ed. and transl. A. Wood, Yale University Press, New Haven – London 2002.

Kant I., *Groundwork for the Metaphysics of Morals*, transl. J. Benneth, 2008. Retrieved from http://www.earlymoderntexts.com/pdf/kantgw.pdf [24.05.2013].

Kant I., *The Critique of Pure Reason*, transl. J. M. B. Meiklejohn, Pennsylvania 2010. Retrieved from http://www2.hn.psu.edu/faculty/jmanis/kant/Critique-Pure-Reason.pdf [3.04. 2013].

Kaufmann A., *G. Radbruch – Leben und Werk*, Gustav Radbruch Gesamtausgabe (RGA), vol. I, C. F. Müller Verlag, Heidelberg 1987–2003.

Kaufmann A., *Gustav Radbruch. Rechtsdenker, Philosoph, Sozialdemokrat*, Serie Piper Porträt, München – Zürich 1987.

Keasey C. B., "The Influence of Opinion-Agreement and Qualitative Supportive Reasoning in the Evaluation of Moral Judgments," *Journal of Personality and Social Psychology*, 1974, no. 30, pp. 477–482.

Kelsen H., *Reine Rechtslehre. Einleitung in die rechtswissenschaftliche Problematik*, Studienausgabe der 1. Auflage 1934, ed. M. Jestaedt, Mohr Siebeck, Tübingen 1934[1], 2008.

Kiesow R. M., Korte M. (eds.), *Emotionales Gesetzbuch. Dekalog der Gefühle*, Böhlau Verlag, Köln – Weimar – Wien 2005.

Knoch D., Leone A. P., Meyer K., Treyer V., Fehr E., "Diminishing Reciprocal Fairness by Disrupting the Right Prefrontal Cortex," *Science Express*, 5.10.2006. Retrieved from www.sciencexpress.org/5_October_2006 [12.04.2010].

Kohlberg L., "Development of Moral Character and Moral Ideology," in M. L. Hoffman, L. W. Hoffman (eds.), *Review of child development research*, vol. I, Russel Sage Foundation, New York 1964, pp. 381–431.

Kohlberg L., "Education for Justice. A Modern Statement of the Platonic View," in N. F. Sizer, T. R. Sizer (eds.), *Moral Education: Five Lectures*, Harvard University Press, Cambridge, MA 1970, pp. 57–83.

Kohlberg L., *Essays on Moral Development*, vol. I: *The Philosophy of Moral Development*, Harper and Row, San Francisco 1984.

Kohlberg L., *Essays on Moral Development*, vol. II: *The Psychology of Moral Development*, Harper and Row, San Francisco 1984.

Kohlberg L., "From is to Ought: How to Commit the Naturalistic Fallacy and Get Away with it in Study of Moral Development," in T. Mischel (ed.), *Cognitive Development and Epistemology*, Academic Press, New York 1971, pp. 151–235.

Kohlberg L., "High School Democracy and Education for a Just Society," in R. Mosher (ed.), *Moral Education. A First Generation of Research and Development*, Praeger, New York 1980, pp. 20–57.

Kohlberg L., "Moral Education for a Society in Moral Transition," *Educational Leadership*, October 1975, pp. 46–54.

Kohlberg L., "Resolving Moral Conflicts Within the Just Community," in C. Gibb Harding (ed.), *Moral Dilemmas*, Precedent Publishing, Chicago 1985, pp. 71–98.

Kohlberg L., *The Development of Modes of Moral Thinking and Choice in the Years Ten to Sixteen*, unpublished doctoral dissertation, University of Chicago, 1958.

Larenz K., *Methodenlehre der Rechtswissenschaft*, Nomos, Heidelberg – Berlin 1975.

Lévinas E., *Ethics and Infinity. Conversations with Philippe Nemo*, transl. R. Cohen, Duquesne University Press, Pittsburg 1985.

Lévinas E., *Totality and Infinity. An Essay on Exteriority*, transl. A. Lingis, Martinus Nijhoff Publishers, The Hague – Boston – London 1979.

Lind G., "Cultural Differences in Moral Judgment Competence? A Study of West and East European University Students," *Behavior Science Research*, 1986, no. 20, pp. 208–225.

Lind G., *Gewalt als die niedrigste Ebene der Konfliktlösung*. Paper presented at the 10th Conference of Peace Psychology, University of Konstanz, 13–15.06.1997.

Lind G., "Growth and Regression in Cognitive-Moral Development," in C.G. Harding (ed.), *Moral Dilemmas*, Precedent Publishing, Chicago 1985, pp. 99–114.

Lind G., *Inhalt und Struktur des moralischen Urteilens. Theoretische, methodologische und empirische Untersuchungen zur Urteils- und Demokratiekompetenz bei Studierenden*, Universität Konstanz, 1985.

Lind G., *Ist Moral lehrbar? Ergebnisse der modernen moralpsychologischen Forschung*, 2nd edition, Logos Verlag, Berlin 2002.

Lind G., "Measuring Moral judgment: A Review of 'The Measurement of Moral Judgment' by Anne Colby and Lawrence Kohlberg," *Human Development*, 1989, no. 32, pp. 388–397.

Lind G., "Moral Competence and Education in Democratic Society," in G. Zecha, P. Weingartner (eds.), *Conscience: An Interdisciplinary Approach*, Reidel, Dordrecht 1987, pp. 37–43.

Lind G., "Moral Education. A Dual-Aspect Theory," in E. Kiel, K. Zierer (eds.), *Gestaltung Basisunterricht*, English hand-out, 2010.

Lind G., *Moral ist lehrbar. Handbuch zur Theorie und Praxis moralischer und demokratischer Bildung*, 2nd supplemented edition, Oldenburg – München 2009².

Lind G., "Moral Regression in Medical Students and Their Learning Environment," *Revista Brasileira de Educaçaõ Médica*, 2000, vol. 24 (3), pp. 24–33.

Lind G., "Rekonstruktion des Kohlberg-Ansatzes: Das Zwei-Aspekte-Modell der Moralentwicklung," in F. Oser, W. Althof (eds.), *Moralische Selbstbestimmung*, Klett-Cotta, Stuttgart 1992, pp. 204–208.

Lind G., "Teaching Students To Speak Up and To Listen To Others: Cultivating Moral Democratic Competencies," in D. E. Lund, P. R. Carr (eds.), *Doing Democracy and Social Justice in Education: Political literacy for all students*, Peter Lang, New York 2008, pp. 185–220.

Lind G., "The Importance of Role-Taking Opportunities for Self-Sustaining Moral Development," *Journal of Research in Education*, 2000, vol. 10 (1), pp. 9–15.

Lind G., "The Meaning and Measurement of Moral Judgment Competence Revisited. A Dual-Aspect Model," in D. Fasko, W. Willis (eds.), *Contemporary Philosophical and Psychological Perspectives on Moral Development and Education*, Hampton Press, Cresskill, NJ 2007, pp. 185–220.

Lind G., "The Theory of Moral-Cognitive Development: A Socio-Psychological Assessement by Georg Lind," in G. Lind, H. A. Hartman, R. Wakenhut (eds.), *Moral Judgment and Social Education*, Transaction Publishers, New Brunswick – London 1982¹, 2010².

Lind G., "Wie misst man moralisches Urteil? Probleme und alternative Möglichkeiten der Messung eines komplexen Konstrukts," in G. Portele (ed.), *Sozialisation und Moral*, Beltz, Weinheim 1978, pp. 171–201.

Lind G., *Zur Psychologie gewalttätigen Verhaltens und seiner Prävention*. Retrieved from http://www.uni-konstanz.de/ag-moral/pdf/Lind-1993_Gewalt-Theorien.pdf; 2nd updated edition reprinted in *Ethics in Progress* online, vol. I, 2010, retrieved from www.ethics-inprogress.org [3.05.2013].

Lind G., Hartman H. A., Wakenhut R. (eds.), *Moral Judgment and Social Education*, Transaction Publishers, New Brunswick – London 1982¹, 2010².

Lind G. et al., "Moral Competence and Democratic Personality," in G. Lind, H.A. Hartmann, R. Wakenhut (eds.), *Moral Judgments and Social Education*, Transaction Publishers, New Brunswick – London 1981[1], 2010[2], pp. 55–78.

Lind G. et al., *Moral Development and the Social Environment*, Precedent Publishing, Chicago 1985.

MacCormick N., *H.L.A. Hart*, Stanford University Press, Stanford, CA 1981.

Malcolm N., *Ludwig Wittgenstein. A Memoir*, Oxford University Press, Oxford 1958.

Marmor A., *Positive Law and Objective Values*, Clarendon Press, Oxford 2001.

Marquard O., *Skepsis und Zustimmung*, Reclam, Stuttgart 1996.

Marsal E., "A German Framework for Philosophizing with Children. The Five Finger Method Model of Ekkehard Martens," in E. Marsal. T. Dobashi, B. Weber (eds.), *Children Philosophize Worldwide. Theoretical and Practical Concepts*, Peter Lang, Frankfurt am Main – Berlin – Bruxelles – New York – Oxford – Wien 2009, pp. 503–512.

Modgil S., Modgil C. (eds.), *Lawrence Kohlberg: Consensus and Controvercy*, Falsici, London 1985.

Moll J., Oliveira-Souza R. de, Zahn R., Grafman J., "The Cognitive Neuroscience of Moral Emotions," in W. Sinnot-Armstrong (ed.), *Moral Psychology*, A Bradford Book, Cambridge, MA – London 2008, pp. 1–17.

Nowak E., Schrader D., Zizek B. (eds.), *Educating Competencies for Democracy*, Peter Lang, Frankfurt am Main 2013.

Nowak E., Urbańska A., "Can the Konstanz Method of Dilemma Discussion Support an Emotional-Cognitive Balance in Aggressive Juveniles?," *Journal of Strategy and Decision Making*, October 2011, pp. 77–85.

Nussbaum M., "Emotions as Judgments of Value," *The Yale Journal of Criticism*, 1992, vol. 1 (5), pp. 201–212

Nussbaum M., "Emotions as Judgments of Value and Importance," in R.C. Solomon (ed.), *Thinking About Feeling. Contemporary Philosophers on Emotions*, Oxford University Press, New York 2004.

Oakeshott M., *The Voice of Liberal Learning*, Yale University Press, New Haven – London 1989.

O'Connor Drury M., *The Danger of Words and Writings on Wittgenstein*, Thoemmes Press, Bristol 2003.

Oser F., "Cognitive Stages of Interaction in Moral Discourse," in W. Kurtines, J. Gewirtz (eds.), *Morality, Moral Behavior, and Moral Development*, Wiley & Sons, New York 1984.

Outhwaite W., *Habermas. A Critical Introduction*, 2nd edition, Stanford University Press, Stanford, CA 2009.

Overgaard S., *Wittgenstein and Other Minds. Rethinking Subjectivity and Intersubjectivity with Wittgenstein, Lévinas, and Husserl*, Routledge, New York 2007.

Overlach F., *Sprache des Schmerzes – sprechen über Schmerzen. Eine grammatisch-semantische gesprächsanalytische Untersuchung von Schmerzausdrücken im Deutschen*, Walter de Gruyter, Berlin – New York 2008.

Piaget J., "Inconscient affectif et inconscient cognitif," *Raison Présente*, 1971, no. 19, pp. 11–20.

Piaget J., "Intelligence and Affectivity," transl. T.A. Brown, C.E. Kaegi, *Annual Reviews*, Palo Alto, CA 1981.

Piaget J., *Psychologie et pédagogie*, Denoël, Paris 1969.

Piaget J., "The Affective Unconscious and The Cognitive Unconscious," in B. Inhelder, H.H. Chipman (eds.), *Piaget and His School*, Springer, New York 1976, pp. 63–71.

Piotrowska I., Sobeski M., "The Primitive," *Journal of Aesthetics and Art Criticism*, 1942, vol. 1 (4), pp. 12–21.

Plügge H., *Wohlbefinden und Missbefinden. Beiträge zu einer medizinischen Anthropologie*, Max Niemeyer Verlag, Tübingen 1962.

Prehn K., Wartenburger I., Mériau K., Scheibe Ch., Goodenough O.R. et al., "Individual Differences in Moral Judgment Influence Neural Correlates of Socio-Normative Judgments," *Scan*, 2008, no. 3, pp. 33–46. Retrieved from doi: 10/scan/nsm037 [17.06.2009].

Price J.M., Dodge K.A., "Reactive and Proactive Aggression in Childhood: Relations to Peer Status Social Context Dimensions," *Journal of Abnormal Child Psychology*, 1989, vol. 17, pp. 455–471.

Pulkkinen L., "Proactive and Reactive Aggression in Early Adolescence as Precursor to Anti- and Prosocial Behavior in Young Adults," *Aggressive Behavior*, 1996, vol. 22, pp. 241–257.

Radbruch G., *Bildungs- und Religionspolitik*, Gustav Radbuch-Gesamtausgabe (RGA), vol. 13, C.F. Müller Verlag, Heidelberg 1987–2003.

Radbruch G., *Der Mensch im Recht*, Vandenhoeck Ruprecht, Göttingen 1961.

Radbruch G., "Fünf Minuten Rechtsphilosophie," in G. Radbruch, *Rechtsphilosophie*, eds. R. Dreier, S. Paulson, 2nd edition, C.F. Müller Verlag, Heidelberg 1945[1], 2003.

Radbruch G., "Five Minutes of Legal Philosophy," *Oxford Journal of Legal Studies*, 1945[1], 2006, vol. 26.

Radbruch G., "Gesetzliches Unrecht und übergesetzliches Recht," in G. Radbruch, *Rechtsphilosophie*, eds. R. Dreier, S. Paulson, 2nd edition, C.F. Müller Verlag, Heidelberg 1946[1], 2003.

Radbruch G., *Politische Schriften aus der Weimarer Zeit. Bildungs- und Religionspolitik*, Gustav Radbuch-Gesamtausgabe (RGA), vol. II, C.F. Müller Verlag, Heidelberg 1993.

Radbruch G., *Rechtsphilosophie. Studienausgabe*, eds. R. Dreier, S.L. Paulson, C.F. Müller Verlag, Heidelberg 2003.

Radbruch G., "Statutory Lawlessness and Supra-Statutory Law," *Oxford Journal of Legal Studies*, 1946[1], 2006, vol. 26.

Raine A., Dodge K., Loeber R., Gatzke-Kopp L., Lynam D., Reynolds C., Stouthamer-Loeber M., Liu J., "The Reactive–Proactive Aggression Questionnaire: Differential Correlates of Reactive and Proactive Aggression in Adolescent Boys," *Aggressive Behavior*, 2006, vol. 32, pp. 159–171.

Ratcliffe M., *Feelings of Being. Phenomenology, Psychiatry, and the Sense of Reality*, Oxford University Press, New York 2007.

Richardson D.R. et al., "Relationship Between Perspective-Taking and Non-Aggressive Responding in the Face of an Attack," *Journal of Personality*, 1988, no. 66 (2), pp. 235–256.

Ricoeur P., *Critique and Conviction*, transl. K. Blamey, Polity Press, New York 1998.

Ricoeur P., *Oneself as Another*, transl. K. Blamey, University of Chicago Press, Chicago 1992.

Ricoeur P., *The Course of Recognition*, transl. D. Pellauer, Harvard University Press, Cambridge, MA 2005.

Roberts W., Strayer J., "Empathy, Emotional Expressiveness, and Prosocial Behaviour," *Child Development*, 1996, no. 67 (2), pp. 449–470.

Ron N. J., "The Moral Reasoning of Juvenile Delinquents: A Meta-Analysis," *Journal of Abnormal Child Psychology*, 1990, no. 18 (3).

Rorty A., *Explaining Emotions*, University of California Press, Berkeley – Los Angeles – London 1980.

Rosen M., *Dignity. Its History and Meaning*, Harvard University Press, Cambridge, MA – London 2012.

Rothman D. R., *Strangers at the Bedside. A History of How Law and Bioethics Transformed Medical Decision Making*, Basic Books, A Division of Harper Collins Publishers, New York 1991.

Sachse R., *Therapeutische Beziehungsgestaltung*, Hogrefe, Göttingen – Bern – Wien – Toronto – Seattle – Oxford – Prag 2006.

Schillinger-Agati M., *Learning Environment and Moral Development: How University Education Fosters Moral Judgment Competence in Brazil and two German-Speaking Countries*, Shaker, Aachen 2006.

Schillinger-Agati M., Lind G., *Moral Competence, Role-Taking and Higher Education: A Cross-Cultural Pilot Study*. Paper presented at the 27th Annual Meeting of the AME, Vancouver 2001.

Schore A. N., *Affect Regulation and the Origin of the Self*, Lawrence Erlbaum Associate Publishers, Hillsdale, NJ 1994.

Schöne-Seifert B., Talbot D., Opolka U., Ach J. S. (eds.), *Neuro-Enhancement. Ethik vor neuen Herausforderungen*, Paderborn 2009.

Schrader W. H., "Autonomie und Interpersonalität," in M. J. Siemek (ed.), *Natur, Kunst, Freiheit*, Fichte-Studien Supplementa, vol. 10, Rodopi, Amsterdam – Atlanta 1998, pp. 17–30.

Selman R. L., "Taking Another's Perspective: Role-Taking Development in Early Childhood," *Child Development*, 1971, no. 42, pp. 721–734.

Selman R. L., *The Growth of Interpersonal Understanding*, Academic Press, New York – London – Toronto – Sydney – San Francisco 1980.

Sharp A. M., "The Classroom Community of Inquiry and the Education of the Emotions," in D. Camhy (ed.), *Philosophical Foundations of Innovative Learning*, Academia Verlag, Sankt Augustin 2007.

Siemek M. J., "Freiheit, Recht, Gerechtigkeit," in M. J. Siemek (ed.), *Natur, Kunst, Freiheit*, Fichte-Studien Supplementa, vol. 10, Rodopi, Amsterdam – Atlanta 1998, pp. 1–16.

Singer P., *The Expanding Circle. Ethics, Evolution and the Moral Progress*, Princeton University Press, Princeton 1981[1], 2011[2].

Sinnot-Armstrong W. (ed.), *Moral Psychology*, vol. III: *The Neuroscience of Morality: Emotion, Brain Disorders, and Development*, The MIT Press, Cambridge, MA – London 2008.

Smith A., *The Theory of Moral Sentiments*, Metalibri, Saõ Paulo 2006.

Sobeski M., *Myśl a marmur* [Thought vs. Marble], PWN, Warsaw 1959.

Sobeski M., *Wybór pism estetycznych* [Selected Writings on Aesthetics], Universitas, Cracow 2010.

Solomon R. C., *Not Passions' Slave. Emotions and Choice*, Oxford University Press, New York 2007.

Solomon R. C., *Thinking about Feeling*, Oxford University Press, New York 2004.

Souza R. de, *The Rationality of the Emotion*, The MIT Press, Cambridge, MA – London 1987.

Sprinthall N. A., Reiman A. J., Thies-Sprinthall L., "Role-Taking and Reflection: Promoting the Conceptual and Moral Development of Teachers," *Learning and Individual Differences*, 1993, vol. 5 (4), pp. 283–299.

Stamm I., *Zwischen Neurobiologie und Sozialethik*, Verlag der Universität Oldenburg, Oldenburg 2007.

Voegelin E., *Rasse und Staat*, Verlag von J. C. B. Mohr (Paul Siebeck), Tübingen 1933.

Vygotsky L. S., *Mind in Society. The Development of Higher Psychological Processes*, Harvard University Press, Cambridge, MA 1978.

Vygotsky L. S., *Thought and Language*, newely revised, ed. and transl. by A. Kozulin, The MIT Press, Cambridge, MA 1986.

Wierciński A., *Hermeneutics Between Philosophy and Theology. The Imperative to Think the Incommensurable*, LIT Verlag, Münster 2010.

Wittgenstein L., *Culture and Value*, ed. G. H. von Wright in colaboration with H. Nyman, rev. A. Pichler, transl. P. Winch, Blackwell Publishers, Oxford – Malden 2004.

Wrobel S., "Es ist notwendig und wir werden es machen. Basta! Legitimationsstrategien in sozialpolitischen Reformdebatten," in G. Drews-Sylla, E. Dütschke, H. Leontiy, E. Polledri (eds.), *Konstruierte Normalitäten – normale Abweichungen*, VS Research Verlag für Sozialwissenschaften Springer, Wiesbaden 2010, pp. 243–258.

Wunder K., *How Ethical Standards Can Be Put Into Practice: Ethical Decision Making in Neonatology Intensive Care*. Paper presented at the 7th International Symposium Moral Competence and Behavior, 25–26.06.2013, Konstanz (Germany).

Zachariah B., "On Not Understanding the Stranger: Histories, Collective Victimhood and the Futility of Postcolonialism," in B. Weber, K. Herb, E. Marsal, T. Dobashi, P. Schweitzer (eds.), *Cultural Politics and Identity. The Public Space of Recognition*, LIT Verlag, Zürich – Berlin 2011, pp. 101–116.

Zajadło J., *Dziedzictwo przeszłości. Gustaw Radbruch: portret filozofa, prawnika, polityka i humanisty* [Heritage of the Past. Gustav Radbruch Portrayed as Philosopher, Lawyer, Politician and Humanist], Arche, Gdańsk 2007.

Zajadło J., *Formuła Radbrucha* [Radbruch's Formula], Arche: Gdańsk 2001.

Zajonc A., "Cognitive-Affective Connections in Teaching and Learning: The Relationship Between Love and Knowledge," *Journal of Cognitive Affective Learning*, 2006, no. 3 (1), pp. 1–9. Retrieved from: https://www.jcal.emory.edu//viewarticle.php?id=82layout=html [20.05.2013].

Zirk-Sadowski M., "Soft Kelsenism Versus Multicentrism: Some Remarks on Theoretical Foundations of European Law," in M. Zirk-Sadowski, M. Golecki, B. Wojciechowski (eds.), *Multicentrism as an Emerging Paradigm in Legal Theory*, Peter Lang, Frankfurt am Main 2009.

Zong Uk T., *Der Weg des rechtsphilosophischen Relativismus bei Gustav Radbruch*, Röhrscheid Verlag, Bonn 1967.

Index of persons

* References to footnotes are in italics.